Hands-On Deep Learning with R

A practical guide to designing, building, and improving neural network models using R

Michael Pawlus
Rodger Devine

BIRMINGHAM - MUMBAI

Hands-On Deep Learning with R

Commissioning Editor: Veena Pagare
Acquisition Editor: Ali Abidi
Content Development Editor: Joseph Sunil
Senior Editor: Roshan Kumar
Technical Editor: Manikandan Kurup
Copy Editor: Safis Editing
Project Coordinator: Aishwarya Mohan
Proofreader: Safis Editing
Indexer: Priyanka Dhadke
Production Designer: Aparna Bhagat

First published: April 2020

Production reference: 1230420

Published by Packt Publishing Ltd.
Livery Place
35 Livery Street
Birmingham
B3 2PB, UK.

ISBN 978-1-78899-683-9

www.packt.com

I dedicate this book to my grandma, Shirley Pawlus, who passed away during the writing process. I know she would have loved seeing this in print.

Also my parents, Mike and Cathy, who lead by example in showing the value of living a life where integrity and a strong work ethic are absolute requirements at all times.

My incredible wife, Sheila Newton, for patiently supporting me and giving me the time and space to write. My amazing children, Esme and Grayson, for being constant sources of joy and inspiration.

My siblings, Brad and Nicole, two of the funniest people on the planet. Their incredible families: my sister-in-law Mai, brother-in-law Jeff, nieces and nephews Ilo, Moni, Noka, Otis, and Oscar.

I also wish to express my gratitude to my friends and co-workers involved throughout this process who provided me with encouragement, motivation, and opportunities for growth: Steph Vaver, Molly Schmied, Megan Stanley, Justin Fincher, Maureen Henry, Jordan Zivoder, Skye Wanstrath, Don Callahan, Jon Gerckens, Danielle Huskey, Courtney Moore, Natasha Morrison, Christy Myers, Mike Parry, Doug Plummer, Sam Sheth, Staci Hostetler, Ashutosh Nandeshwar, Susan Engel, Jing Zhou, Ritu Jain, Rodger Devine, Jessica Cho, Christine Van Dort, Maria Barrera, Jaime Miranda, James Sinclair, Joe Gonzales, Steve Grimes, Rich Majerus, Mirabai Auer, John Gough, Marianne Pelletier, Jen Filla, Emma Hinke, Barron Cato, Jake Tolbert, Sam Wren, Brett Lantz, Carrick Davis, Mark Egge, John Gormaly, Mary Darrow, Martin Lane, Tom Flood, Julie Pape, Judy Hurley, Karen Heil, Alexis Renwanz, Daniel Berumen, Anna Snyder, Morgan Green, Stuart Kirk, Greg Bennett, Satkartar Khalsa, November Project Columbus, November Project LA, the entire November Project Family, Scott Stanislav, Brian McDonald, Jen McDonald, Ryan Laird, Will Rein, Tony Kempski, Andy Nelson, and I'm sure there are others besides. If I forgot, you know who you are and please forgive me. I am thankful to have crossed paths with so many phenomenal humans. This is for all of you.

– Michael Pawlus

I would like to dedicate this book to my father, Rodger A. Devine, for always encouraging me to share knowledge to help others, and my beloved piano teacher, Katherine Teves, for inspiring me to see the forest for the trees and tap into my creativity to solve problems.

Many thanks to all of my friends, family, colleagues, teachers, and mentors for their inspiration, encouragement, and support throughout the process of writing this book, including Alessio Frenda, Amy Turbes, Anita Lawson, Andrew Mortensen, Anne Brownlee, Anthony Maddox, Apra Community and Staff, Ariane Reister, Ashley Budd, Ashutosh Nandeshwar, Barron Cato, Bond Lammey, Bob Burdenski, Bob Jones, Brett Lantz, Caroline Chang, Carrie White, Carrick Davis, Caroline Oblack, CASE DRIVE/planning committee and staff, Chandra Montgomery, Cheryl Williams, Christina Hendershaw, Christine Van Dort, Crystal Taylor, the Dornsife Advancement Team, Emily DeYoung, Emily Walsh, Emma Hinke, Fabian Primera, Gareth Griffin, Heather Campbell, Heather Grieg, Henry Lau, Hui Cha "Kim" Devine, Jaime Miranda, James Sinclair, James Cheng, Jarrod Van Kirk, Jay Dillon, Jeff Kelley, Jennifer Cunningham, Jennifer Maccormack, Jennifer Liu-Cooper, Jill Meister, Jing Zhou, Jo Theodosopoulos, Joe Person, John Taylor, Josh Birkholz, Josh Jacobson, Karen Isble, Kate Weber, Kevin Coates, Kevin Corbett, Kevin Jones, Kim "McData" McDade, Kim Jacobson, Lauren Dixson, Laurent "Lo" de Janvry, Leah Nickel, Linda Pavich, Lindsey Nadeau, Liz Regan Jones, Liz Rejman, Mandy Simon, Maria Barrera, Marianne Pelletier, Marissa Todd, Mark Egge, Megan Doud, Melissa Bank-Stepno, Michael Pawlus, Milagro "Misa" Lobato, Nathan Gulick, Nedra Newton-Jones, Nicole Ferguson, OCL Cohort 13, Pat Tobey, Patrick Franklin, Paul Worster, Peter Wylie, the Public Exchange "Tiger" Team, Qiaozhu Mei, Rich Majerus, Robin Rone, Rose Romani, Ryan Donnelly, Salijo Hendershaw, Sam Jones, Sarah Barr, Sarah Daly, Shahan Sanossian, Shalonda Martin, Steve Grimes, Susan Engel, Susan Hayes McQueen, Tadd and Nayiri Mullinix, Tanya Kern, Terri Devine, Todd Osborn, Tracey Church, U-M School of Information, USC Advancement, Will Winston, and countless others.

Together, we can go further.

– Rodger Devine

Packt>

Packt.com

Subscribe to our online digital library for full access to over 7,000 books and videos, as well as industry leading tools to help you plan your personal development and advance your career. For more information, please visit our website.

Why subscribe?

- Spend less time learning and more time coding with practical eBooks and Videos from over 4,000 industry professionals

- Improve your learning with Skill Plans built especially for you

- Get a free eBook or video every month

- Fully searchable for easy access to vital information

- Copy and paste, print, and bookmark content

Did you know that Packt offers eBook versions of every book published, with PDF and ePub files available? You can upgrade to the eBook version at www.packt.com and as a print book customer, you are entitled to a discount on the eBook copy. Get in touch with us at customercare@packtpub.com for more details.

At www.packt.com, you can also read a collection of free technical articles, sign up for a range of free newsletters, and receive exclusive discounts and offers on Packt books and eBooks.

Contributors

About the authors

Michael Pawlus is a data scientist at The Ohio State University, where he is currently part of the team responsible for building the data science infrastructure for the advancement department, while also heading up the implementation of innovative projects there. Prior to this, Michael was a data scientist at the University of Southern California. In addition to this work, Michael has chaired data science education conferences, published articles on the role of data science within fundraising, and currently serves on committees where he is focused on providing a wider variety of educational offerings as well as increasing the diversity of content creators in this space. He holds degrees from Grand Valley State University and the University of Sheffield.

> *I want to thank everyone who has supported and encouraged me throughout the writing of this book, especially my wife, Sheila, for going out of her way to give me the time and space to finish this project.*

Rodger Devine is the Associate Dean of External Affairs for Strategy and Innovation at the USC Dornsife College of Letters, Arts, and Sciences. Rodger's portfolio includes advancement operations, BI, leadership annual giving, program innovation, prospect development, and strategic information management. Prior to USC, Rodger served as the Director of Information, Analytics, and Annual Giving at the Michigan Ross School of Business. He brings with him nearly 20 years of experience in software engineering, IT operations, BI, project management, organizational development, and leadership. Rodger completed his masters in data science at the University of Michigan and is a doctoral student in the OCL program at the USC Rossier School of Education.

> *Thanks to all of my friends, family, colleagues, and mentors for their continued support, patience, and encouragement throughout the process of writing this book, especially Alessio Frenda, Joe Person, Kim Jacobson, and Todd Osborn.*

About the reviewers

Over the last 12 years, **Sray Agrawal** has been working as a data scientist and acquiring experience in a variety of domains. He has had experience of working in BFSI, e-commerce, retail, telecommunications, hospitality, travel, education, real estate, entertainment, and in many others sectors besides. He is currently working for Publicis Sapient as a data scientist, based in London. His expertise lies in predictive modeling, forecasting, and advanced machine learning. He possesses a deep understanding of algorithms and advanced statistics. He has a background in management and economics and has undertaken a masters-equivalent program in data science and analytics. He is also a certified predictive modeler from SAS. His current areas of interest are fair and explainable machine learning.

Oleg Okun is a machine learning expert and an author/editor of four books and numerous journal articles and conference papers. During his more than 25+ years in work, he has been employed in both academia and industry, in his mother country, Belarus, and abroad (Finland, Sweden, and Germany). His work experience includes document image analysis, fingerprint biometrics, bioinformatics, online/offline marketing analytics, and credit scoring analytics. He is interested in all aspects of distributed machine learning and the Internet of Things. He currently lives and works in Hamburg, Germany, and is about to start a new job as a chief architect of intelligent systems. His favorite programming languages are Python, R, and Scala.

Packt is searching for authors like you

If you're interested in becoming an author for Packt, please visit authors.packtpub.com and apply today. We have worked with thousands of developers and tech professionals, just like you, to help them share their insight with the global tech community. You can make a general application, apply for a specific hot topic that we are recruiting an author for, or submit your own idea.

Table of Contents

Section 3: Reinforcement Learning

Preface

Deep learning enables efficient and accurate learning from massive amounts of data. Deep learning is being adopted by numerous industries at an increasing pace since it can help solve a number of challenges that cannot easily be solved by means of traditional machine learning techniques.

Developers working with R will be able to put their knowledge to work with this practical guide to deep learning. This book provides a hands-on approach to implementation and associated methodologies that will have you up and running and productive in no time. Complete with step-by-step explanations of essential concepts and practical examples, you will begin by exploring deep learning in general, including an overview of deep learning advantages and architecture. You will explore the architecture of various deep learning algorithms and understand their applicable fields. You will also learn how to build deep learning models, optimize hyperparameters, and evaluate model performance.

By the end of this book, you will be able to build and deploy your own deep learning models and applications using deep learning frameworks and algorithms specific to your problem.

Who this book is for

The target audience of this book is data analysts, machine learning engineers, and data scientists who are familiar with machine learning and want to consolidate their knowledge of deep learning or make their machine learning applications more efficient using R. We assume that the reader has a programming background with at least some common machine learning techniques and previous experience or familiarity with R.

What this book covers

Chapter 1, *Machine Learning Basics*, reviews all the essential elements of machine learning. This quick refresher is important as we move into deep learning, a subset of machine learning, which shares a number of common terms and methods.

Chapter 2, *Setting Up R for Deep Learning*, summarizes the common frameworks and algorithms for deep learning and reinforced deep learning in R. You will become familiar with the common libraries, including MXNet, H2O, and Keras, and learn how to install each library in R.

Chapter 3, *Artificial Neural Networks*, teaches you about artificial neural networks, which make up the base building block for all deep learning. You will build a simple artificial neural network and learn how all of its components combine to solve complex problems.

Chapter 4, *CNNs for Image Recognition*, demonstrates how to use convolutional neural networks for image recognition. We will briefly cover why these deep learning networks are superior to shallow nets. The remainder of the chapter will cover the components of a convolutional neural network with considerations for making the most appropriate choice.

Chapter 5, *Multilayer Perceptron Neural Networks for Signal Detection*, shows how to build a multilayer perceptron neural network for signal detection. You will learn the architecture of multilayer perceptron neural networks, and also learn how to prepare data, define hidden layers and neurons, and train a model using a backpropagation algorithm in R.

Chapter 6, *Neural Collaborative Filtering Using Embeddings*, explains how to build a neural collaborative filtering recommender system using layered embeddings. You will learn how to use the custom Keras API, construct an architecture with user-item embedding layers, and train a practical recommender system using implicit ratings.

Chapter 7, *Deep Learning for Natural Language Processing*, explains how to create document summaries. The chapter begins with removing parts of documents that should not be considered and tokenizing the remaining text. Afterward, embeddings are applied and clusters are created. These clusters are then used to make document summaries. We will also learn to code a **Restricted Boltzmann Machine (RBM)** along with defining Gibbs Sampling, Contrastive Divergence, and Free Energy for the algorithm. The chapter will conclude with compiling multiple RBMs to create a deep belief network.

Chapter 8, *Long Short-Term Memory Networks for Stock Forecasting*, shows how to use **long short-term memory (LSTM)** RNN networks for predictive analytics. You will learn how to prepare sequence data for LSTM and how to build a predictive model with LSTM.

Chapter 9, *Generative Adversarial Networks for Faces*, describes the main components and applications of **generative adversarial networks (GANs)**. You will learn the common applications of generative adversarial networks and how to build a face generation model with GANs.

Chapter 10, *Reinforcement Learning for Gaming*, demonstrates the reinforcement learning method on a tic-tac-toe game. You will learn the concept and implementation of reinforcement learning in a highly customizable framework. Moreover, you will also learn how to create an agent that plays the best action for each game step and how to implement reinforcement learning in R.

Chapter 11, *Deep Q-Learning for Maze Solving*, shows us how to use R to implement reinforcement learning techniques within a maze environment. In particular, we will create an agent to solve a maze by training an agent to perform actions and to learn from failed attempts.

To get the most out of this book

We assume you are comfortable and have a working familiarity with downloading and installing software on your computer, including R and additional R library packages from CRAN or GitHub. We also assume some baseline familiarity with independently troubleshooting and resolving packaging dependencies (as needed) based on R Studio console output. You will need a version of R and R Studio installed on your computer—the latest version, if possible.

All code examples have been tested using R version 3.6.3 on macOS X 10.11 (El Capitan) and higher. This code should work with future version releases, too, although this may require some of the deep learning R software packages listed in Chapter 2, *Setting Up R for Deep Learning*, to be updated.

Hardware/software covered in the book	OS requirements
64-bit for Intel Mac	macOS X 10.11 (El Capitan) and higher
R version 3.6.3	macOS X 10.11 (El Capitan) and higher
R Studio Desktop 1.2.5033 (Orange Blossom 330255dd)	R version 3.0.1+

Once you have installed R (https://www.r-project.org) and R Studio Desktop (https://rstudio.com/products/rstudio/download/) on your computer, you should be ready to install the additional deep learning software packages outlined in Chapter 2, *Setting Up R for Deep Learning*.

If you are using the digital version of this book, we advise you to type the code yourself or access the code via the GitHub repository (link available in the next section). Doing so will help you avoid any potential errors related to the copying and pasting of code.

Download the example code files

You can download the example code files for this book from your account at www.packt.com. If you purchased this book elsewhere, you can visit www.packtpub.com/support and register to have the files emailed directly to you.

You can download the code files by following these steps:

1. Log in or register at www.packt.com.
2. Select the **Support** tab.
3. Click on **Code Downloads**.
4. Enter the name of the book in the **Search** box and follow the onscreen instructions.

Once the file is downloaded, please make sure that you unzip or extract the folder using the latest version of:

- WinRAR/7-Zip for Windows
- Zipeg/iZip/UnRarX for Mac
- 7-Zip/PeaZip for Linux

The code bundle for the book is also hosted on GitHub at https://github.com/ PacktPublishing/Hands-on-Deep-Learning-with-R. In case there's an update to the code, it will be updated on the existing GitHub repository.

We also have other code bundles from our rich catalog of books and videos available at https://github.com/PacktPublishing/. Check them out!

Download the color images

We also provide a PDF file that has color images of the screenshots/diagrams used in this book. You can download it here: https://static.packt-cdn.com/downloads/ 9781788996839_ColorImages.pdf

Conventions used

There are a number of text conventions used throughout this book.

CodeInText: Indicates code words in text, database table names, folder names, filenames, file extensions, pathnames, dummy URLs, user input, and Twitter handles. Here is an example: "The linear_fits function is then used again to draw one more line."

A block of code is set as follows:

```
linear_fits <- function(w, to_add = TRUE, line_type = 1) {curve(-w[1] /
w[2] * x - w[3] / w[2], xlim = c(-1, 2), ylim = c(-1, 2), col = "black",lty
= line_type, lwd = 2, xlab = "Input Value A", ylab = "Input Value B", add =
to_add)}
```

When we wish to draw your attention to a particular part of a code block, the relevant lines or items are set in bold:

```
results <- softmax(c(2,3,6,9))
results

[1] 0.0008658387 0.0023535935 0.0472731888 0.9495073791
```

Bold: Indicates a new term, an important word, or words that you see on screen. For example, words in menus or dialog boxes appear in the text like this. Here is an example: "One potential problem with ReLU is known as **dying ReLU**, where, since the function assigns a zero value to all negative values, signals can get dropped completely before reaching the output node."

Warnings or important notes appear like this.

Tips and tricks appear like this.

Get in touch

Feedback from our readers is always welcome.

General feedback: If you have questions about any aspect of this book, mention the book title in the subject of your message and email us at customercare@packtpub.com.

Errata: Although we have taken every care to ensure the accuracy of our content, mistakes do happen. If you have found a mistake in this book, we would be grateful if you would report this to us. Please visit www.packtpub.com/support/errata, selecting your book, clicking on the Errata Submission Form link, and entering the details.

Piracy: If you come across any illegal copies of our works in any form on the internet, we would be grateful if you would provide us with the location address or website name. Please contact us at copyright@packt.com with a link to the material.

If you are interested in becoming an author: If there is a topic that you have expertise in, and you are interested in either writing or contributing to a book, please visit authors.packtpub.com.

Reviews

Please leave a review. Once you have read and used this book, why not leave a review on the site that you purchased it from? Potential readers can then see and use your unbiased opinion to make purchase decisions. We at Packt can understand what you think about our products and our authors can see your feedback on their book. Thank you!

For more information about Packt, please visit `packt.com`.

Section 1: Deep Learning Basics

This section provides a brief overview of deep learning as it relates to machine learning. In this section of the book, you will learn how to get set up to do deep learning in R and build your first neural network, which is the building block of all the deep learning to follow.

This section comprises the following chapters:

- Chapter 1, *Machine Learning Basics*
- Chapter 2, *Setting Up R for Deep Learning*
- Chapter 3, *Artificial Neural Networks*

Machine Learning Basics **1**

Welcome to *Hands-On Deep Learning with R*! This book will take you through all of the steps that are necessary to code deep learning models using the R statistical programming language. It begins with simple examples as the first step for those just getting started, along with a review of the foundational elements of deep learning for those with more experience. As you progress through this book, you will learn how to code increasingly complex deep learning solutions for a wide variety of tasks. However, regardless of the complexity, each chapter will carefully detail each step. This is so that all topics and concepts can be fully comprehended and the reason for every line of code is completely explained.

In this chapter, we will go through a quick overview of the machine learning process as it will form a base for the subsequent chapters of this book. We will look at processing a dataset to review techniques such as handling outliers and missing values. We will learn how to model data to brush up on the process of predicting an outcome and evaluating the results, and we will also review the most suitable metrics for various problems. We will look at improving a model using parameter tuning, feature engineering, and ensembling, and we will learn when to use different machine learning algorithms based on the task to solve.

This chapter will cover the following topics:

- An overview of machine learning
- Preparing data for modeling
- Training a model on prepared data
- Evaluating model results
- Improving model results
- Reviewing different algorithms

An overview of machine learning

All deep learning is machine learning, but not all machine learning is deep learning. Throughout this book, we will focus on processes and techniques that are specific to deep learning in R. However, all the core principles of machine learning are essential to understand before we can move on to explore deep learning.

Deep learning is marked as a special subset of machine learning based on the use of neural networks that mimic brain activity behavior. The learning is referred to as being deep because, during the modeling process, the data is manipulated by a number of hidden layers. In this type of modeling, specific information is gathered from each layer. For example, one layer may find the edges of images while another finds particular hues.

Notable applications for this type of machine learning include the following:

- Image recognition (including facial recognition)
- Signal detection
- Recommendation systems
- Document summarization
- Topic modeling
- Forecasting
- Solving games
- Moving an object through space, for example, self-driving cars

All of these topics will be covered throughout the course of this book. All of these topics implement deep learning and neural networks, which are primarily used for classification and regression.

Preparing data for modeling

One of the benefits of deep learning is that it largely removes the need for feature engineering, which you may be used to with machine learning. That being said, the data still needs to be prepared before we begin modeling. Let's review the following goals to prepare data for modeling:

- Remove no-information and extremely low-information variables
- Identify dates and extract date parts
- Handle missing values
- Handle outliers

In this chapter, we will be investigating air quality data using data provided by the London Air Quality Network. Specifically, we will look at readings for nitrogen dioxide in the area of Tower Hamlets (Mile End Road) during 2018. This is a very small dataset with only a few features and approximately 35,000 observations. We are using a limited dataset here so that all of our code, even our modeling, runs quickly. That said, the dataset fits well for the process that we will explore. It requires some, but not an inordinate amount of, initial cleaning and preparation. In addition to this, it is suitable to use for decision tree-based modeling, which will be a useful form of machine learning to review as we start to apply deep learning models in future chapters.

Our first step will be to do some cursory data exploration to see what data cleaning and preparation steps will be necessary. R has some really helpful convenience packages for this type of exploratory data analysis. Let's do a quick review by looking at some important areas of exploratory data analysis using the following series of code blocks:

1. We will start by loading our data and libraries. To do this, we will use the base R `library()` function to load all of the libraries that we will need. If there are any libraries listed that you do not have installed, use the `install.packages()` function to install these libraries. We will also use the `read_csv()` function from the `readr` package to load in the data. We load libraries and data using the following code:

   ```
   library(tidyverse)
   library(lubridate)
   library(xgboost)
   library(Metrics)
   library(DataExplorer)
   library(caret)
   la_no2 <- readr::read_csv("data/LondonAir_TH_MER_NO2.csv")
   ```

   Packages are included before the functions are called; therefore, this gives us an understanding of where and why each package is being used. As shown in the preceding code block, the following packages will be used in this chapter:

   - `tidyverse`: This suite of packages will be used extensively. In this case, the `dplyr` package is used in this chapter for data wrangling, for instance, looking at aggregate values or adding and removing columns and rows.
   - `lubridate`: This will be used to easily extract details from a column holding values with a date data type.
   - `xgboost`: This will be the model that we will use for our data.

- `Metrics`: This will be used to evaluate our model.
- `DataExplorer`: This will be used for generating exploratory data analysis plots.
- `caret`: This will be used when tuning our model as it provides a convenient method for performing a grid search of hyperparameters.

2. Next, we will view the structure of the data using the `str` function, which provides details on the data object class and dimensions and column-specific details on the data type, along with some sample values, as shown in the following code:

```
utils::str(la_no2)
```

After running the code, we will see the following printed to our console:

```
> utils::str(la_no2)
Classes 'tbl_df', 'tbl' and 'data.frame':        35040 obs. of  6 variables:
 $ Site                 : chr  "TH2" "TH2" "TH2" "TH2" ...
 $ Species              : chr  "NO2" "NO2" "NO2" "NO2" ...
 $ ReadingDateTime      : chr  "01/01/2018 00:00" "01/01/2018 00:15" "01/0
:45" ...
 $ Value                : num  28 28 28 28 29.2 29.2 29.2 29.2 25.7 25.7 .
 $ Units                : chr  "ug m-3" "ug m-3" "ug m-3" "ug m-3" ...
 $ Provisional or Ratified: chr  "R" "R" "R" "R" ...
```

3. All of this data is from the same site, with readings for the same species of pollutants, and we can conclude that the unit of measure will likely be consistent throughout as well. If this is the case, we can remove these columns as they provide no informational value. Even if we did not know the first variable would always be the same, we can start to see this pattern from the results of the structure (`str`) function. We can confirm that this is the case, though, by running the following code, using the `group_by` and `summarise` functions from the `dplyr` package:

```
la_no2 %>% dplyr::group_by(Units, Site, Species) %>%
dplyr::summarise(count = n())
```

After running the preceding code, we will see the following printed to our console:

```
> la_no2 %>% dplyr::group_by(Units, Site, Species) %>% dplyr::summarise(count = n())
# A tibble: 1 x 4
# Groups:   Units, Site [?]
  Units Site  Species count
  <chr> <chr> <chr>   <int>
1 ug m-3 TH2   NO2     35040
```

We have confirmed that the `Site`, `Species`, and `Units` values are always the same, so we can remove them from the data as they will provide no information. We can also see that the actual reading values are stored as character strings and we have dates stored that way as well. In its current form, the `date` field exhibits a characteristic known as high cardinality, which is to say that there are a large number of unique values. When we see this, we will usually want to act on these types of columns so that they have fewer distinct values. In this case, the technique is clear because we know that this should be a date value.

4. In the code that follows, we will use the `dplyr select` function to remove the columns that we don't want to keep. We will use the `dplyr mutate` function along with functions from the `lubridate` package to transform the variables we have identified. After transforming the data, we can remove the old character string date column and the full date column as we will use the atomized date values going forward. We remove the columns we don't need and break the converted date field into its component parts using the following code:

```
la_no2 <- la_no2 %>%
dplyr::select(c(-Site,-Species,-Units)) %>%
  dplyr::mutate(
    Value = as.numeric(Value),
    reading_date = lubridate::dmy_hm(ReadingDateTime),
    reading_year = lubridate::year(reading_date),
    reading_month = lubridate::month(reading_date),
    reading_day = lubridate::day(reading_date),
    reading_hour = lubridate::hour(reading_date),
    reading_minute = lubridate::minute(reading_date)
  ) %>%
  dplyr::select(c(-ReadingDateTime, -reading_date))
```

Before running the preceding code, we should note that the dataframe in our **Environment** pane looks like the following screenshot:

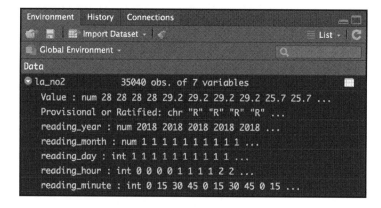

After running the code, we can note the differences to the dataframe, which should now look like the following screenshot:

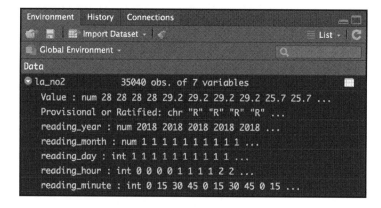

As you can see, the columns that contained only one value have been removed, and the data column now occupies five columns with one for each of the date and time parts.

5. Next, we will use the `DataExplorer` package to explore any missing values. There are numerous ways in which we summarize the number and proportion of missing values in a given data object. Of these, the `plot_missing()` function offers a count and percentage of missing values along with a visualization—all from one function call. We plot missing values using the following line of code:

```
DataExplorer::plot_missing(la_no2)
```

After running this code, a plot is produced. In your **Viewer** pane, you should see the following plot:

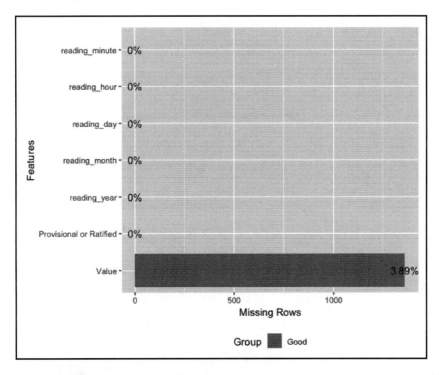

As you can see, there are no missing values among the independent variables. However, among the target variable class, there are around 1,500 missing values, accounting for 3.89% of the column.

6. Since we have missing values, we should consider whether any action should be taken. In this case, we will simply remove these rows as there are not many of them, and the portion of the data with no missing values will still be representative of the entire dataset. While, in this case, the values are simply removed, there are a number of options available to handle missing values. A summary of possible actions is presented later on in this chapter. To remove the rows with missing values, we run the following line of code:

```
la_no2 <- la_no2 %>% filter(!is.na(Value))
```

7. We will also run a check on our discrete variable as well just to see the distribution of values among the categories present in this column. Again, the `DataExplorer` package offers a convenient function for this, which will provide a plot for the discrete values present noting the frequency of each. We generate this plot with the `plot_bar` function using the following line of code:

```
DataExplorer::plot_bar(la_no2)
```

After running the preceding function, we are able to view the following visualization, which clearly shows that there are more **Ratified** results than **Provisional** results. From reading the documentation for this dataset, the **Ratified** results are verified and can be trusted to be accurate, while the **Provisional** results may not be as accurate. Let's take a look at the output:

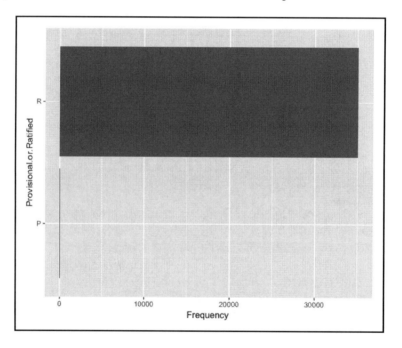

We created a plot in order to quickly see the distribution of values among the discrete terms in the **Provisional or Ratified** column. We can also create a table using the following code to get more specific details:

```
la_no2 %>% dplyr::group_by(`Provisional or Ratified`) %>%
dplyr::summarise(count = n())
```

The preceding code uses the group_by function to group rows based on the values present in the Provisional or Ratified column. It then uses the summarise function, along with setting the count argument equal to n(), to calculate the number of rows containing each of the discrete values from the Provisional or Ratified column. Running the preceding code will print the output to your console, as follows:

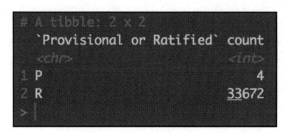

8. Since there are very few values marked as Provisional, we will just remove these rows. To do so, we will first use the filter function, which is used to remove rows based on a particular condition. In this case, we will filter the data so that only rows with an 'R' value in the Provisional or Ratified column will remain, as shown here:

```
la_no2 <- la_no2 %>%
  dplyr::filter(
    `Provisional or Ratified` == 'R'
  )
```

9. Next, we will remove the Provisional or Ratified column since it only holds one unique value. To do this, we will use the select() function, which is used to remove columns in a similar way to how a filter is used to remove rows. Here, the select() function is called and the argument passed to the function is -`Provisional or Ratified`, which will remove this column. Alternatively, all of the other column names, aside from Provisional or Ratified, could be passed in as an argument. The select() function works by either using the columns to include or the columns to exclude. In this case, it is faster to note the column to exclude, which is why this choice was made. Please refer to the following code:

```
la_no2 <- la_no2 %>%
  dplyr::select(-`Provisional or Ratified`)
```

10. Earlier, we noted that all of our data is from the year 2018. Now that our date data is broken up into component parts, we should only see one value in the `reading_year` column. One way to test whether this is the case is to use the `range()` function. We check for the minimum and maximum values in the `reading_year` column by running the following code:

```
range(la_no2$reading_year)
```

Running the preceding code will result in values being printed to our console. Your console should look like this:

We can see from the results of our call to the `range()` function that, in fact, the `reading_year` column only includes one value. With this being the case, we can use the `select()` function to remove the `reading_year` column with the help of the following code:

```
la_no2 <- la_no2 %>%
  dplyr::select(-reading_year)
```

11. Next, we can do a histogram check of continuous variables to look for outliers. To accomplish this, we will once again use the `DataExplorer` package. This time, we will use the `plot_histogram` function to visualize the continuous values for all of the columns with these types of values, as shown in the following code block:

```
DataExplorer::plot_histogram(la_no2)
```

After running the preceding code, five plots are generated displaying the frequency for continuous values among the five columns that have these types of values. Your **Viewer** pane should look like the following:

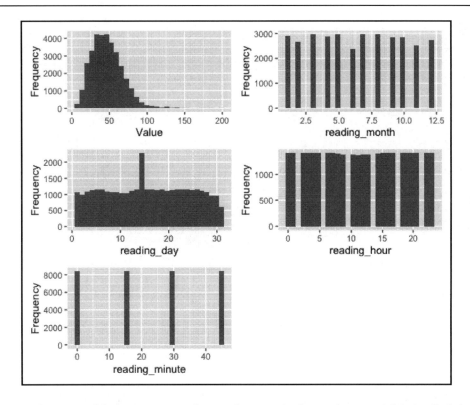

In the preceding output, we do see that our independent variable is slightly right-skewed, and, as a result, we could take some action on the outlier values. If there was a more dramatic skew, then we could apply a log transformation. As there are not many, we could also remove these values if we thought they were noisy. However, for now, we will just leave them in the data. If, in the end, our model is performing poorly, then it would be worthwhile to perform some outlier treatment to see whether this improves performance.

12. Lastly, let's do a correlation check. We will again use the `DataExplorer` package, and this time we will use the `plot_correlation()` function. To generate a correlation plot, we run the following line of code:

```
DataExplorer::plot_correlation(la_no2)
```

Running the preceding line of code will generate a plot. The plot uses blue and red colors to denote negative and positive correlations, respectively. These colors will not be present in the diagram in this book; however, you can still see the correlation values. After running the preceding code, you will see a plot in your **Viewer** pane, which looks like the following:

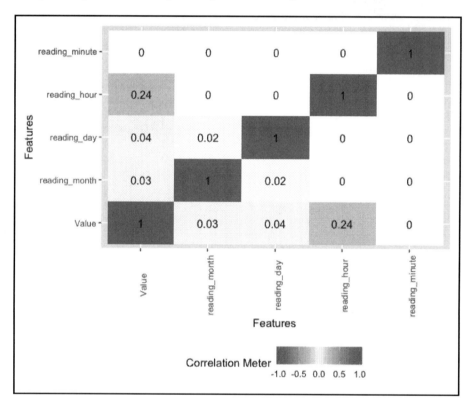

From this plot, we can see that the pollutant value does have some correlation with the `reading_hour` feature, and less correlation with the `reading_day` and `reading_month` features, suggesting that there is a higher trend throughout the day for when this pollutant is being produced than in the week, month, or year. The main objective of this plot is to look for independent variables that are highly correlated as it might suggest that these variables are conveying the same information, and, in that case, we may want to remove one or combine them in some way.

We now have a dataset that is properly preprocessed and ready for modeling. The correlation plot shows that the variables are not significantly correlated. Of course, this is not surprising as the remaining variables simply describe discrete moments in time.

The date value was converted from a string that provided no informational value to a date value further split into date parts represented as numeric data. All columns that contained only one value were removed as they provided no information. The few rows marked as provisional values were removed since there were not many of these, and, in the description of the data, there were warnings about the validity of pollutant measures marked this way. Lastly, rows containing null values for the predictor variable were removed. This was done because there were not many of these; however, there are other tactics we could have taken in this situation. We have noted them in the following section.

Handling missing values

In the preprocessing work that we just completed, we decided to remove missing values. This is an option when there are very few cases that contain missing values and, in this example, this was true. However, other situations may require different approaches to handling missing values. Here are some common options in addition to deleting rows and columns:

- **Imputation with a measure of centrality (mean/median/mode)**: Use one of the measures of centrality to fill in the missing values. This can work well if you have normally distributed numeric data. Modal imputation can also be used on non-numeric data by selecting the most frequent value to replace the missing values.
- **Tweak for the missing values**: You can use the known values to impute the missing values. Examples of this approach include using regression with linear data or the **k-nearest neighbor (KNN)** algorithm to assign a value based on similarity to known values in the feature space.
- **Replace it with a constant value**: The missing value can also be replaced with a constant value outside the range of values present or not already present in the categorical data. The advantage here is that it will become clear later on whether these missing values have any informational value, as they will be clearly set to the side. This is in contrast to imputing with a measure of centrality where the final result will be some missing values now containing the imputed value, while some equal values will have actually already been present in the data. In this case, it becomes difficult to know which values were missing values and which were the values already present in the data.

Training a model on prepared data

Now that the data is ready, we will split it into train and test sets and run a simple model. The objective at this point is not to try to achieve the best performance, but rather to get some type of a benchmark result to use in the future as we try to improve our model.

Train and test data

When we build predictive models, we need to create two separate sets of data with the help of the following segments. One is used by the model to learn the task and the other is used to test how well the model learned the task. Here are the types of data that we will look at:

- **Train data**: The segment of the data used to fit the model. The model has access to the explainer variables or independent variables, which are the selected columns, to describe a record in your data, as well as the target variable or dependent variable. That is the value we are trying to predict during the training process using this dataset. This segment should usually be between 50% and 80% of your total data.

- **Test data**: The segment of the data used to evaluate the model results. The model should never have access to this data during the learning process and should never see the target variable. This dataset is used to test what the model has learned about the dependent variables. After fitting our model during the training phase, we now use this model to predict values on the test set. During this phase, only we have the correct answers; the independent variable, that is, the model, never has access to these values. After the model makes its predictions, we can evaluate how well the model performed by comparing the predicted values to the actual correct values.

- **Validation data**: Validation data is a portion of the training dataset that the model uses to refine hyperparameters. As the varying values are selected for the hyperparameters, the model makes checks against the validation set and uses the results gathered during this process to select the values for the hyperparameters that produce the best performing models.

- **Cross-validation**: One potential issue that can arise when we use only one train and test set is that the model will learn about specific descriptive features that are particular to this segment of the data. What the model learns may not generalize well when applied to other data in the future. This is known as overfitting. To mitigate this problem, we can use a process known as cross-validation. In a simple example, we can do an 80/20 split of the data where 20% is held for test data and we can model and test on this split. We can then create a separate 80/20 split and do the same modeling and testing. We can repeat this process 5 times with 5 different test sets—each composed of a different fifth of the data. This exact type of cross-validation is known as 5-fold cross-validation. After all of the iterations are completed, we can check whether the results are consistent for each. And, if so, we can feel more confident that our model is not overfitting and use this to generalize on more data.

Choosing an algorithm

For this task, we will use `xgboost`, which is a very popular implementation of the gradient tree boosting algorithm. The reason this works so well is that each model iteration learns from the results of the previous model. This model uses boosting for iterative learning in contrast to bagging. Both of these ensembling techniques can be used to compensate for a known weakness in tree-based learners, which has to do with overfitting to the training data.

One simple difference between bagging and boosting is that, with bagging, full trees are grown and then the results are averaged, while, with boosting, each iteration of the tree model learns from the model before it. This is an important concept, as this idea of an algorithm that incorporates an additive function with information gained after modeling on the residuals of the previous model will be used in deep learning as we move forward.

Here, we will explore the power of this type of machine learning algorithm on this simple example. Additionally, we will pay particular attention to how what we learn here is relevant for more complex examples in the subsequent chapters. We will use the following code to train an `xgboost` model:

1. We start the process of fitting a model to our data by partitioning our data into train and test sets, using the following code:

```
set.seed(1)
partition <- sample(nrow(la_no2), 0.75*nrow(la_no2), replace=FALSE)
train <- la_no2[partition,]
test <- la_no2[-partition,]
```

```
target <- train$Value

dtrain <- xgboost::xgb.DMatrix(data = as.matrix(train), label=
target)
dtest <- xgboost::xgb.DMatrix(data = as.matrix(test))
```

In the preceding code, we started with the `set.seed()` function. This is because aspects of this modeling process involve pseudorandomness, and setting the seed ensures that the same values are used for these elements every time, so we can consistently produce the same results.

We split the data into training data, which we will model on, and a test set to check whether our predictions are accurate. We do this by getting a random sample of row index values, which we store in the vector labeled `partition`, and use them to subset our data. In addition, after partitioning, we split out the target variable and store this in a vector.

Then, we convert our data into a dense matrix so that it is in the proper format to be passed to the `xgboost` algorithm.

2. Following this, we will create a list of parameters. Some of these values are required for the analysis that we will be doing and others are just starting values chosen arbitrarily. For those values, later on, we will look at ways to more scientifically choose them. We prepare our initial parameter list using the following code:

```
params <-list(
   objective = "reg:linear",
   booster = "gbtree",
   eval_metric = "rmse",
   eta=0.1,
   subsample=0.8,
   colsample_bytree=0.75,
   print_every_n = 10,
   verbose = TRUE
)
```

In the preceding code, the required values in this list include the following:

- `objective = "reg:linear"`: This is used to define the task objective as linear regression. Here, we are conducting a regression task seeking the value of nitrogen dioxide.
- `booster = "gbtree"`: This tells us that we will use gradient tree boosting to choose the best model for predicting results.

- `eval_metric = "rmse"`: This tells us that we will use the **Root Mean Squared Error (RMSE)** to evaluate the success of our model. Later on, we will look at why this is the most appropriate choice, along with some of the other options we can use here for other tasks.

Next, these are the variables where we are arbitrarily choosing starting values:

- `eta=0.1`: This is used to define the learning rate. To begin, it makes sense to use a larger number; however, as we move forward, we will want to use a smaller learning rate and additional rounds to improve performance.
- `subsample=0.8`: This tells us that, for each tree, we will use 80% of the rows from the data.
- `col_subsample=0.75`: This tells us that, for each tree, we will use 75% of the columns from the data.

These are the parameters that do not impact the model and only impact how we review the results of the model:

- `print_every_n = 10`: This is used to state that the evaluation scores should be printed after every 10 rounds.
- `verbose = TRUE`: This is used to denote that the evaluation scores should be printed to the console so that they can be seen by the end user during the model run.

3. Now that we have the parameters defined, we will run the model using the following code:

```
xgb <- xgboost::xgb.train(
  params = params,
  data = dtrain,
  nrounds = 100
)
```

When we run the model, we bring in the list of parameters that we previously defined, that is, the model should be run against the training dataset and we choose to run the model for 100 rounds. This means that we will grow 100 trees. This is, again, an arbitrary value. Later, we will look at ways to discover the optimal number of rounds. Then, we predict the test dataset using the model that we just defined. For our train dataset, the algorithm knows the correct value and uses this to adjust the model.

4. In the next section, we will apply the model to the test data where the model no longer has access to the correct values, and, without this knowledge, the model uses the independent variables to make predictions for the target variable. Please refer to the following code block:

```
pred <- predict(xgb, dtest)
```

When we run the preceding code, we take the data from the dense matrix, labeled `dtest`, and run it through our model labeled `xgb`. The model takes the tree splits that were calculated during training and applies them to the new data to make predictions. The predictions are stored in a vector called `pred`.

5. Lastly, we will use the RMSE function to check model performance. For this evaluation metric, the closer it is to zero, the better, as this is a measure of the difference between true values and predicted values. To evaluate the performance of our model, we run the following line of code:

```
Metrics::rmse(test$Value,XGBpred)
```

After running the preceding code, we will see a value printed to our console. Your console should look like the following output:

```
> Metrics::rmse(test$Value,pred)
[1] 0.05389282
```

From our quick and simple model, we have achieved an RMSE score of 0.054. Soon, we will make some changes to the model parameters to try to improve our score. Before that, let's take a quick look at all of the different evaluation metrics that we can use in addition to RMSE while also taking a deep dive into explaining how RMSE works.

Evaluating model results

We only know whether a model is successful if we can measure it, and it is worthwhile taking a moment to remember which metrics to use in which scenarios. Take, for example, a credit card fraud dataset where there is a large imbalance in the target variable because there will only be a, relatively, few cases of fraud among many non-fraudulent cases.

If we use a metric that just measures the percentage of the target variable that we predict successfully, then we will not be evaluating our model in a very helpful way. In this case, to keep the math simple, let's imagine we have 10,000 cases and only 10 of them are fraudulent accounts. If we predict that all cases are not fraudulent, then we will have 99.9% accuracy. This is very accurate, but it is not very helpful. Here is a review of the different metrics and when to use them.

Machine learning metrics

Choosing the wrong metric will make it very difficult to evaluate performance and, as a result, improve our model. Therefore, it is very important to choose the right metric. Let's take a look at the following machine learning metrics:

- **Accuracy**: The simplest evaluation metric is accuracy. Accuracy measures the difference between the predicted value and the actual value. This metric is easy to interpret and communicate; however, as we mentioned earlier, it doesn't measure performance well when used to evaluate a highly unbalanced target variable, for example.
- **Confusion Matrix**: The confusion matrix provides a convenient way to display classification accuracy along with Type I and Type II errors. The combined view of these four related metrics can be especially informative in deciding where to focus our efforts during the tuning process. It can also help mark cases where other metrics may be more helpful. When there are too many values in the majority class, then a metric that is designed for use with class imbalances, such as log-loss, should be employed.
- **Mean Absolute Error** (**MAE**): This metric takes the difference between the predicted value and the actual value and calculates the mean value of these errors. This metric is simple to interpret and is useful when there is no need to apply an additional penalty to large errors. If an error that is three times larger than another error is three times as bad, then this is a good metric to use. However, there are many cases where an error that is three times larger than another error is much more than three times as bad, and this results in adding an additional penalty, which can be accomplished with the next metric.
- **RMSE**: This metric takes the square of the error for every prediction, the difference between the predicted value and the actual value, sums these squared errors, and then takes the square root of the sums. In this case, if the squaring has even a few highly inaccurate predictions, it will result in a sizable penalty and a higher value on this error metric. We can see how this would help in our preceding example and why we have chosen to use RMSE. This metric is used for regression.

- **Area Under the Curve** (**AUC**): The AUC refers to the *Area under the Receiver-Operator Curve*. In this model, your target variable needs to be a value expressing the confidence or probability that a row belongs to the positive or negative target condition. To make this more concrete, AUC can be used when your task is to predict how likely someone is to make a given purchase. Clearly, from this explanation, we can see that AUC is a metric for classification.
- **Logarithmic Loss** (**Log-Loss**): The log-loss evaluation metric rewards confident predictions more than AUC and penalizes neutral predictions. This is important when we have an imbalanced target dataset and finding the minority class is critical. Having an extra penalty on incorrect guesses helps us get to the model that better predicts these minority class members correctly. Log-loss is also better for multiclass models where the target variable is not binary.

Improving model results

Since we have a regression problem, we now know why we chose RMSE, and we have a baseline metric of performance, we can begin to work on improving our model. Every model will have its own different way of improving results; however, we can generalize slightly. Feature engineering helps to improve model performance; however, since this type of work is less important with deep learning, we will not focus on that here. Also, we have already used feature engineering to generate our date and time parts. In addition, we can run our model for longer at a slower learning rate and we can tune hyperparameters. In order to find the best values using this type of model improvement method, we will use a technique called **grid search** to look at a range of values for a number of different fields.

Let's search for the optimal number of rounds. Using the cross-validation version of `xgboost` through the R interface, we can train our model again on our default hyperparameter settings. This time, instead of choosing 100 rounds, we will use the functionality within `xgboost` to determine the optimal number of trees to grow. Using cross-validation, the model can evaluate the error rate at the end of every round, and we will use the `early_stopping_rounds` feature so that the model stops growing additional trees after a given number of attempts, when it no longer continues to decrease the error rate.

Let's take a look at the following code, which determines the number of rounds or number of trees that produces the lowest error rate given the default setting:

```
xgb_cv <- xgboost::xgb.cv(
  params = params,
  data = dtrain,
  nrounds = 10000,
```

```
nfold = 5,
showsd = T,
stratified = T,
print_every_n = 100,
early_stopping_rounds = 25,
maximize = F)
```

After we run the preceding code, we will see model performance metrics printing to the console as the model runs. The beginning of this report on the console should look like the following screenshot:

```
[1]      train-rmse:45.919647+0.063184    test-rmse:45.919886+0.256939
Multiple eval metrics are present. Will use test_rmse for early stopping.
Will train until test_rmse hasn't improved in 25 rounds.

[101]    train-rmse:0.063975+0.000527    test-rmse:0.068940+0.000908
[201]    train-rmse:0.042611+0.000869    test-rmse:0.046707+0.001828
[301]    train-rmse:0.031549+0.000307    test-rmse:0.035700+0.001520
[401]    train-rmse:0.024728+0.000432    test-rmse:0.028956+0.001782
[501]    train-rmse:0.019792+0.000269    test-rmse:0.024302+0.001766
[601]    train-rmse:0.015852+0.000179    test-rmse:0.020667+0.001924
[701]    train-rmse:0.012949+0.000287    test-rmse:0.018038+0.002138
[801]    train-rmse:0.010725+0.000294    test-rmse:0.016161+0.002342
```

Here, we can see that our model performance is improving rapidly, and we have confirmation that our model will stop training when the model hasn't improved for 25 rounds.

When your model reaches the optimal number of runs, your console should look like the following screenshot:

```
[2701]   train-rmse:0.000920+0.000042    test-rmse:0.010240+0.003410
[2801]   train-rmse:0.000876+0.000035    test-rmse:0.010233+0.003413
[2901]   train-rmse:0.000840+0.000031    test-rmse:0.010225+0.003415
[3001]   train-rmse:0.000818+0.000028    test-rmse:0.010221+0.003417
[3101]   train-rmse:0.000798+0.000025    test-rmse:0.010218+0.003418
[3201]   train-rmse:0.000782+0.000023    test-rmse:0.010214+0.003420
Stopping. Best iteration:
[3205]   train-rmse:0.000781+0.000023    test-rmse:0.010214+0.003420
```

Here, we can see that the model performance is improving more slowly and that the model has stopped because it was no longer improving. The report that is printed out to the console also identifies the best performing round.

Breaking down everything that is happening in the preceding example, we again train an `xgboost` model on the same data with the same parameters as we did previously. However, we set the number of rounds to be much higher. In order to find the best iteration, we need enough rounds so that the model doesn't stop growing trees before finding the optimal number of trees. In this case, the best iteration occurs at around 3,205; so, if we had set the number of rounds at 1,000, for example, the modeling process would have completed after growing 1,000 trees. However, we still would not know the number of rounds that produces the lowest error rate, which is why we set the number of rounds to be so high.

The following is the list of settings being used in the preceding code. Let's take a look at the purpose of using each of these settings:

- `nfold`: This is the number of folds or how many partitions to make in the data for cross-validation. Here, we use 5, which utilizes the alternating 80/20 split referenced earlier.
- `showsd`: This shows the standard deviation in order to note the variation among the results from the different combinations of folds. This is important to ensure the model works well on all sets of data and will generalize well when used on future data.
- `stratified`: This ensures that each fold of data contains the same proportion of the target class.
- `print_every_n`: This tells us how often to print the results of the cross-validation to the console.
- `early_stopping_rounds`: This is a value that decides when the model should stop growing trees. You can use this value to check whether performance has improved during the given number of rounds. The process will stop when the model no longer improves while growing trees to the limit of rounds set.
- `maximize`: This notes whether the evaluation metric is one where improvement involves maximizing the score or minimizing the score.

Now, let's do a grid search on select hyperparameters. As the name implies, a grid search will model for all defined hyperparameter value combinations. Using this technique, we can adjust a few settings that will control how the model grows trees and then evaluate which settings provide the best performance. A complete list of all of the tunable hyperparameters for `xgboost` is included with the package documentation. For this example, we will focus on the following three hyperparameters:

- `max_depth`: This is the maximum depth of the tree. Since we only have 4 features, we will try depths of 2, 3, and 4.
- `gamma`: This is the minimum loss reduction needed to continue creating splits. Setting this level higher will create shallower trees as nodes that contribute less to reducing the error rate are not further divided. We will try values of 0, 0.5, and 1.
- `min_child_weight`: This is the number of instances needed to grow a node. If there are fewer instances than the threshold, then the tree will discontinue partitioning from this node. The higher this number, the more shallow trees that will be grown. For this example, we will try values of 1, 3, and 5.

We will now go through all the code required to perform a grid search to tune our parameters to the optimal values in order to improve model performance:

1. Our first step will be to define our search grid by assigning the vector of values, mentioned previously, to their respective hyperparameter within the parameter grid. We define the values we will try for our hyperparameters by running the following code:

```
xgb_grid <- expand.grid(
  nrounds = 500,
  eta = 0.01,
  max_depth = c(2,3,4),
  gamma = c(0,0.5,1),
  colsample_bytree = 0.75,
  min_child_weight = c(1,3,5),
  subsample = 0.8
)
```

As shown in the preceding code, for expediency, we will set the number of rounds to 500. Though, you could use the rounds found by searching for the best iteration previously in a real-world situation.

When including `eta` in your grid search, also remember to include `nrounds` as you will need more rounds as the learning rate decreases.

2. After this, we will use the `trainControl` function within `caret` to define how we want to handle this parameter search. For this, we will list the code and then walk through the settings selected. There are many additional settings for `trainControl`; however, we are focusing on a select few for this chapter. We set how we will train our model using the following code:

```
xgb_tc = caret::trainControl(
  method = "cv",
  number = 5,
  search = "grid",
  returnResamp = "final",
  savePredictions = "final",
  verboseIter = TRUE,
  allowParallel = TRUE
)
```

The `method` and `number` parameters for this function simply define our cross-validation strategy, which will be 5-fold again, as used previously. We will use a grid search to go through all possible combinations among the parameter settings defined in the last section of code. The next two parameters are used to save the resample and prediction details for the best iteration after modeling on all combinations. Lastly, we set `verboseIter` to TRUE to print iteration details to the console, and `allowParallel` is set to TRUE to use parallel processing to increase computational speed.

3. With the grid search values in place and the search strategy defined, we now run the model again using every possible hyperparameter combination. We then train our model while employing a grid search of our hyperparameters using the settings from the first two steps:

```
xgb_param_tune = caret::train(
  x = dtrain,
  y = target,
  trControl = xgb_tc,
  tuneGrid = xgb_grid,
  method = "xgbTree",
  verbose = TRUE
)
```

After running this code, we will see a report printing to our console that is similar to when we ran our model the first time. Your console should look like the following screenshot:

```
+ Fold5: eta=0.01, max_depth=4, gamma=1.0, colsample_bytree=0.75, min_child_weight=1, subsample=0.8, nro
unds=500
- Fold5: eta=0.01, max_depth=4, gamma=1.0, colsample_bytree=0.75, min_child_weight=1, subsample=0.8, nro
unds=500
+ Fold5: eta=0.01, max_depth=4, gamma=1.0, colsample_bytree=0.75, min_child_weight=3, subsample=0.8, nro
unds=500
- Fold5: eta=0.01, max_depth=4, gamma=1.0, colsample_bytree=0.75, min_child_weight=3, subsample=0.8, nro
unds=500
+ Fold5: eta=0.01, max_depth=4, gamma=1.0, colsample_bytree=0.75, min_child_weight=5, subsample=0.8, nro
unds=500
- Fold5: eta=0.01, max_depth=4, gamma=1.0, colsample_bytree=0.75, min_child_weight=5, subsample=0.8, nro
unds=500
Aggregating results
Selecting tuning parameters
Fitting nrounds = 500, max_depth = 4, eta = 0.01, gamma = 0, colsample_bytree = 0.75, min_child_weight =
1, subsample = 0.8 on full training set
```

The report shows the current fold and current parameter setting as the model goes through all combinations on all five different splits of the data. In the preceding screenshot, we see a test of all `min_child_weight` options holding everything else constant on the fifth split of the data. In the end, we see the best tuning parameters being selected.

In this situation, the best depth is using all of the features, which is not surprising given the lack of features. The best minimum child weight is 1, which means that even sparsely populated nodes still hold important information for our model. The best gamma value is 0, which is the default value. As this value rises, it places a slight constraint on the error rate improvement needed by each node before splitting. In this case, after our grid search, we are largely left with the default values; yet, we can see the process by which we would choose alternatives to these defaults if they helped to improve model performance.

4. Now that we know the best hyperparameter settings, we can plug them back into the model that we ran before and see whether there is any improvement. We train our model using the parameters and iteration count that we found optimizes performance by running the following code:

```
params <-list(
    objective = "reg:linear",
    booster = "gbtree",
    eval_metric = "rmse",
    eta=0.01,
```

```
        subsample=0.8,
        colsample_bytree=0.75,
        max_depth = 4,
        min_child_weight = 1,
        gamma = 1
    )
xgb <- xgboost::xgb.train(
    params = params,
    data = dtrain,
    nrounds = 3162,
    print_every_n = 10,
    verbose = TRUE,
    maximize = FALSE
)

pred <- stats::predict(xgb, dtest)
Metrics::rmse(test$Value,pred)
```

When we run the preceding code, we train our model and make predictions, like we did earlier, and we also run the line of code to calculate the RMSE value. When we run this line, we will see a value printed to our console. Your console should look like the following screenshot:

```
> Metrics::rmse(test$Value,pred)
[1] 0.02155505
```

From the results of calculating the error rate, we can see that the score has changed from 0.054 to 0.022, which is an improvement from our first attempt. Using this data, with limited features, we may think that a time series model would have been a better choice; however, with only 1 year of data, a time series approach wouldn't catch any late seasonality effects that are not already present. This type of modeling creates a map for future years and shows that missing data can be predicted by simply using the date and time values for known data. This means that we can estimate NO2 values for future years. After collecting several years of data, a time series approach could then be used to make predictions that take into account year over year trends, in addition to the seasonality information captured here.

We used xgboost, which is a popular tree boosting algorithm, to predict pollution levels in an area of London. Earlier, we walked through creating a simple model to establish a benchmark. We then looked at how we should measure performance. Then, we took steps that improved performance. While we selected xgboost for this task, there are other machine learning algorithms that we could choose from, which we will review next.

Reviewing different algorithms

We have raced through machine learning relatively quickly, as we wanted to focus on the underlying concepts that will follow along with us as we head into deep learning. As such, we cannot offer a comprehensive explanation of all machine learning techniques; however, we will quickly review the different algorithm types here, as this will be helpful to remember going forward.

We'll do a quick review of the following machine learning algorithms:

- **Decision Trees**: A decision tree is a simple model that makes up the base learners of many more complex algorithms. A decision tree simply splits a dataset at a given variable and notes the proportion of the target class that exists in the splits. For example, if we were to predict who is more likely to enjoy playing with baby toys, then a split on age would likely show that the split of the data containing just those under the age of 3 has a high percentage of true results in the `target` variable, that is, a high proportion that does enjoy this type of activity, while those who are older would likely not enjoy this.

- **Random Forests**: Random forests are similar to `xgboost`, which was used in this brief machine learning overview. A notable distinction between random forests and `xgboost` is that random forests build full decision trees. This makes up the set of base learners. The results from these simple base learner models are then averaged together to arrive at predictions that are better than any base learner. This technique is known as bagging. In contrast, `xgboost` uses boosting, which includes what it has learned from building previous base learners as it applies additional decision trees to the data. While both are useful and powerful ways to ensemble results and improve performance, we have chosen to focus on `xgboost` in this example because this idea of carrying forward information learned from the previous iteration is also present in deep learning.

- **Logistic Regression and Support Vector Machines (SVM)**: SVMs separate features in n-dimensional space with a line that is the farthest from the two closest points in that space. This boundary is then applied to the test data and points on one side are classified one way, while points on the other are classified as a member of the other class. This is similar to logistic regression, with the main difference being that logistic regression evaluates all data points, while SVM just includes the points nearest to the line used to split the data. In addition, logistic regression works better when there are fewer explainer variables, and SVM works better when the dataset contains a larger number of dimensions. SVM will seek to find a line that divides all features, while logistic regression will use a combination of best-fitting, but not perfect, lines to estimate the probability that a data point belongs to a particular member of the target variable.

- **KNN and k-means**: These are two ways to create clusters within our data. KNN is a supervised learning technique. Using this method, the model plots the points on a *k*-dimensional feature space. When new points are introduced during the training process, the model identifies the class for the nearest neighbors to the new point and assigns this class to this record. By contrast, *k*-means is an unsupervised learning technique that finds centroids in the feature space such that *k* clusters can be created where each point is classified based on the minimum distance to a given centroid.
- **GBM and LightGBM**: Aside from `xgboost`, GBM and LightGBM also provide a means to generate predictions using a boosting mechanism for improving model performance between iterations. **Gradient Boosting Machines (GBM)** is the precursor to `xgboost` and LightGBM. It largely operates the same way by using a boosting ensemble technique on decision tree base learners; however, it is more primitive in its approach. GBM grows full trees using all features, while `xgboost` and LightGBM have different ways to reduce the number of splits that take place, which speed up how fast trees can be grown.

The biggest difference between `xgboost` and LightGBM is that, where `xgboost` grows a new level for every tree after computing the feature splits, LightGBM will just grow the level below the most predictive leaf. This leaf-wise splitting offers superior speed advantages over the level-wise splitting used by `xgboost`. Also, with the focus on single leaf splits, the model can better find the values that minimize error compared with splitting into entire levels, which can lead to better performance. LightGBM may overtake `xgboost` as the go-to model for practitioners; however, for now, `xgboost` is still more widely used, which is why it was selected for this brief overview.

Summary

In this chapter, we referred to a raw dataset, explored the data, and took the necessary preprocessing steps to get the data ready for modeling. We performed data type transformations to convert numbers and dates being stored as character strings into numeric and date value columns, respectively. In addition, we performed some feature engineering by breaking up the date value into its component parts. After completing preprocessing, we modeled our data. We followed an approach that included creating a baseline model and then tuning hyperparameters to improve our initial score. We used early stopping rounds and grid searches to identify hyperparameter values that produced the best results. After modifying our model-based results from our tuning procedures, we noticed much better performance.

All of the aspects of machine learning that were discussed in this chapter will be used in the subsequent chapters too. We will need to get our data ready for modeling, and we will need to know how we can improve model performance by adjusting its settings. In addition, we have been focusing on a decision tree ensembling model in xgboost because our work with neural networks in upcoming chapters will be similar. We will need to consider efficiency and performance just as we did with xgboost, by adjusting how trees are grown.

This review of machine learning provides the foundation for stepping into deep learning. We begin, in the next chapter, with installing and exploring the packages used.

Setting Up R for Deep Learning 2

In this book, we will primarily use the following libraries for deep learning: **H2O**, **MXNet**, and **Keras**. We will also use the **Restricted Boltzmann Machine** (**RBM**) package specifically for RBMs and **deep belief networks** (**DBNs**). In addition, we will conclude the book by using the `ReinforcementLearning` package.

In this chapter, we will install all of the previously listed packages. Each package can be used to train deep learning models in R. However, each has its particular strengths and weaknesses. We will explore the underlying architecture for each of these packages, which will help us to understand how they execute code. The packages have been created to allow R programmers to perform deep learning, with the exception of `RBM` and `ReinforcementLearning`, which are not written natively in R. This does have important implications for us to consider, starting with ensuring that we have all the necessary dependencies in order to install the packages.

This chapter will cover the following main topics:

- Installing the packages
- Preparing a sample dataset
- Exploring Keras
- Exploring H2O
- Reinforcement learning and RBM
- Deep learning library comparison

Technical requirements

You can find the code files used in this chapter at https://github.com/PacktPublishing/Hands-on-Deep-Learning-with-R.

Installing the packages

Some packages can be directly installed from CRAN or GitHub, while H2O and MXNet are a bit more complex. We will start with the packages that are the most straightforward to install and then move on to those that are more complex.

Installing ReinforcementLearning

You can install ReinforcementLearning by using install.packages, since there is a CRAN release for this package, with the following line of code:

```
install.packages("ReinforcementLearning")
```

Installing RBM

The RBM package is only available on GitHub and is not available on CRAN, so the installation here is slightly different. First, you will need to install the devtools package if you do not already have it installed on your system. Next, use the install_github() function from the devtools package in place of install.packages in order to install the RBM package, as in the following code:

```
install.packages("devtools")
library(devtools)
install_github("TimoMatzen/RBM")
```

Installing Keras

Installing Keras is similar to the way that we installed RBM, with one subtle, but important, difference. After running install_github() function to download and install the package, you run install_keras() to complete the installation. From the Keras documentation, calling install_keras() function is not required if you would prefer to install Keras yourself.

If you choose this route, the R package will find the version that you have installed. For this book, we will use `install_keras()` to complete installation, as in the following code:

```
devtools::install_github("rstudio/keras")
library(keras)

install_keras()
```

If you would prefer to install the GPU version, then just make one change when calling the function, as follows:

```
## for the gpu version :
install_keras(gpu=TRUE)
```

Running `install_keras()` will install Keras and TensorFlow in a virtual environment by default, except on a Windows machine where—at the time of writing—this is not supported, in which case a `conda` environment will be used and Anaconda will need to be installed on the Windows machine beforehand. By default, the CPU version of TensorFlow and the latest release of Keras will be installed; an optional argument can be added in order to install the GPU version, as in the preceding code. For this book, we will accept the default values and run `install_keras`.

If you have a machine with multiple versions of Python, you may discover some issues. If the Python instance that you wish to use is not declared, then R will attempt to find Python by first looking in common locations such as `usr/bin` and `usr/local/bin`.

When using Keras, you will likely want to point to the Python instance in your TensorFlow virtual environment. By default, the virtual environment will be called `r-tensorflow`. You can tell R the version of Python you would like to use by using the `use_python()` function from the `reticulate` package. Within the function, simply note the path to the instance of Python in the virtual environment. On my machine, this looks as follows:

```
use_python('/Users/pawlus/.virtualenvs/r-tensorflow/bin/python')
```

This should look similar on your machine.

Once R has the path to the right instance of Python, the code that we will introduce later in this chapter should work. However, if you are not referencing the correct version of Python, you will encounter errors and the code will not run.

Installing H2O

For H2O, we will use the installation instructions from the H2O website. Using this approach, we will first search for any previous installations of H2O and remove those. Next, `RCurl` and `jsonlite` are installed and, after this, H2O is installed from the AWS S3 bucket containing the latest release. This is accomplished by simply making a change to the location of the repository when obtaining the package files, which, by default, is a CRAN server. We install H2O by running the following code:

```
if ("package:h2o" %in% search()) { detach("package:h2o", unload=TRUE) }
if ("h2o" %in% rownames(installed.packages())) { remove.packages("h2o") }

pkgs <- c("RCurl","jsonlite")
for (pkg in pkgs) {
  if (! (pkg %in% rownames(installed.packages()))) { install.packages(pkg)
}
}

install.packages("h2o", type="source",
repos=(c("http://h2o-release.s3.amazonaws.com/h2o/latest_stable_R")))
```

Installing MXNet

There are multiple ways to install MXNet. The following code is the easiest installation instruction for setting up the CPU version of MXNet:

```
cran <- getOption("repos")
cran["dmlc"] <-
"https://apache-mxnet.s3-accelerate.dualstack.amazonaws.com/R/CRAN/"
options(repos = cran)
install.packages("mxnet")
```

For the GPU support, use the following installation code:

```
cran <- getOption("repos")
cran["dmlc"] <-
"https://apache-mxnet.s3-accelerate.dualstack.amazonaws.com/R/CRAN/GPU/cu92
"
options(repos = cran)
install.packages("mxnet")
```

OpenCV and OpenBLAS are required to use MXNet. If you need to install these, you can do so through one of the following options.

For macOS X, Homebrew can be used to install these libraries:

1. If Homebrew is not already installed, installation instructions can be found at `https://brew.sh/`.

2. With Homebrew available, open a Terminal window and install the libraries using the following commands:

```
brew install opencv
brew install openblas
```

3. Finally, as shown here, create a symbolic link to ensure that the latest version of OpenBLAS is being used:

```
ln -sf /usr/local/opt/openblas/lib/libopenblas.dylib
/usr/local/opt/openblas/lib/libopenblasp-r0.3.1.dylib
```

For Windows, the process is slightly more involved and so the details will not be noted in this book:

- To install OpenCV, follow the instructions found at `https://docs.opencv.org/3.4.3/d3/d52/tutorial_windows_install.html`.
- To install OpenBLAS, follow the instructions found at `https://github.com/xianyi/OpenBLAS/wiki/How-to-use-OpenBLAS-in-Microsoft-Visual-Studio`.

With OpenCV and OpenBLAS installed, the preceding lines should work to download and install the MXNet package. However, if you run into errors while trying to load the library, then it may be necessary to build the MXNet package and then create the R package. The instructions to complete this are very clear and detailed, but they are too long to include in this book:

- **For macOS X**: `https://mxnet.incubator.apache.org/versions/master/install/osx_setup.html`
- **For Windows**: `https://mxnet.incubator.apache.org/versions/master/install/windows_setup.html`

If there are still issues when downloading and installing the package after following the steps needed to build the MXNet library and the R bindings, this could be due to a number of possible reasons, many of which have been documented. Unfortunately, trying to work through all the possible installation scenarios and issues is outside the scope of this book. However, to use MXNet for learning purposes, it is possible to use a kernel from the Kaggle website, where MXNet is available.

Preparing a sample dataset

For Keras, H2O, and MXNet, we will use the adult census dataset, which uses U.S. Census data to predict whether someone makes more or less than USD50,000 a year. We will perform the data preparation for the Keras and MXNet examples here, so we are not repeating the same code in both examples:

1. In the following code, we will load the data and label the two datasets to prepare for combining them:

```
library(tidyverse)
library(caret)

train <- read.csv("adult_processed_train.csv")
train <- train %>% dplyr::mutate(dataset = "train")
test <- read.csv("adult_processed_test.csv")
test <- test %>% dplyr::mutate(dataset = "test")
```

As a result of running the preceding code, we will now have our libraries loaded and ready to use. We also have the `train` and `test` data loaded, which can now be seen in the `Environment` pane.

2. Next, we will combine the datasets so we can make some changes to all the data at the same time. We will use the `complete.cases` function to remove rows with `NA` for the sake of simplicity for these examples. We will also remove white space around the character terms so that terms such as `Male` and `Male ` are both treated as the same term. Let's have a look at the following code:

```
all <- rbind(train,test)

all <- all[complete.cases(all),]

all <- all %>%
    mutate_if(~is.factor(.),~trimws(.))
```

3. We will now perform some extra pre-processing steps on the `train` dataset. First, we use the `filter()` function to extract the `train` data from the combined data frame labeled `all`. After that, we will extract the `target` column as a vector and then remove the `target` and `label` columns. We isolate the `train` data and `train` target variables using the following code:

```
train <- all %>% filter(dataset == "train")
train_target <- as.numeric(factor(train$target))
train <- train %>% select(-target, -dataset)
```

4. We will now separate the columns with numeric values and those with character values so that we can encode the character value column to prepare for a completely numeric matrix. We separate the numeric and character columns using the following code:

```
train_chars <- train %>%
  select_if(is.character)

train_ints <- train %>%
  select_if(is.integer)
```

5. Next, we will use the `dummyVars()` function from `caret` to pivot the character values within a column into separate columns and we will indicate whether a character string is present in the row by assigning 1 to the row. If the character string is not present, then the column will contain 0 for that row. We perform this one-hot encoding step by running the following code:

```
ohe <- caret::dummyVars(" ~ .", data = train_chars)
train_ohe <- data.frame(predict(ohe, newdata = train_chars))
```

6. After transforming the data, we will now bind the two datasets back together with the following line of code:

```
train <- cbind(train_ints,train_ohe)
```

7. We will then repeat the same steps for the `test` dataset by running the following code:

```
test <- all %>% filter(dataset == "test")
test_target <- as.numeric(factor(test$target))
test <- test %>% select(-target, -dataset)

test_chars <- test %>%
  select_if(is.character)

test_ints <- test %>%
  select_if(is.integer)

ohe <- caret::dummyVars(" ~ .", data = test_chars)
test_ohe <- data.frame(predict(ohe, newdata = test_chars))

test <- cbind(test_ints,test_ohe)
```

8. When we created our target vector, it converted the factor values to 1 and 2. However, we would like this to be 1 and 0, so we will subtract 1 from the vector, as in the following code:

```
train_target <- train_target-1
test_target <- test_target-1
```

9. The last step is to clean up one column from the train dataset because it is not present in the test dataset. We remove this particular column by running the following line of code:

```
train <- train %>% select(-native.countryHoland.Netherlands)
```

Now that we have loaded and prepared this dataset, we can use it in the next step to demonstrate some preliminary examples using all the packages that we have installed. At this point, our goal is to take a look at the syntax and ensure that the code can run and that the libraries are installed correctly. In later chapters, we will go into more depth about each package.

Exploring Keras

Keras was created and is maintained by Francois Chollet. Keras lays claim to being designed for humans, so common use cases are simple to execute and the syntax is clear and comprehensible. Keras is made to work with a number of lower-level deep learning languages and, in this book, Keras will be the interface that we use to utilize a number of popular deep learning backends, including TensorFlow.

Available functions

Keras offers support for a broad array of deep learning methods, including the following:

- **Recurrent neural networks (RNNs)**
- **Long short-term memory (LSTM)** networks
- **Convolutional neural networks (CNNs)**
- **Multilayer perceptrons (MLPs)**
- **Variable autoencoders**

This is not an exhaustive list and further support is available for additional methods. However, these are what will be covered in the later chapters of this book.

A Keras example

In this example, we will train a multilayer perceptron on the adult census dataset that we just prepared. This example is included to introduce the syntax of the package and to show that a basic exercise can be completed without an excessive amount of code:

 If you have multiple versions of Python installed on your system, then this can become an issue. Use the `reticulate` package and the `use_python()` function to define the path to the Python instance that you would like to use; for example, `use_python(usr/local/bin/python3)`. You can also use `RETICULATE_PYTHON` within your `.Rprofile` file to set the path to the Python instance that R should use.

1. To begin, we will load the `tensorflow` and `keras` libraries, as shown:

```
library(tensorflow)
library(keras)
```

2. Next, we will convert our datasets into matrices, as shown:

```
train <- as.matrix(train)
test <- as.matrix(test)
```

3. Now, we can create a sequential model, which will move through each layer in succession. We will have one layer and then we will compile the results. We define our model by running the following code:

```
model <- keras_model_sequential()

model %>%
   layer_dense(units=35, activation = 'relu')

model %>% keras::compile(loss='binary_crossentropy',
                         optimizer='adam',
                         metrics='accuracy')
```

4. In the previous step, we defined our model and now, in the following code, we will fit this model to our training dataset:

```
history <- model%>%
   fit(train,
       train_target,
       epoch=10,
      batch=16,
       validation_split = 0.15)
```

5. Finally, we can evaluate our model by comparing our model results to the `test` target values. We evaluate model performance by running the following code:

```
model%>%
    keras::evaluate(test,test_target)
```

This is the general syntax for `keras`. As we have shown, it is compatible with piping and has a syntax that will be familiar to R programmers. Next, we will look at an example using the MXNet package.

Exploring MXNet

MXNet is a deep learning library designed by the Apache Software Foundation. It supports both imperative and symbolic programming. It is designed for speed by serializing functions with dependencies while running functions with no dependencies in parallel. It provides compatibility with CPU and GPU processors.

Available functions

MXNet provides the means to run a very extensive list of deep learning methods, including the following:

- CNN
- RNN
- GAN
- LSTM
- Autoencoders
- RBM/DBN
- Reinforcement learning

Getting started with MXNet

For MXNet, we will use the same prepared adult census dataset. We will also use a multilayer perceptron as our model. Fitting a model using MXNet will be quite familiar to you if you are familiar with fitting a model using a number of other common machine learning packages:

1. First, we will load the MXNet package with the following line of code:

   ```
   library(mxnet)
   ```

2. Then, we will define our multilayer perceptron. A seed value is set for reproducibility purposes. Afterward, the training data is converted to a data matrix and passed as an argument to the model, along with the training target values, as shown:

   ```
   mx.set.seed(0)

   model <- mx.mlp(data.matrix(train), train_target, hidden_node=10,
   out_node=2, out_activation="softmax",
                   num.round=10, array.batch.size=20,
   learning.rate=0.05, momentum=0.8,
                   eval.metric=mx.metric.accuracy)
   ```

3. Next, we will make our predictions by applying the model to a data matrix version of the test data, as in the following code:

   ```
   preds = predict(model, data.matrix(test))
   ```

4. We can then use a confusion matrix to evaluate performance, with the adjusted target class on the *y*-axis and the predicted results on the *x*-axis, as shown:

   ```
   pred.label = max.col(t(preds))-1
   table(pred.label, test_target)
   ```

The syntax for MXNet should look familiar to those with experience with doing machine learning coding in R. The function to train the model takes in descriptive and target data, as well as captures values for a number of options, just like using RandomForest or XGBoost.

The options are slightly different and we will cover how to best assign values to these arguments in a later chapter. However, the syntax is quite similar to the syntax used for other machine learning libraries in R. Next, we will write the code to train a minimal model using H2O.

Exploring H2O

H2O has been around longer than Keras and MXNet and is still used widely. It makes use of Java and MapReduce in-memory compression to handle big datasets. H2O is used for many machine learning tasks and also supports deep learning. In particular, H2O provides native support for feedforward artificial neural networks (multilayer perceptrons). H2O performs automatic data preparation and missing value handling. Loading data requires the use of a special data type: H2OFrame.

Available functions

H2O only natively supports feedforward neural networks. Compared with the other main packages for deep learning, this creates an obvious limitation for this library. However, this is a very common deep learning implementation. In addition, H2O allows for large objects to be stored outside memory in the H2O cluster. For these reasons, H2O is still a valuable library to know about when studying deep learning.

An H2O example

For this example, we will again use the adult census dataset to predict income. As with our Keras example, this will be kept extremely minimal and we will cover just enough to illustrate the syntax for working with H2O, as well as the design nuances that differ from other packages:

1. The first major difference when working with H2O is that we must explicitly initialize our H2O session, which will generate a Java Virtual Machine instance and connect it with R. This is accomplished with the following lines of code:

```
# load H2O package
library(h2o)

# start H2O
h2o::h2o.init()
```

2. Loading data to use with H2O requires converting the data to `H2OFrame`. `H2OFrame` is very similar to data frames, with the major distinction having to do with where the object is stored. While data frames are held in memory, `H2OFrame` is stored on the H2O cluster. This feature can be an advantage with very large datasets. In the following example, we will convert the data into the proper format using a two-step process. First, we load the data by reading `csv` in the usual way. Second, we will convert the data frames to `H2OFrame`. We convert our data into the proper format using the following code:

```
## load data
train <- read.csv("adult_processed_train.csv")
test <- read.csv("adult_processed_test.csv")

# load data on H2o
train <- as.h2o(train)
test <- as.h2o(test)
```

3. For this example, we will perform some imputation as the sole pre-processing step. In this step, we will replace all missing values and we will use `mean` for numeric data and `mode` for factor data. In H2O, setting `column = 0` will apply the function to the entire frame. Of note is that the function is called on the data; however, it is not necessary to assign the results to a new object as the imputations will be directly reflected in the data passed through as an argument to the function. It is also worth highlighting that in H2O, we can pass a vector to the method argument and it will be used for every variable in this case by first checking whether the first method can be used and, if not, moving on to the second method. Pre-processing this data is accomplished by running the following lines of code:

```
## pre-process
h2o.impute(train, column = 0, method = c("mean", "mode"))
h2o.impute(test, column = 0, method = c("mean", "mode"))
```

4. In addition, in this step, we will define the `dependent` and `independent` variables. The `dependent` variable is held in the `target` column, while all the remaining columns contain the `independent` variables, which will be used for predicting the `target` variable during this task:

```
#set dependent and independent variables
target <- "target"
predictors <- colnames(train)[1:14]
```

5. With all of the preparation steps complete, we can now create a minimal model. The H2O `deeplearning` function will create a feedforward artificial neural network. In this example, just the minimum required to run the model will be included. However, this function can accept 80 to 90 arguments and we will cover many of these in the later chapters. In the following code, we provide a name for our model, identify the training data, set a seed for reproducibility through replicating pseudo-random numbers involved in the model, define the `dependent` and `independent` variables, and note the number of times the model should be run and how the data should be cut for each round:

```
#train the model - without hidden layer
model <- h2o.deeplearning(model_id = "h2o_dl_example"
                          ,training_frame = train
                          ,seed = 321
                          ,y = target
                          ,x = predictors
                          ,epochs = 10
                          ,nfolds = 5)
```

6. After running the model, the performance can be evaluated on the out-of-fold samples using the following line of code:

```
h2o.performance(model, xval = TRUE)
```

7. Finally, when our model is complete, the cluster must be explicitly shut down just as it was initialized. The following function will close the current `h2o` instance:

```
h2o::h2o.shutdown()
```

We can observe the following in this example:

- The syntax for H2O varies quite a bit from other machine learning libraries.
- First, we need to initiate the Java Virtual Machine and we need to store our data in special data containers with this package.
- In addition, we can see that imputation happens by running the function on a data object without assigning the changes back to an object.
- We can see that we also need to include all the independent variable column names, which is slightly different from other models.
- All of this is to say that H2O may feel a little unfamiliar as you use it. It is also limited in terms of the algorithms available. However, the ability to work with larger datasets is a definite advantage to this package.

Now that we have looked at the comprehensive deep learning packages, we will focus on packages written with R that perform a specific modeling task or a limited set of tasks.

Exploring ReinforcementLearning and RBM

The `ReinforcementLearning` and `RBM` packages differ from the libraries already covered in two important ways: first, they are specialized packages that have functions for only one specific deep learning task instead of attempting to support myriad deep learning options, and second, they are completely written in R and have no additional language dependencies. This can be an advantage as the complexity of the previous libraries means that the packages can break when changes happen outside the package. The support pages for these libraries are full of examples of installation FAQs and troubleshooting instructions, as well as some cases where a given package may suddenly stop working or become deprecated. In these cases, we encourage you to continue searching CRAN and other sites as the R community is well known for its dynamic, evolving, and robust support and development.

Reinforcement learning example

In this example, we will create a sample environment for reinforcement learning. The concept of reinforcement learning will be explored in more detail in a later chapter. For this example, we will generate a series of states and actions, along with the reward for taking those actions, that is, whether taking the action led to the desired result or a negative consequence. Afterward, we will define how our agent should respond or learn from actions. Once all of this has been defined, we will run the program and the agent will navigate through the environment to learn to solve the task. We will define and run a minimal reinforcement learning example by running the following code:

```
library(ReinforcementLearning)

data <- sampleGridSequence(N = 1000)

control <- list(alpha = 0.1, gamma = 0.1, epsilon = 0.1)

model <- ReinforcementLearning(data, s = "State", a = "Action", r =
"Reward", s_new = "NextState", control = control)

print(model)
```

We can see the following in this example:

- The syntax is very familiar and similar to many other R packages that we might use. In addition, we can see that we can complete a simple reinforcement learning task using a minimal amount of code.
- In the GitHub repository for the package, all of the functions are written in R, which provides the convenience to explore the possible reasons for issues if they arrive. This also alleviates any concerns over dependencies on additional languages present in the more complex packages noted previously.

An RBM example

Here is a simple example using the RBM package. RBMs can be created using the MXNet library. However, we include this package in this book to note when it makes the most sense to train an RBM model using MXNet and when a standalone implementation of the algorithm may be a better fit.

In the following example, we assign the train Fashion MNIST dataset to an object, create an RBM model on this data, and then make a prediction using the modeled results. A detailed exploration of how the RBM algorithm achieves this outcome and suggested applications are included in a future chapter. We will see how simply we can train this model and use it for prediction with a familiar syntax by running the following code:

```
library(RBM)

data(Fashion)

train <- Fashion$trainX
train_label <- Fashion$trainY

rbmModel <- RBM(x = t(train), y = train_label, n.iter = 500, n.hidden =
200, size.minibatch = 10)

test <- Fashion$testX
test_label <- Fashion$testY

PredictRBM(test = t(test), labels = test_label, model = rbmModel)
```

As with the `ReinforcementLearning` package, the following applies:

- RBM is written entirely in R, so exploring the code in the repository is an excellent way to better understand how this particular technique works.
- Also, as noted before, if you only need to train a model using RBM, then using a standalone package can be a great way to avoid having to load too many unnecessary functions, as is the case when using a library such as MXNet.
- Both comprehensive packages and standalone packages have their place in a deep learning workflow, so this book will highlight the advantages and disadvantages of each of them.

Comparing the deep learning libraries

When comparing the three comprehensive machine learning libraries highlighted in this chapter (Keras, H2O, and MXNet), there are three primary differences: external language dependencies, functions, and syntax (ease of use and cognitive load). We will now cover each of these main differences in turn.

The first major difference between the three packages is the external language dependencies for each. As mentioned earlier, none of these packages are written in R. What this means is that you will need additional languages installed on your machine in order for these packages to work. It also means that you cannot easily look at the source documentation to see how a particular function works or why you are receiving a certain error (unless you know one of the languages, of course). The packages are written using the following languages: Keras in Python, H2O in Java, and MXNet in C#.

The next major difference has to do with the types of models that can be implemented from each package. You can use all three packages to train a feedforward model, such as a multilayer perceptron, where all hidden layers are fully connected layers. Keras and MXNet allow you to train deep learning models that include different types of hidden layers, as well as feedback loops between layers. These include RNNs, LSTMs, and CNNs. MXNet offers support for additional algorithms, including GANs, RBMs/DBNs, and reinforcement learning.

The last major difference has to do with the syntax for the model. Some use a very familiar syntax, which, in turn, makes them easier to learn and use. There is less for you to remember when the code resembles other R code that you use for other purposes. To this end, Keras has a very familiar syntax. It is modular, which means every function performs a discrete step within the overall model and all the functions can be piped together.

This closely resembles the way that `tidyverse` functions are chained together for data preparation. MXNet follows a syntax similar to other machine learning packages, where a dataset and target variable vector are passed to the function to train the model, along with numerous additional arguments that control how the model is created. The syntax for H2O deviates the furthest from common R programming conventions. It requires a cluster to be initialized ahead of any modeling. Data must also be stored in specific data objects and some functions operate on a data object just by calling a function on that object without assigning the results to a new object, as in typical R programming.

Aside from these differences, Keras also provides a means for using TensorFlow, while H2O allows larger objects to be stored out of memory. As noted, MXNet has the most robust offering of deep learning algorithms. As we can see, each package has its advantages and, throughout this book, we will explore them in depth and note the most suitable use cases and applications along the way.

Summary

Having completed this chapter, you should now have all of the libraries that will be used in this book installed. In addition, you should be familiar with the syntax for each of them, and you should have seen a preliminary example of how to train a model using each one. We also explored some of the differences between the deep learning libraries, noting their strengths as well as their limitations. The three main packages (Keras, MXNet, and H2O) are widely used for deep learning in industry and academia, and an understanding of these will enable you to tackle a number of deep learning problems. We are now ready to explore them all in more depth. However, before we do, we will review neural networks—the building block for all deep learning.

In the following chapter, you will learn about artificial neural networks, which comprise the base building block for all deep learning. We will not use these deep learning libraries yet in the next chapter; however, the basics of how neural networks are coded will be critical as we move forward. Everything we cover in the next chapter will carry forward and be useful as we code examples of deep learning models. All deep learning cases are variations of the basic neural network, which we will learn how to create in the next chapter.

3
Artificial Neural Networks

In this chapter, you will learn about artificial neural networks, which forms the foundation for all deep learning. We will discuss what makes deep learning different from other forms of machine learning and then spend time diving into some of its specific and special features.

By the end of this chapter, we will have learned what makes deep learning a special subset of machine learning. We'll have an understanding of neural networks, how they mimic the brain, and the benefits of hidden layers for discrete element detection. We'll create a feedforward neural network, noting the role of the activation function in determining variable weights.

This chapter will cover the following topics:

- Contrasting deep learning with machine learning
- Comparing neural networks and the human brain
- Understanding the role of hidden layers
- Creating a feedforward network
- Augmenting our neural network with backpropagation

Technical requirements

For the source code of this chapter, please refer to the GitHub link at `https://github.com/PacktPublishing/Hands-on-Deep-Learning-with-R`.

Contrasting deep learning with machine learning

One key strength of deep learning not shared by other forms of ML is its ability to factor the way variables are related. For instance, if we think back to when we were first learning about animals, then we could imagine a simple task where we are given five images of cats and five images of dogs; later, when we were shown a new image, we would be able to determine whether it was a cat or dog using the patterns that we detected from the previous images that we studied. In our example, it was the images that were to be classified as either cats or dogs. We can consider this example as a training set, and will use the same terminology for the classification of images. Mentally, our brain tries to match the images with the patterns that form the features of these two different species so that we can differentiate between them. This is what happens in deep learning as well.

Today, we would find the preceding example task to be quite simple; however, think of how a computer would have to learn this:

- It needs to account for the ways that features are related for dogs compared with cats and it needs to do this wherever an animal appears in a photo, however much of the image is taken up by the animal.
- For this, we cannot use the standard machine-learning approach where all input is used without consideration for how it is related. The placement and proximity of pixels in two-dimensional space must be considered, so we can already see how a simple task for humans is already more complex for a machine.
- Furthermore, just evaluating the input data in the form of two-dimensional arrays is not enough. The machine also needs the multiple hidden layer architecture present in deep learning to identify multiple different patterns among the data arrays. That is to say, the pure signal won't be as helpful as the relationship between given signals that are near each other.
- Each layer will identify the presence of a different aspect of the image from basic shape detection to the length and steepness of color gradients.

When performing a simple regression or classification task, we apply a weight to each variable and then use this to predict an outcome. With deep learning, there is a middle step where artificial neurons or units are created using all the variables. This step creates new features that are a combination of all variables with varying weights applied. This activity happens in what is known as a hidden layer. After this, the signal is passed on to another hidden layer and the same process happens again.

Each layer will learn a different aspect from the input. Let's look at an example of this:

- The first layer creates neurons based on the overall size of the object in the image by applying different weights to the negative and positive space.
- In the second layer, the neurons may be created based on the shape and size of the ears and nose.
- In this way, the different characteristics of cats and dogs are captured among the entirety of the hidden layers.

The weights are assigned randomly at first. This is then checked against the actual answers. After several attempts, the model learns that adjusting weights in a given direction produces better results, and so it will continue to adjust the weights in the same direction until the chosen error rate is minimized.

Once this is complete and the weights are learned, a new input can be introduced. The model will multiply all variables by the learned weights at every neuron and each neuron will use an activation function that determines whether to activate or fire and send the signal forward to the next layer. We will go into more detail on the various activation functions later in the chapter. For now, let's just say that a calculation occurs at each neuron, after which a final value is produced at the output node. In this case, the probability is that the image is either a dog or a cat.

In this illustration, we may begin to see the power of neural networks and deep learning. The model is not evaluating the variables in isolation but rather in concert. By contrast, regression models calculate weights for each individual variable separately. Regression models can use interaction terms to calculate weights for combinations of variables; however, even this doesn't consider all variables in the same way as neural networks that evaluate all variables at all neurons. The neurons created from all the variables are then used to define the next set of neurons in the next layer. In this way, the entirety of the feature space is considered and is then partitioned based on themes that emerge after evaluating all variables.

Comparing neural networks and the human brain

Let's consider how a human brain learns in order to see the ways in which a neural network is similar and the ways in which it is different.

Our brain contains a large number of neurons, and each neuron is connected to thousands of nearby neurons. As these neurons receive signals, they fire if the input contains a certain amount of a given color or a certain amount of a given texture. After millions of these interconnected neurons fire, the brain interprets the incoming signal as a certain class.

Of course, these connections are not set permanently but rather change dynamically as we continue to have experiences, notice patterns, and discover relationships. If we try a new fruit for the first time and discover that it is really sour, then all the attributes that help us recognize this fruit are connected with things that we know are sour. In the future, whether we will want to experience eating this fruit again or not will depend on how much we want to experience this sour taste.

Another example that shows how the neural network in our brain constantly evolves focuses on the types of activities that we find enjoyable. For instance, have you ever wondered why babies find shaking a simple toy enjoyable while we do not? In our brains, novelty is rewarded by the release of opioids; however, as a given piece of stimulus becomes less surprising, a smaller number of neurons are needed to interpret this experience, resulting in a less intense response as fewer neurons are firing. In this way, we see the dynamic nature of the neural connections in our brains, which are in constant flux.

When we discuss the connections between neurons, we are specifically speaking of the synapses between neurons. Artificial neural networks seek to mimic the type of learning done by the human brain by creating a massive web of connections between constructed neurons and an output node or nodes, in a crude approximation of the brain's neurons. Just as the synapses that connect neurons in our brain can get stronger or weaker, the weights between neurons can change during the training process.

However, unlike the human brain, simple artificial neural networks like those that we are studying in this chapter do not start with any inherited weights and connections. They begin with a random assignment of weights and connections. Also, while the weights can change during the training process, this does not continue during the application of the model. At this phase, the weights that were derived during the training process are applied and there isn't a continual adjustment. This can be contrasted with the human brain. The neural networks in our brains do behave similarly to artificial neural networks; however, the adjustments to how neurons are connected update constantly. Lastly, the human brain has billions of neurons and trillions of connections, while artificial neural networks like those we will build shortly have much fewer.

While there are some significant differences between the way a brain learns and the way an artificial neural network learns, by sharing a similar design structure, the artificial neural network is capable of solving some extremely complex tasks. This idea has continued to develop and improve, and throughout the course of this book, we will see just how powerful this idea has been for data science.

Utilizing bias and activation functions within hidden layers

When we described deep learning earlier, we noted that the defining characteristic is the presence of hidden layers comprised of neurons that contain the weighted sum of all predictor variables in a dataset. We just addressed how this array of interconnected neurons is modeled after the human brain. Now let's take a deeper dive into what is happening in these hidden layers where neurons are created.

At this point, we can deduce the following:

- We understand that all variables receive a coefficient at random for each neuron based on how many units we want to create in each layer.
- The algorithm then continues to make changes to these coefficients until it minimizes the error rate.
- However, there is one additional coefficient present during this process of passing weighted values to the neurons, and that is known as the bias function.

The bias function can simply be thought of as a means of adjusting the shape of the line separating the data laterally. For now, let's simply imagine that a straight diagonal line is drawn to separate data points in two-dimensional space. In the following example, no matter how we adjust the slope of the line, we cannot find a line that bisects the triangles and circles:

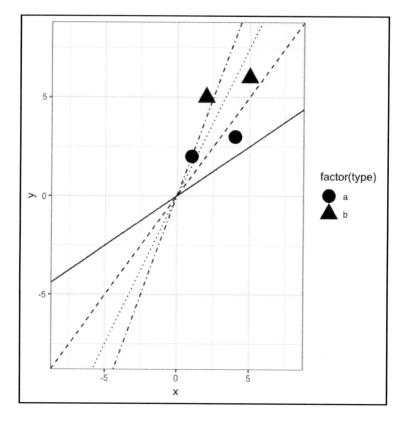

However, if we adjust the line slightly so that it intercepts the *y*-axis above the center of the plot, then we can fit a line between the two classes of points. This is what the bias function does. It adjusts the intercept point to allow for a better fitting line:

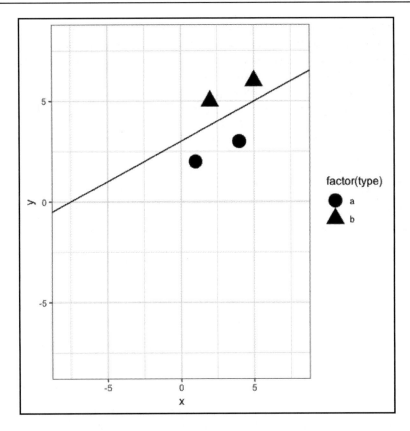

The bias function is a coefficient that adjusts the line along the *x*-axis in this way to account for situations where the data requires the line to intersect the point where **y** is equal to **0** and **x** perhaps equals **5**.

All the weighted units and the bias function value are summed within the neuron and plotted along a linearly divided space. Calculating where a point is located relative to this line determines whether the neuron activates or switches on and continues to send a signal forward or if it switches off. Neural networks that use this type of function as a threshold to determine what happens with an incoming signal are referred to as perceptrons and are the earliest form of artificial neural network created.

However, as neural networks have evolved, it has become clearer that using a linear model to separate data would not work in all circumstances. As a result, there are now a number of available functions that can take place within the neuron to determine whether the signal should continue or stop as it passes through. These gate functions are referred to as activation functions, as they simulate the process of a neuron within the brain being triggered to fire or activate and send a signal to a connected neuron or not. At this point, let's explore the variety of activation functions available.

Surveying activation functions

The activation functions are the last piece of the neural network that we have not covered in depth yet. To review what we know so far, in a neural network, we start with an input, as we would with any machine-learning modeling exercise. This data consists of a dependent target variable that we would like to predict and any number of independent predictor variables that are to be used for this prediction task.

During the training process, the independent variables are weighted and combined in simulated neurons. A bias function is also applied during this step and this constant value is combined with the weighted independent variable values. At this point, an activation function evaluates an aggregation of the values and if it is above a set threshold limit, then the neuron fires and the signal is passed forward to additional hidden layers, if they exist, or to the output node.

Let's consider the simplest activation function, which is a Heaviside or binary step function. This can be imagined visually as two horizontal lines that act as the threshold limits on either side of a vertical line splitting the data so that the shape is like that of a step. If the value is on the horizontal line at 1, then the signal progresses; otherwise, the neuron doesn't fire. We also previously mentioned how a diagonal line could be used at this step to linearly separate points. When points cannot be separated by either of these simple activation functions, then we can use nonlinear alternatives, which we will look at next.

Exploring the sigmoid function

The sigmoid function is the classic S-shaped function. This function works especially well for logistic regression tasks. While most of the results will be classified by the tails on either side of the curve, there is an area in the middle for capturing uncertainty about some of the data. The drawback of this shape is that the gradient is almost zero at the extremes, so the model may not be able to continue to learn as the points get towards either side.

The sigmoid function also contains a derivative value, which means that we can use this function along with backpropagation to update the weights after the variables pass through additional layers. We will explore backpropagation more in the final parts of this chapter.

Another advantage of the sigmoid function is that it confines values between 0 and 1 so that the values are conveniently bound.

The `sigmoid` function can be defined simply using R code:

```
sigmoid = function(x) {
   1 / (1 + exp(-x))
}
```

In this function, we can see that the dynamic value is the exponent of negative x.

Let's use this sigmoid function on a sequence of values between −10 and 10:

1. To start, we will create a `tibble` containing two columns. One column will contain the sequence of numbers and the other will use the results of passing this sequence of values as arguments through the `sigmoid` function:

   ```
   vals <- tibble(x = seq(-10, 10, 1), sigmoid_x = sigmoid(seq(-10,
   10, 1)))
   ```

2. Next, we set up the base of our plot by using the `ggplot()` function and passing in the data objects and defining the values that will be used along the x- and y-axes. In this case, we use the sequence of values between −10 and 10 along the x-axis and the results of passing these values through the sigmoid function along the y-axis:

   ```
   p <- ggplot(vals, aes(x, sigmoid_x))
   ```

3. We will now add the points and use the `stat_function` feature to connect the points and display the sigmoid shape:

   ```
   p <- p + geom_point()
   p + stat_function(fun = sigmoid, n = 1000)
   ```

If we now look at this shape, we can see why this type of activation function works so well for logistic regression. Using the `sigmoid` function to transform our values has pushed most of the values close to the extremes of 0 or 1:

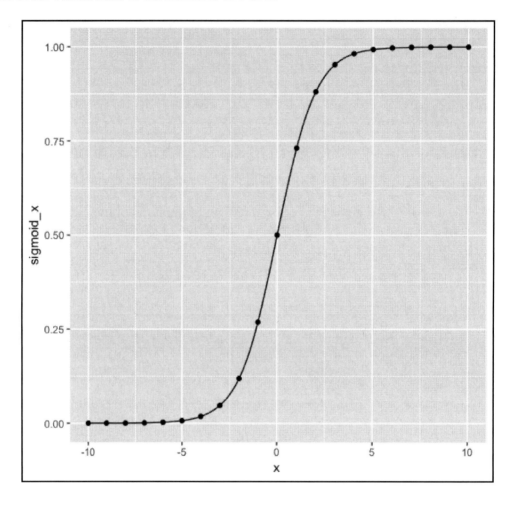

Investigating the hyperbolic tangent function

The hyperbolic tangent function, which is also known as **tanh**, is very similar to the sigmoid function; however, the lower bound of the curve is in negative space to better handle data containing negative values.

Aside from this one difference, everything else about the hyperbolic tangent function is the same as the sigmoid function, and like the sigmoid function, the hyperbolic tangent contains a derivative element and can be used with backpropagation.

Since tanh is bounded between -1 and 1, the gradient is larger and the derivative is more pronounced. Being bounded means that tanh is centered around 0, which can be advantageous in a model with a large number of hidden layers as the results from a layer are easier for the next layer to use.

Let's use the same sequence of values and plot the values after passing all of these values through the hyperbolic tangent function, which is included with base R and can be called using `tanh()`:

1. As we did in the preceding sigmoid example, we will create a `tibble` with the values in our sequence and the transformed values:

   ```
   vals <- tibble(x = seq(-10, 10, 1), tanh_x = tanh(seq(-10, 10, 1)))
   ```

2. We then set up the base of our plot by passing the dataset along with the values to use for the *x*-axis and the *y*-axis to the `ggplot()` function:

   ```
   p <- ggplot(vals, aes(x, tanh_x))
   ```

3. Lastly, we again add our points and use the `stat_function` feature to connect the dots and display our shape:

   ```
   p <- p + geom_point()
   p + stat_function(fun = tanh, n = 1000)
   ```

As we look at this shape, we can see that it is a very similar shape to the sigmoid shape that we just plotted; however, note that the y-axis now has a range from -1 to 1 rather than 0 to 1, as was the case with the sigmoid shape. As a result, the values are pushed even further to the extremes and negative values remain negative after transformation:

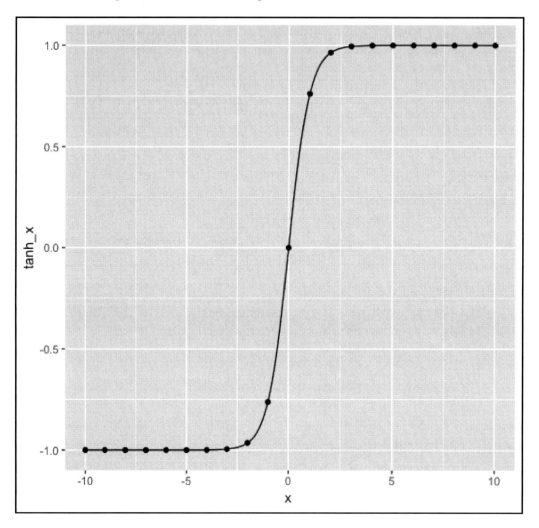

Plotting the rectified linear units activation function

Rectified Linear Units (ReLU) is a hybrid function that fits a line for positive values of x while assigning any negative values of x with a value of 0. Even though one half of this function is linear, the shape is nonlinear and carries with it all the advantages of nonlinearity, such as being able to use the derivative for backpropagation.

Unlike the previous two activation functions, it has no upper bound. This lack of a constraint can be helpful to avoid the issue with the sigmoid or tanh function, where the gradient becomes very gradual near the extremes and provides little information to help the model continue to learn. Another major advantage of ReLU is how it leads to sparsity in the neural network because of the drop off at the center point. Using signoid or tanh, very few output values from the function will be zero, which means that the activation functions will fire, leading to a dense network. By contrast, ReLU results in far more output values of zero, leading to fewer neurons firing and a much sparser network.

ReLU will learn faster than sigmoid and tanh because of its simplicity. The ReLU function results in more zero values than sigmoid or tanh, which will improve the speed of the training process; however, since we no longer know the unaltered value for these points, they cannot be updated during backpropagation later. This can be an issue if weights would otherwise be adjusted to pass along relevant information during backpropagation; however, it is no longer possible once the derivative is set to zero.

Let's write some code to visualize the ReLU function:

1. First, we will define the function. It is simply defined so that if a value for x is greater than 0, then it sets x equal to y, and creates a line with a slope of 1; otherwise, it sets y to x and creates a horizontal line on the x-axis. This can be coded like this:

```
relu <- function(x){dplyr::if_else(x > 0, x, 0)}
```

2. Next, let's create our dataset again using the same sequence of numbers as before and the transformed values after passing this sequence through our ReLU function:

```
vals <- tibble(x = seq(-10, 10, 1), relu_x = relu(seq(-10, 10, 1)))
```

3. Lastly, let's plot these points and connect them to display the shape of this activation function:

```
p <- ggplot(vals, aes(x, relu_x))
p <- p + geom_point()
p + geom_line()
```

Now, as we look at this shape, we can see its strengths. Having no upper bounds provides the model with more information than sigmoid, where the gradient becomes very minimal near the extremes. In addition, converting all negative values to 0 results in a much more sparse neural network and faster training time:

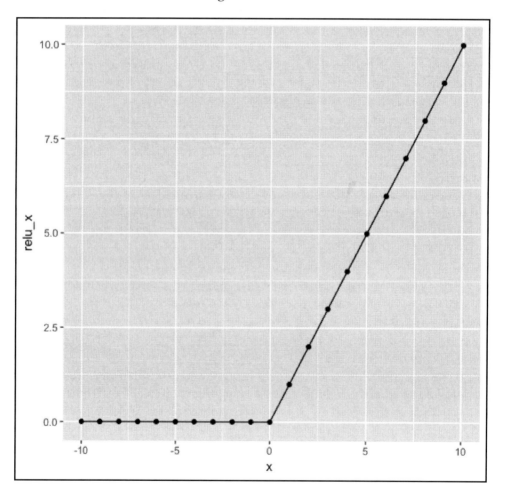

Calculating the Leaky ReLU activation function

One potential problem with ReLU is known as **dying ReLU**, where, since the function assigns a zero value for all negative values, signals can get dropped completely before reaching the output node. One way to try to solve this issue is to use Leaky ReLU, which assigns a small alpha value when numbers are negative so that the signal is not completely lost. Once this constant is applied, the values that would otherwise have been zero now have a small slope. This keeps the neuron from being fully deactivated so that information can still be passed on to improve the model.

Let's create a simple example of the Leaky ReLU activation function:

1. We start by defining the function. We will do this in the exact same way as the ReLU function, except that instead of assigning a 0 to all negative values, we will instead multiply by a constant to provide a small slope:

   ```
   leaky_relu <- function(x,a){dplyr::if_else(x > 0, x, x*a)}
   ```

2. After this, we create the dataset with the sequence of values that we have been using in these examples, along with the transformed values:

   ```
   vals <- tibble(x = seq(-10, 10, 1), leaky_relu_x =
   leaky_relu(seq(-10, 10, 1),0.01))
   ```

3. Lastly, we plot these points to display the shape of this activation function:

   ```
   p <- ggplot(vals, aes(x, leaky_relu_x))
   p <- p + geom_point()
   p + geom_line()
   ```

When we look at this shape, we can see why this alternative to ReLU is preferable sometimes. Having the slight slope for negative values of **x** combats the dying ReLU problem where the neural network becomes too sparse and doesn't have the data needed to converge around a prediction:

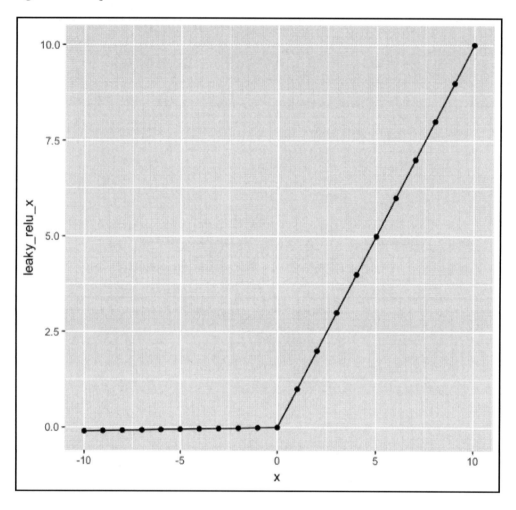

Defining the swish activation function

Swish is a more recently developed activation function that aims to leverage the strengths of ReLU while also addressing some of its shortcomings. Swish, like ReLU, has a lower bound and no upper bound, which is a strength as it can still deactivate neurons while preventing values from being forced to converge around an upper bound. However, unlike ReLU, the lower bound is still curved, and what's more notable is that the line is nonmonotonic, which means that as values for x decrease, the value for y can increase. This is an important feature that prevents the dying neuron problem as the derivative can continue to be modified across iterations.

Let's investigate the shape of this activation function:

1. Let's start by defining the function, as we did in other examples. The formula simply takes a value and multiplies it by the result of passing the exact same value through the sigmoid function:

   ```
   swish <- function(x){x * sigmoid(x)}
   ```

2. After this, we will create our dataset again with the same sequence of values that we have used previously and a corresponding set of transformed values:

   ```
   vals <- tibble(x = seq(-10, 10, 1), swish_x = swish(seq(-10, 10, 1)))
   ```

3. Finally, we can plot these points to display the shape of this function:

   ```
   p <- ggplot(vals, aes(x, swish_x))
   p <- p + geom_point()
   p + geom_line()
   ```

As we look at this shape, we will see that, like ReLU, it has a lower bound and no upper bound; however, unlike ReLU and all other activation functions, it is nonmonotonic—that is, we can see that the values for y when x is negative first decrease and then increase. This feature has been shown to be especially beneficial as neural networks get progressively deeper:

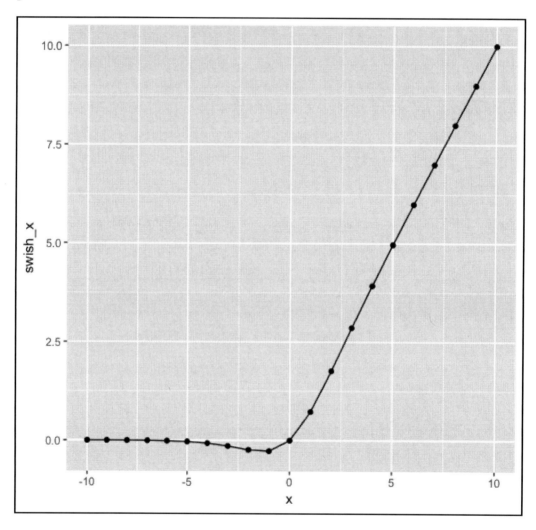

Predicting class likelihood with softmax

The `softmax()` function is needed when there is more than one target variable. Softmax will create probabilities that a particular set of input variables belongs to each class. After these results are calculated, they can be used to assign input rows to one of the possible target classes. Let's explore this activation function with a slightly different example:

1. We will start by defining the function:

```
softmax <- function(x) {exp(x) / sum(exp(x))}
```

2. Next, let's pass a vector of values to the function:

```
results <- softmax(c(2,3,6,9))
results
```

```
[1]  0.0008658387  0.0023535935  0.0472731888  0.9495073791
```

3. Let's confirm that the sum of these transformed values equals 1:

```
sum(results)
```

```
[1] 1
```

We can see that this function will take a set of values and calculate a probability that each is a value we are trying to predict so that the sum of all probabilities is 1. This can be used to select the most likely value among a set of more than two values for a given target.

Creating a feedforward network

With an understanding of neural networks, we will now build some simple examples. First, we will create the functions needed to create a very simple neural network ourselves to better understand what is happening during the modeling process. Afterward, we will use the `neuralnet` package to build a neural network that solves a task using a simple dataset.

Writing a neural network with Base R

For this example, we will use Base R to create a very simple neural network from scratch to better understand exactly what is happening at each step. In order to complete this task we will do the following:

- Define the activation function for the neurons in our model
- Create a function that shows the line after every iteration of learning the weights
- Make some test data and plot these data values
- Update weights using the results of the previous attempt

We will use the following steps to do so:

1. First, we code the Heaviside (binary) step activation function to start. We will recall that this function evaluates the input and if this value is greater than zero, then the output value of the function is 1; otherwise, the value is 0. We can express this logic in code using the following lines of code:

   ```
   artificial_neuron <- function(input) {  as.vector(ifelse(input %*%
   weights > 0, 1, 0))
   }
   ```

2. Next, we can create the function for drawing the line using random weights at first and then the learned weight as we iterate over and update the values passed to the expression portion of the curve function, as shown here:

   ```
   linear_fits <- function(w, to_add = TRUE, line_type = 1) {curve(-
   w[1] / w[2] * x - w[3] / w[2], xlim = c(-1, 2), ylim = c(-1, 2),
   col = "black",lty = line_type, lwd = 2, xlab = "Input Value A",
   ylab = "Input Value B", add = to_add)}
   ```

   In the expression equation, we can see that everything is relative to x. In this case, if we just ran curve((x)), then we would get a line at exactly 45 degrees so that the x and y were always equal and the slope of the line was 1. In the preceding code, we use the weights to change the slope of the line relative to x. The remainder just defines the plot and the line and the add argument is used to declare whether the new line produced by the curve function should be added to the plot in addition to the line or lines already there.

3. With these functions defined, we can now assign some initial values for the input, output, learning rate, and weights. The input values are a set of *x* and *y* coordinates along with a constant value. The output values are just binary flags, in this case, denoting whether the input variable is or is not a member of the target class. Lastly, some random weights are included to initialize the model, along with a learning rate that will be used for updating weights at every iteration:

```
input <- matrix(c(1, 0,
                  0, 0,
                  1, 1,
                  0, 1), ncol = 2, byrow = TRUE)
input <- cbind(input, 1)
output <- c(0, 1, 0, 1)
weights <- c(0.12, 0.18, 0.24)
learning_rate <- 0.2
```

4. Next, we can add our first line, which is the guess using the random weights along with our output points. We would like to arrive at a line that completely bisects the two points that belong to the target class from the two points that do not. To start, we apply our initial random weights to the expression equation within the `linear_fits()` function to create an initial slope. The `points()` function adds our points with squares to the two points that are part of the target class and circles for the points that are not part of this class:

```
linear_fits(weights, to_add = FALSE)
points(input[ , 1:2], pch = (output + 21))
```

As we can tell from the following plot that is generated by the preceding code, this first line is extremely far from bisecting the two classes:

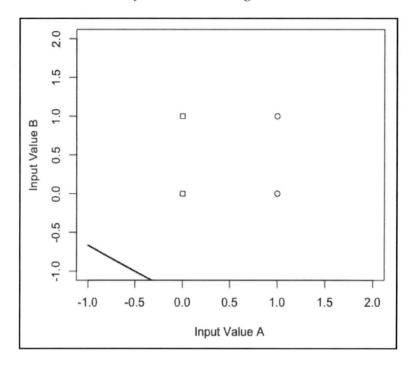

4. Now, we will begin to update the weights by using the values from the corresponding input and output values. First, the weights are updated by the learning rate. The smaller this number is, the more gradual the changes will be. This is multiplied by the target class value minus the product of the result of the artificial neuron function, which again is either 0 or 1 since we are using the binary step activation function and the first input values. The `linear_fits()` function is then used again to draw one more line:

```
weights <- weights + learning_rate * (output[1] -
artificial_neuron(input[1, ])) * input[1, ]
linear_fits(weights)
```

Using the `linear_fits()` function, we have created a new line that is closer to bisecting the classes, and yet it is not yet completely dividing the points as we would like:

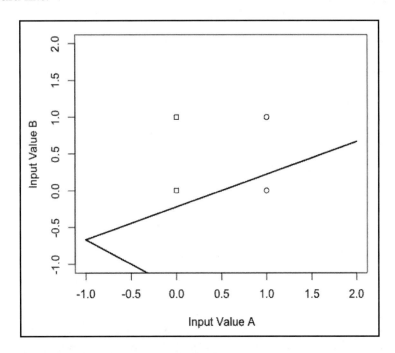

5. This same operation is repeated for the remainder of the input and output values. A different line type is used for the last plot because, as we will see, this line solves the problem and finds a slope that separates the two classes. The third line is drawn next:

```
weights <- weights + learning_rate * (output[2] -
artificial_neuron(input[2, ])) * input[2, ]
linear_fits(weights)
```

Here, the third line completely overlaps the second line:

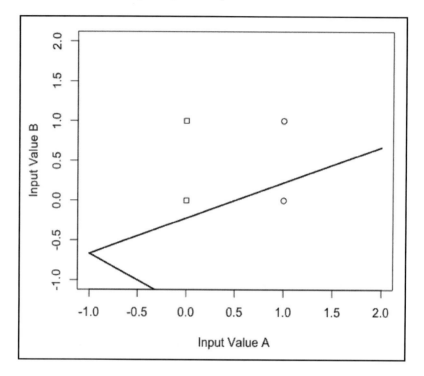

6. The next code is used to draw the fourth line:

```
weights <- weights + learning_rate * (output[3] -
artificial_neuron(input[3, ])) * input[3, ]
linear_fits(weights)
```

The fourth line deviates further away from bisecting the points than the second or the third line:

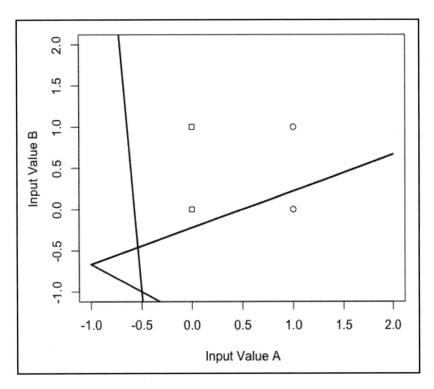

7. The final line is created using the following line of code:

```
weights <- weights + learning_rate * (output[4] -
artificial_neuron(input[4, ])) * input[4, ]
linear_fits(weights, line_type = 2)
```

We see here that the dotted line successfully bisects the square points and separates them from the circular points:

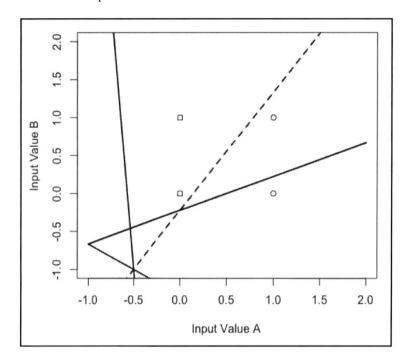

In this minimal example, we can see what is happening when we fit a neural network. The model attempts to separate different classes of variables just like in other machine-learning models. In this case, during every iteration, the weights are updated depending on whether the neuron fires along with the constant change introduced by the learning rate value. Through this process, the goal is to reduce the error rate. In this case, we did not define a formal error rate as we could clearly see when the line successfully divided the classes. In the next example, we will step away from the underlying math and focus on optimizing a slightly more complex neural network using an open source dataset.

Creating a model with Wisconsin cancer data

For this example, we will use the breast cancer dataset from the University of Wisconsin. Details on this dataset can be found at the UCI Machine Learning Repository at `http://archive.ics.uci.edu/ml/datasets/breast+cancer+wisconsin+%28diagnostic%29`.

1. The dataset can be loaded using the following lines of code:

```
library(tidyverse)

wbdc <-
readr::read_csv("http://archive.ics.uci.edu/ml/machine-learning-dat
abases/breast-cancer-wisconsin/wdbc.data", col_names = FALSE)
```

2. After loading the data, we will encode the target variable by converting the column from a character column with two character values that indicate whether or not there were signs of malignancy to a numeric data type holding binary values. For this type of neural network, we will need all values to be numeric, including the target variable:

```
wbdc <- wbdc %>%
    dplyr::mutate(target = dplyr::if_else(X2 == "M", 1, 0)) %>%
    dplyr::select(-X2)
```

3. Next, we will scale and standardize all of our predictor values. As we mentioned, all data needs to be numeric for the neural network, and by scaling and standardizing the data, we will increase performance by giving the activation functions a set of values that are all constrained within the same boundaries:

```
wbdc <- wbdc %>% dplyr::mutate_at(vars(-X1, -target), funs((. -
min(.))/(max(.) - min(.)) ))
```

4. Next, we will partition to train and test, just like in our machine learning example. We will use the ID column in X1 for splitting the data in this step; however, afterward, we can drop this column. Here, we will use a `tidyverse` approach to simplify the process:

```
train <- wbdc %>% dplyr::sample_frac(.8)
test  <- dplyr::anti_join(wbdc, train, by = 'X1')

test <- test %>% dplyr::select(-X1)
train <- train  %>% dplyr::select(-X1)
```

5. Our last data preparation step is to extract all the actual correct responses from the test data and then remove this column from the test dataset. This vector of values will be used to calculate performance after modeling:

```
actual <- test$target
test <- test %>% dplyr::select(-target)
```

The data is now completely prepared and ready for modeling with a neural network.

6. Next, we need to create the formula syntax for the `neuralnet` package, which is a dependent variable ~. This is similar to the syntax for fitting a linear model with R. All independent variables can be connected with the + sign between each one; however, when there are many independent variables, then it would be very tedious to write the name for every column, even in this example, where the column names are just X followed by a number. Fortunately, there is a way to expedite this process, which we will use in the following steps. First, we will get the names for all of the columns in our train set and then, using paste and collapse, we will create the string of independent variables to go on the other side of our formula from the dependent variable:

```
n <- names(train)
formula <- as.formula(paste("target ~", paste(n[!n == "target"],
collapse = " + ", sep = "")))
```

7. With this set, we can now fit our model. In this case, we will keep the model fairly simple, only using a few of the arguments available for this function. Specifically, we include the formula that we just created, defining the dependent and independent variables. Next, we indicate that the model will be fit to the train data. Choosing the correct number of layers and units per layer involves trying a few combinations and comparing performance. In this case, we start with two layers containing about half as many units as there are variables. Lastly, we note that the activation function should be logistic, which is the sigmoid function, and that we are not performing a linear operation:

```
net <- neuralnet::neuralnet(formula,
                data = train,
                hidden = c(15,15),
                linear.output = FALSE,
                act.fct = "logistic"
                )
```

8. With the modeling process complete, we can now use our model to make predictions. With the `neuralnet` package, we use the `compute()` function to generate these prediction values:

```
prediction_list <- neuralnet::compute(net, test)
```

9. When we pass the model and the test dataset through the `compute()` function, we are given a list. The list contains details about the neurons within the model, along with the predicted values. In this case, we just want the predicted values, so we will pull these from the list. In addition, we will create a set of binary predictions. The binary predictions are created by changing values to 1, if the predicted probability is greater than 0.5; otherwise, the value is changed to a 0. We will use each set of predictions for two different model evaluation methods:

```
predictions <- as.vector(prediction_list$net.result)
binary_predictions <- dplyr::if_else(predictions > 0.5, 1, 0)
```

10. Using our binary predictions, we can easily calculate basic model accuracy—that is, we will sum the number of cases where the binary predicted value matches the actual value and divide that number by the total number of actual values:

```
sum(binary_predictions == actual)/length(actual)
```

Here, we see that the accuracy is 92.98%, so our basic neural net has performed quite well on this data.

11. We can also look at the breakdown for this accuracy value by using a confusion matrix. The simplest way to produce a confusion matrix is to use the `confusionMatrix()` function, which is part of the `caret` package. This function requires a table containing the predicted valued and the actual values as an argument. In this case, we need to use our binary predictions as the results need to fit into one of four categories, and as such, levels of granularity are not permitted:

```
results_table <- table(binary_predictions, actual)
library(caret)
caret::confusionMatrix(results_table)

# Confusion Matrix and Statistics
#
# actual
# binary_predictions  0  1
# 0 67   2
# 1  1  44
#
```

```
# Accuracy : 0.9737
# 95% CI : (0.925, 0.9945)
# No Information Rate : 0.5965
# P-Value [Acc > NIR] : <2e-16
#
# Kappa : 0.9451
# Mcnemar's Test P-Value : 1
#
# Sensitivity : 0.9853
# Specificity : 0.9565
# Pos Pred Value : 0.9710
# Neg Pred Value : 0.9778
# Prevalence : 0.5965
# Detection Rate : 0.5877
# Detection Prevalence : 0.6053
# Balanced Accuracy : 0.9709
#
# 'Positive' Class : 0
```

12. After calling this function, we see that we are provided with a two by two grid containing the results. The confusion matrix has categorized our predictions into the following four outcomes:

   - **True positives**: Values of 1 correctly predicted to be 1. The actual test target variable contains the value we are predicting and we correctly predicted it.
   - **Type I errors**: Values of 0 incorrectly predicted to be values of 1. The actual test target variable does not have the value we are predicting; however, we predicted that it will. Also referred to as a false positive.
   - **Type II errors**: Values of 1 incorrectly predicted to be values of 0. The actual test target variable does have the value we are predicting; however, we predicted that it will not. Also referred to as a false negative.
   - **True negatives**: Values of 0 correctly predicted to be 0. The actual test target variable does not contain the value we are predicting and we correctly predicted that it would not have it.

It also includes a number of other statistical measures that are outside the scope of this chapter; however, we can note that the accuracy is included and the value matches the value that we just calculated ourselves.

In addition to using our binary prediction to calculate accuracy, we can also use our probabilities so that we take into account the level of certainty for each outcome. In order to measure performance using these values, we will use the AUC, or area under the curve, score. This compares the probabilities for true positive cases with the probabilities for false positive cases. The final result is a measure of the confidence that positive values are positive and that negative values are negative, or in this case, that negative values are not incorrectly labeled positive with high confidence.

13. To calculate the AUC score, we can use the `auc()` function, which is part of the `Metrics` package. The function takes two arguments—a vector of actual values and a vector of predicted probabilities that a record should be classified as the target variable based on the model's interpretation of the independent variable for that row:

```
library(Metrics)
Metrics::auc(actual, predictions)
```

The AUC score of 0.987 is even stronger than the accuracy score calculated previously.

This model is already working very well at solving the prediction task using this dataset; however, we will now try to add a backpropagation step and see if we can improve performance further.

Augmenting our neural network with backpropagation

At this point, we have a working neural network. For this simple example, we will add one additional feature of neural networks that can improve performance, which is backpropagation. A neural network can learn to solve a task by multiplying the variable by values so that the variables are weighted as they pass through hidden layers. The backpropagation step allows the model to traverse back through layers and adjust the weights that were learned during previous steps:

1. In practical terms, this step is quite straightforward to implement. We simply declare that we will use the backpropagation algorithm and indicate the learning rate, which controls how much the weights are adjusted. In general, this learning rate value should be very low.

In the following example, we have to do the following:

- The `threshold` value and `stepmax` value have to be changed as the model failed to converge using the default values.
- The `threshold` argument defines the value that the error rate must reach before the model stops and the `stepmax` argument defines the number of iterations the model will run before stopping.

By changing these values, you can program the model to run longer and stop sooner, both of which will help if you run into an error when converging:

```
bp_net <- neuralnet::neuralnet(formula,
                    data = train,
                    hidden = c(15,15),
                    linear.output = FALSE,
                    act.fct = "logistic",
                    algorithm = "backprop",
                    learningrate = 0.00001,
                    threshold = 0.3,
                    stepmax = 1e6
)
```

2. After running this new version of the model, we can run the same steps again to assess performance. First, we will run `compute` on the new model to get new predictions. We will once again create a vector of probabilities and binary predictions, and as a first step, we will create the table of binary prediction values and actual values and pass this to the `confusionMatrix()` function. We will skip calculating the accuracy this time around as it is included in the output from the call to the `confusionMatrix()` function:

```
prediction_list <- neuralnet::compute(bp_net, test)
predictions <- as.vector(prediction_list$net.result)
binary_predictions <- dplyr::if_else(predictions > 0.5, 1, 0)
results_table <- table(binary_predictions, actual)
caret::confusionMatrix(results_table)
```

3. Our accuracy has improved, increasing from 92.98% to 94.74%. Let's now check our AUC score. Again, we simply pass the actual values and predicted probabilities to the `auc()` function:

```
Metrics::auc(actual, predictions)
```

Our AUC score has improved, increasing from 0.987 to 0.993, so we can see that backpropagation does improve model performance.

That being said, what exactly is happening during this step?

- The backpropagation step takes the derivative of the error rate and uses this to update weights based on results.
- The derivative is just the rate at which the current weights impact the error rate. So if the derivative rate is 7, then changing the weights by a single unit will result in a change to the error rate that is 7 times larger.
- Using just a feedforward neural network, we can update the initial weights based on the final derivative value; however, using backpropagation, we can update the weights at every neuron.
- Using information about how previous changes have impacted the derivative, this step either increases or decreases the weights.
- The learning rate is applied so that changes are never dramatic but rather smooth and gradual. This process can continue until the error rate is minimized.

Summary

In this chapter, we learned that deep learning is differentiated from other machine-learning algorithms because of the use of multiple hidden layers. This network of hidden layers, which are composed of artificial neurons, was designed to mimic the way our brain processes input signals to interpret our environment. The units within the hidden layers take in all the independent variables and apply some weights to these variables. In this way, each neuron classifies the combination of input values in different ways.

From understanding the architecture of this type of machine learning from a high level, we then took a deeper dive into the actual process of converting the input to predictions using this approach. We discussed the various activation functions that act as the gate for every neuron, determining whether a signal should be passed to the next layer. We then built two feedforward neural networks—one using base R for a better understanding of what is happening and another using the `neuralnet` package on a larger dataset. Lastly, we applied the backpropagation step to further improve our model.

As stated, the artificial neural network is the fundamental building block for more complex deep learning, and now that we have this understanding, we will move on to creating convolutional neural networks for image recognition in the next chapter.

Section 2: Deep Learning Applications

This section covers various deep learning applications in image processing, natural language processing, recommender systems, and predictive analytics. The reader will learn how to tackle recognition problems including image recognition and signal detection, programmatically summarize documents, conduct topic modeling, and forecast stock market prices.

This section comprises the following chapters:

4
CNNs for Image Recognition

In this chapter, you will learn to use **convolutional neural networks (CNNs)** for image recognition. Convolutional neural networks are a variation of neural networks that are particularly well-suited to image recognition because they take into account the relationship between data points in space.

We will cover how convolutional neural networks differ from the basic feedforward, fully connected neural network that we created in the last chapter. The main difference is that the hidden layers in a CNN are not all fully connected dense layers—CNNs include a number of special layers. One of these is the convolutional layer, which convolves a filter around the image space. The other special layer is a pooling layer, which reduces the size of the input and only persists particular values. We will go into more depth on these layers later in the chapter.

As we learn about these concepts, we will see why they are so critical for image recognition. When we think about classifying images, we know that we need to detect patterns among arrays of pixels and that the neighboring pixels are important for finding certain shapes. By learning more about the convolution layer, you will know how to adjust the filter or lens to detect different patterns depending on your image data. You will also learn how to adjust the pooling layer depending on the size of your data to help make your model run more efficiently.

Specifically, this chapter will cover the following topics:

- Image recognition with shallow nets
- Image recognition with convolutional neural networks
- Enhancing the model with appropriate activation layers
- Choosing the most appropriate activation function
- Selecting optimal epochs using dropout and early stopping

Technical requirements

You can find the code files of this chapter on the GitHub link at https://github.com/PacktPublishing/Hands-on-Deep-Learning-with-R.

Image recognition with shallow nets

Image classifiers can be created without using deep-learning algorithms and methods. To demonstrate, let's use the **Fashion MNIST** dataset, which is an alternative to the MNIST handwriting dataset. The name MNIST stands for the **Modified National Institute of Standards and Technology** database, and as the name suggests, it is a modified version of the original dataset created by the National Institute of Standards and Technology. While MNIST is a series of hand-drawn numbers, Fashion MNIST uses small images of different types of clothing. The clothing in the dataset is labeled with one of ten categories. Fashion MNIST has nothing to do with the National Institute of Standards and Technology; however, the MNIST name carried over since it is well-known as a database to use for image recognition.

Since this dataset is not very large and each image is only 28 x 28 pixels, we can use a machine-learning algorithm, such as RandomForest, to train a classifier. We will train a very simple RandomForest model and achieve surprisingly good results; however, at the end of the chapter, we will discuss why these same results will not scale as the dataset gets larger and the individual images get larger. We will now code our image recognition model using traditional machine-learning methods:

1. We will start by loading the tidyverse suite of packages, as shown in the following code. In this case, we only need readr for reading in the data; however, we will use other packages later. We will also load randomForest for training our model and caret for evaluating our model performance:

```
library(tidyverse)
library(caret)
library(randomForest)
```

The code here will not return any values to the console; however, within the RStudio environment, we will see a checkmark next to these packages in the **Packages** window indicating that they are ready to be used. Your **Packages** pane should look like the following image, which shows that two of three packages have been loaded:

2. Next, we read in the train and test data for the Fashion MNIST dataset with the help of the following code:

```
fm <- readr::read_csv('fashionmnist/fashion-mnist_train.csv')
fm_test <- readr::read_csv('fashionmnist/fashion-mnist_test.csv')
```

This code will place two data objects in our environment called `fm` and `fm_test`. The **Environment** pane should look like the following screenshot:

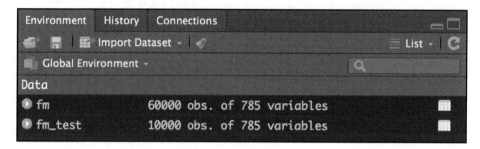

We will use `fm` to train our model. The data from `fm` will be used to compute weights for splits along this tree-based model. We will then use our model, which contains information on how the independent variable values relate to the target variables, to predict target variables for the `fm_test` data using the independent variable values.

3. Next, we will train our model. We set a seed for reproducibility so that we get the same quasirandom numbers every time we run the model, and as such, we always get the same results. We convert the label to a factor. The label, in this case, is an integer between 0 and 9; however, we do not want the model to treat these values numerically. Instead, they should be treated as different categories. The remaining columns aside from the label are all pixel values. We use ~. to denote that we will use all the remaining columns (all the pixel values) as independent variables for our model. We will grow 10 trees because this is simply an example that image classification can be done this way. Lastly, we will choose 5 variables at random during every split in our tree. We will train our `RandomForest` model in this way using the following code:

```
set.seed(0)

rf_model <- randomForest::randomForest(as.factor(label)~.,
data = fm,
ntree=10,
mtry=5)
```

When we execute the code, the model will run, which can take several minutes. During this time, we will be unable to execute any code in the console. We can see that the model is now in our environment. The following screenshot shows some of the details contained in the model object:

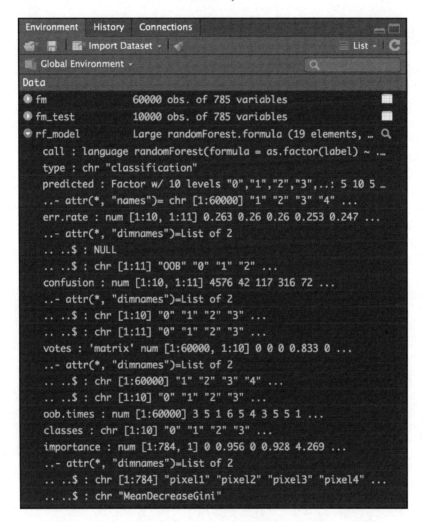

We can use this model object to make predictions on new data.

4. We then use our model to make predictions on the test dataset and use the `ConfusionMatrix` function to evaluate performance. The following code will populate the vector of predicted values and then evaluate the accuracy of the predictions:

```
pred <- predict(rf_model, fm_test, type="response")

caret::confusionMatrix(as.factor(fm_test$label), pred)

# Accuracy : 0.8457
```

The preceding code will create one last data object, which is a vector that holds the predicted values for each case based on the model being trained on the independent variables for that dataset. We also printed some output to our console with performance metrics. The output that you receive will look like the following screenshot:

```
Confusion Matrix and Statistics

          Reference
Prediction   0   1   2   3   4   5   6   7   8   9
         0 820   2  19  41   7   0  98   0  13   0
         1   5 954   8  23   3   1   5   0   1   0
         2  16   2 749   7 132   1  86   0   7   0
         3  30   8  11 901  34   0  16   0   0   0
         4   2   4 112  44 770   1  64   0   3   0
         5   0   0   0   0   0 928   0  45   7  20
         6 206   1 107  35 114   0 515   0  22   0
         7   0   0   0   0   0  28   0 907   2  63
         8   4   2  10   0   5   4  12   4 959   0
         9   0   1   0   0   0  12   0  53   3 931

Overall Statistics

               Accuracy : 0.8434
                 95% CI : (0.8361, 0.8505)
    No Information Rate : 0.1083
    P-Value [Acc > NIR] : < 2.2e-16

                  Kappa : 0.826
 Mcnemar's Test P-Value : NA
```

The metrics are based on comparing the actual target variables for the test dataset with the predicted values from modeling on the test data.

Surprisingly, this model produced decent results. We have achieved an accuracy of 84.6%. This shows that a simple approach can work for a dataset like this; however, as the data scales up, this type of model will have worse performance.

To understand why, we should first explain how images are stored as data for modeling. When we view a grayscale image, we see lighter and darker areas. In fact, every pixel holds an integer from 0 for white to 255 for black and anywhere in between. These numbers are converted into tones so that we can visualize the image; however, for our purposes, we use these raw pixel values. When modeling with `RandomForest`, each pixel value is compared in isolation with all the other images; however, this is rarely ideal. Usually, we want to look for larger patterns of pixels within each image.

Let's explore how to create a shallow neural network with just one layer. The hidden layer of the neural network will perform a calculation using all input values so that the entire image is considered. We are going to make this a simple binominal classification problem for illustration purposes and use a method to create our neural network that is similar to the method we used in the last chapter. If you completed that chapter, then this will likely look familiar. Completing the previous chapter is not a prerequisite as we will walk through all the steps here:

1. Before starting, we will load two more libraries for the following code: the `neuralnet` package for training our model and the `Metrics` package for evaluation functions. In particular, we will use the AUC metric later to evaluate our model. Both of these libraries can be loaded by running the following lines of code:

   ```
   library(neuralnet)
   library(Metrics)
   ```

This code will not cause anything to happen in the console; however, we will see checks by these packages in the **Package** pane indicating that these packages are ready to use. Your **Packages** pane will look like the following screenshot:

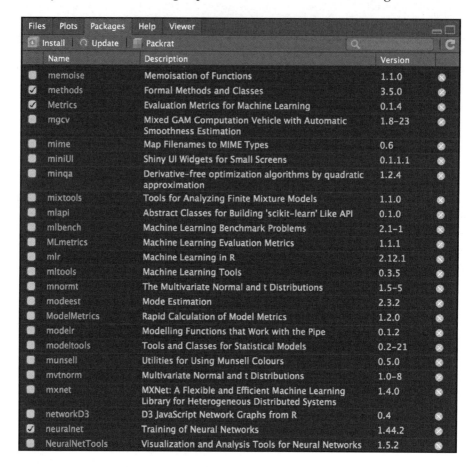

2. First, we will change the **target** column so that it is a simple binary response rather than include all ten categories. This is done so that we can keep this neural network very straightforward, as this is just to create a benchmark for comparing with our CNN later and to show how coding the two styles of neural networks differs. This filtering is accomplished by running the following lines of code:

```
fm <- fm %>% dplyr::filter(label < 2)

fm_test <- fm_test %>% dplyr::filter(label < 2)
```

After running this code, we will see that the size of our data objects has changed and reduced in size as a result of our filtering. You should see that your data objects have changed from having 60,000 and 10,000 observations respectively to 12,000 and 2,000, as shown in the following screenshot:

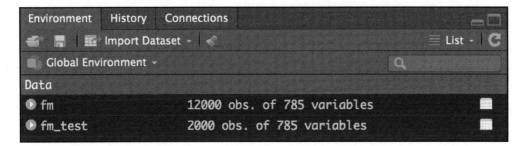

With the data in this format, we are now able to proceed with writing our code as a binary response task.

3. Now, using the following code, we will remove the target variable from the test set and isolate it in a separate vector for evaluation later:

```
test_label <- fm_test$label

fm_test <- fm_test %>% dplyr::select(-label)
```

After running this code you will notice two changes: there is one less variable or column in the `fm_test` object and there is a new data object called `test_label`, which is a vector containing the values that were in the label column of the `fm_test` object. Your **Environment** pane should look like the following screenshot:

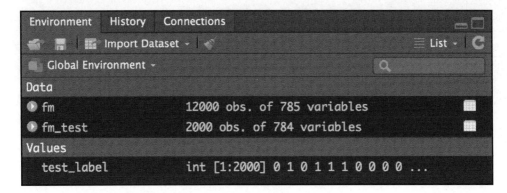

We have made this change because we do not want the label in our test object. In this object, we need to treat the data as if we do not know the true classes so that we can try to predict the classes. We then use the labels from the vector later to evaluate how well we predicted the correct values.

4. Next, we will create the formula for our neural network. Using the `neuralnet` function from the `neuralnet` package, we need our formula to be formatted with the target variable on one side of a tilde (~) and all of our independent variables on the other side connected by plus (+) signs. In the following code, we collect all columns names into a vector n and then use `paste` to concatenate each term from this vector with a plus sign in between:

```
n <- names(fm)
formula <- as.formula(paste("label ~", paste(n[!n == "label"],
collapse = " + ", sep = "")))
```

After running this code, we can see the changes in our **Environment** pane. We will see the vector n that contains all the column names and the `formula` object that has the dependent variable and independent variables placed together in the proper format. Your **Environment** pane should now look like the following screenshot:

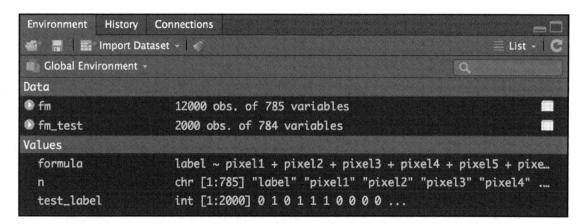

We ran the preceding code in order to create this `formula` object as it is a requirement for training a neural network using the `neuralnet` package.

5. After this, we can write the code to train our model. We will set a seed for reproducibility as we always do with modeling. We will include one hidden layer with the number of units set to approximately one-third the number of predictor variables. We will set the `linear.output` argument to `false` to denote that this will be a classification model. We will also set the activation function to `logistic` because this is a classification problem. We train our model in the way we described earlier using the following code:

```
set.seed(0)

net <- neuralnet::neuralnet(formula,
                            data = fm,
                            hidden = 250,
                            linear.output = FALSE,
                            act.fct = "logistic"
)
```

After running the code, we now have a new object in our **Environment** pane that contains all the details gathered from training our model that can now be applied to make predictions on new data. Your **Environment** pane should contain a model object similar to the one shown in the following screenshot:

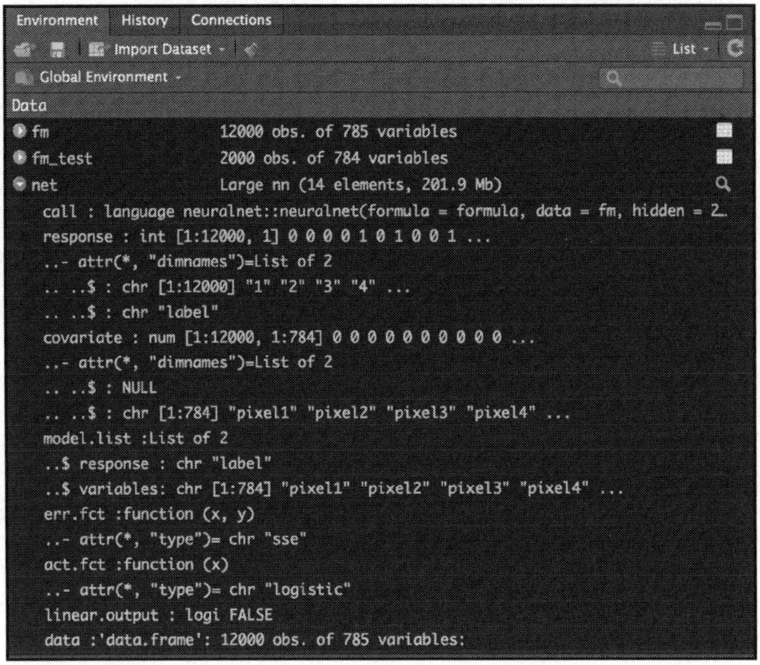

Now that we have run this code, we have a model that we can use to make predictions on our test data.

6. Lastly, we can make our predictions and evaluate our results with the help of the following code:

```
prediction_list <- neuralnet::compute(net, fm_test)
predictions <- as.vector(prediction_list$net.result)

Metrics::auc(test_label, predictions)
```

Running this code will print the accuracy metric to the console. Your console should contain output just like the following image:

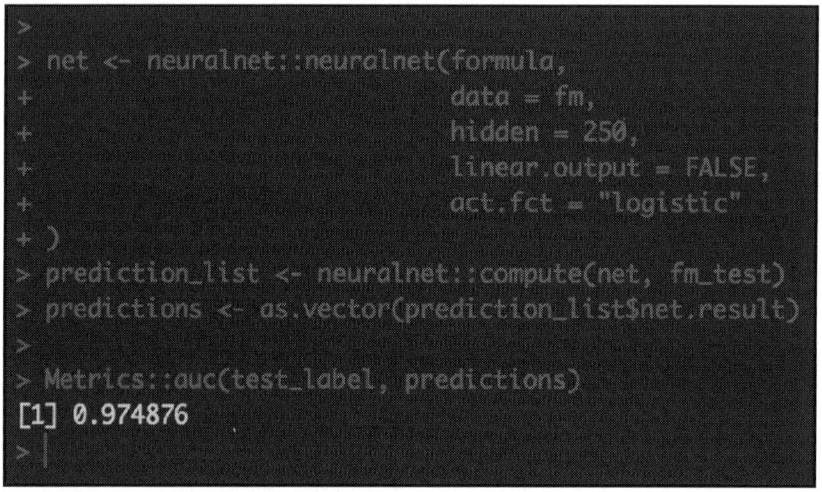

```
>
> net <- neuralnet::neuralnet(formula,
+                              data = fm,
+                              hidden = 250,
+                              linear.output = FALSE,
+                              act.fct = "logistic"
+ )
> prediction_list <- neuralnet::compute(net, fm_test)
> predictions <- as.vector(prediction_list$net.result)
>
> Metrics::auc(test_label, predictions)
[1] 0.974876
>
```

Looking at this output, we see that we have a significant improvement already. Accuracy is now up to 97.487%. When the pixels were considered in concert, it did improve results. We should remember that this model only used two target variables, and the selection of these target variables could also be part of the reason for the significant increase. In any case, with larger images, it is not efficient to push all pixel values to an activation function. This is where convolutional neural networks come in to solve this problem. They are able to look at smaller groupings of pixel values to look for patterns. They also contain a means of reducing dimensionality.

Let's now explore what separates convolutional neural networks from traditional neural networks.

Image recognition with convolutional neural networks

Convolutional neural networks are a special form of neural network. In a traditional neural network, the input is passed to the model as vectors; however, for image data, it is more helpful to have the data arranged as matrices because we want to capture the relationship of the pixel values in two-dimensional space.

Convolutional neural networks are able to capture these two-dimensional relationships through the use of a filter that convolves over the image data. The filter is a matrix with constant values and dimensions that are smaller than the image data. The constant values are multiplied by the underlying values and the sum of the resulting products is passed through to an activation function.

The activation function step, which can also be considered a separate layer, evaluates whether a given pattern is present in an image. In a traditional neural network, the activation layer determines whether the calculated value from the input values exceeds a threshold and should be fed forward in the model. In a convolutional neural network, the activation layer operates in a very similar way; however, because it uses matrix multiplication, it is able to evaluate whether a two-dimensional shape is present in the data.

After the activation layer, the data is further processed by a pooling layer. The function of the pooling layer is to concentrate the signal captured in the previous step while also reducing the dimensionality of the data. The pooling layer will result in a matrix that is smaller than the input data. Often a 2 x 2 pooling layer will be used that reduces the size of the input data by half. In this case, the values within every 2 x 2 section are pooled through some sort of aggregation. These values can be aggregated using any means, such as summing and averaging the values; however, in most cases, the max value is used and this value is passed to the pooling layer.

After the preceding method has been implemented, the processed and reduced image data is flattened and the vectors are then fed forward to essentially a traditional neural network as the last step. Let's start here with just this final step, since we are familiar with using a traditional neural network to model from the previous code. Here, we will see two things: firstly, that we can train a model on image data using just this final step, and secondly, that the syntax is slightly different but generally recognizable when compared with training this type of model using the `neuralnet` package.

We will now code a neural network consisting of fully connected dense hidden layers using the `keras` package:

1. First, we will load the `keras` library and the Fashion MNIST dataset that comes with the package. This is accomplished by running the following code:

```
library(keras)

fashion_mnist <- dataset_fashion_mnist()
```

When we run the preceding code, we will see that we get both the train and test data together in one list object. Your **Environment** pane should now look like the following:

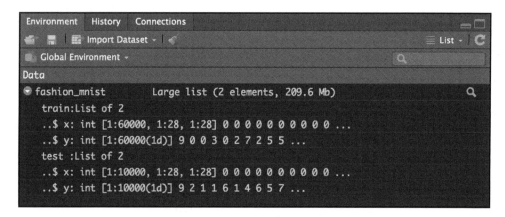

2. Next, we can split the dataset into its component parts. It is conveniently set up so that it is easy to extract the training and test datasets and target variables. In the previous code, we used a version of the Fashion MNIST data that has already been preprocessed so that every pixel was in a separate column; however, in the following code, we will start with a large array of 28 x 28 matrices and demonstrate how to transform this data so that all pixel values for a given image are in the same row. The first step in the process is to separate out the four data objects from the list using the preceding code:

```
train <- fashion_mnist$train$x
train_target <- fashion_mnist$train$y

test <- fashion_mnist$test$x
test_target <- fashion_mnist$test$y
```

When you look at your **Environment** pane now, you will see the image data stored in 28 x 28 matrices and the target variables in vectors within an array. Your **Environment** pane will look like the following:

```
Environment   History   Connections                                    ━ ☐
  📥  📄  📊 Import Dataset ▾  🔍                          ≡ List ▾  C
  🌐 Global Environment ▾                                  🔍
Data
  ⊙ fashion_mnist        Large list (2 elements, 209.6 Mb)          🔍
     train:List of 2
     ..$ x: int [1:60000, 1:28, 1:28] 0 0 0 0 0 0 0 0 0 0 ...
     ..$ y: int [1:60000(1d)] 9 0 0 3 0 2 7 2 5 5 ...
     test :List of 2
     ..$ x: int [1:10000, 1:28, 1:28] 0 0 0 0 0 0 0 0 0 0 ...
     ..$ y: int [1:10000(1d)] 9 2 1 1 6 1 4 6 5 7 ...
Values
  ⊙ test                 Large array (7840000 elements, 29.9 Mb)
     nt [1:10000, 1:28, 1:28] 0 0 0 0 0 0 0 0 0 0 ...
     test_target         int [1:10000(1d)] 9 2 1 1 6 1 4 6 5 7 ...
  ⊙ train                Large array (47040000 elements, 179.4 Mb)
     nt [1:60000, 1:28, 1:28] 0 0 0 0 0 0 0 0 0 0 ...
     train_target        int [1:60000(1d)] 9 0 0 3 0 2 7 2 5 5 ...
```

With our data in this format, we could apply our convolutional filters, which we will do soon; however, at this point, we are going to code a dense, fully connected neural network, and in order to do so, we will need to get all the data to one row per image instead of a two-dimensional matrix per image. Since we need the data in both formats at different stages of coding a convolutional neural network, it is a straightforward conversion process that we will complete in step six.

3. Image data consists of a matrix or matrices of pixel values between 0 and 255. To process this data with our neural network, we need to convert these values to floats between 0 and 1. As shown in the following code, we will use the normalize() convenience function to achieve this result and the range() function to test whether the values are now between 0 and 1:

```
train <- normalize(train)
test <- normalize(test)

range(train)
```

After running this code, we may not see a noticeable change in the **Environment** pane for our data objects; however, when we run the `range()` function, we can see that all values are now between `0` and `1`. The output to your console after running the `range()` function on the data object will look like this:

```
> train <- normalize(train)
> test <- normalize(test)
> range(train)
[1] 0 1
>
```

4. Now we can begin to train our model using the `keras` syntax. In the following code, we begin by declaring that we will be creating a sequential model, which means that data will pass through each subsequent layer in turn:

```
set.seed(0)

model <- keras_model_sequential()
```

Running the preceding code initiates the model object; however, it doesn't contain any data yet. You can see this in your **Environment** pane, which will look like this:

```
Environment   History   Connections
    |  Import Dataset -  |                                    ≡ List -  C
  Global Environment -                                    Q
Data
 fashion_mnist       Large list (2 elements, 209.6 Mb)              Q
    train:List of 2
    ..$ x: int [1:60000, 1:28, 1:28] 0 0 0 0 0 0 0 0 0 0 ...
    ..$ y: int [1:60000(1d)] 9 0 0 3 0 2 7 2 5 5 ...
    test :List of 2
    ..$ x: int [1:10000, 1:28, 1:28] 0 0 0 0 0 0 0 0 0 0 ...
    ..$ y: int [1:10000(1d)] 9 2 1 1 6 1 4 6 5 7 ...
Values
    model
 test                Large array (7840000 elements, 59.8 Mb)
    um [1:10000, 1:28, 1:28] 0 0 0 0 0 0 0 0 0 0 ...
    test_target         int [1:10000(1d)] 9 2 1 1 6 1 4 6 5 7 ...
 train               Large array (47040000 elements, 358.9 Mb)
    um [1:60000, 1:28, 1:28] 0 0 0 0 0 0 0 0 0 0 ...
    train_target        int [1:60000(1d)] 9 0 0 3 0 2 7 2 5 5 ...
```

5. The steps we take next are the final steps of a convolutional neural network and represent the part of the process where the data is converted in such a way that it can be processed by a traditional neural network. The first step will be to define the layer that takes the data from a large array of matrices and transforms the data so that all values for a given image are in one single row. To do this, we use the `layer_flatten()` function and pass the matrix shape in as an argument, as shown here:

```
model %>%
    layer_flatten(input_shape = c(28, 28))
```

The preceding code and the remainder of the steps that define the model will not cause a noticeable change in your R environment. This step adds a layer to the model object, though. This layer flattens our data so that the data for every image will be contained in a single row.

6. We will include one hidden layer as we have done previously. The way this is done in `keras` is to use the `layer_dense` function. We then note how many units we would like our hidden layer to have and the activation function that should be used to decide whether the signal from a unit should feed forward. In this case, we select a unit count that is approximately one-third the size of our total number of independent variable columns and **rectified linear units (ReLU)** as our activation function:

```
model %>%
    layer_dense(units = 256, activation = 'relu')
```

Again, this step produces no output or noticeable change to the environment. This adds one dense, fully connected layer to the model. The layer will contain 256 units or neurons. It will use the ReLU function to determine which signals get sent forward.

7. In the following code, we have 10 possible target classes, so we include 10 units in our output layer, one for each class. Since this is a multinomial classification problem, we use the `softmax` function to compute the probabilities that any given set of image data belongs to one of the 10 classes of clothing:

```
model %>%
    layer_dense(units = 10, activation = 'softmax')
```

This line of code will add the last layer to this current neural network. This will be our output layer, which is another dense, fully connected layer where units are equal to the number of target classes. The `softmax` function will be used at this step to determine the probability that a given set of data belongs to each of the possible target classes. This step again produces no output or change in the R environment.

8. Before moving on to the `compile` step, we need to convert our target vectors to a matrix, which can be done simply with the `to_categorical` functions using the following code:

```
test_target <- to_categorical(test_target)
train_target <- to_categorical(train_target)
```

After running the code, we will see a change in our **Environment** pane. The `target` variable objects that were vectors are now matrices where every row contains a single value equal to `1` at the index point for the class to which it belongs. Your **Environment** pane will now look like this:

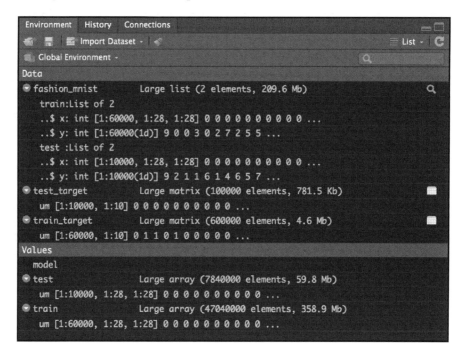

This step is a requirement for training a multinominal classification model with `keras`.

9. The following code is used to define the arguments for the `compile` step. Here, we select the `optimizer`, `loss`, and `evaluation` metrics. The `optimizer` is the algorithm that calculates the error rate between the model results and the actual values to adjust weights. We define the compile portion of the model using the following code:

```
model %>% compile(
  optimizer = 'adam',
  loss = 'categorical_crossentropy',
  metrics = 'categorical_accuracy'
)
```

In the preceding code, we did the following:

- We chose **Adaptive Moment Estimation** (**Adam**). The loss function is the formula that is used to calculate the error rate.
- When working with a multinominal classification problem like this one, the most suitable loss function is categorical crossentropy, which is another term for multiclass log loss.
- In order to use this loss function, the target variable must be stored as a matrix, which is why we performed that data type conversion in the previous step.
- The metrics argument stores the measurement for evaluating model performance, and we used categorical accuracy.

10. The step to fit our model at this point requires just three arguments. We pass in the training dataset, the target variables of the training data, and the number of times we would like the model to run. As shown in the following code, we will choose `10` epochs at this point so that our model finishes running quickly; however, if you have time to run the model for longer, then you will likely get better results. Train a neural network on the train data with the following code:

```
model %>% fit(train, train_target, epochs = 10
```

When we run this code, we will get a printout to our console with the results from every epoch. The output to your console will look like this:

```
Epoch 1/10
60000/60000 [==============================] - 5s 75us/sample - loss: 0.4718 -
categorical_accuracy: 0.8308
Epoch 2/10
60000/60000 [==============================] - 5s 77us/sample - loss: 0.3506 -
categorical_accuracy: 0.8706
Epoch 3/10
60000/60000 [==============================] - 5s 76us/sample - loss: 0.3154 -
categorical_accuracy: 0.8833
Epoch 4/10
60000/60000 [==============================] - 4s 74us/sample - loss: 0.2922 -
categorical_accuracy: 0.8907
Epoch 5/10
60000/60000 [==============================] - 4s 71us/sample - loss: 0.2745 -
categorical_accuracy: 0.8974
Epoch 6/10
60000/60000 [==============================] - 4s 72us/sample - loss: 0.2580 -
categorical_accuracy: 0.9020
Epoch 7/10
60000/60000 [==============================] - 4s 74us/sample - loss: 0.2468 -
categorical_accuracy: 0.9070
Epoch 8/10
60000/60000 [==============================] - 4s 71us/sample - loss: 0.2355 -
categorical_accuracy: 0.9108
Epoch 9/10
60000/60000 [==============================] - 4s 68us/sample - loss: 0.2236 -
categorical_accuracy: 0.9157
Epoch 10/10
60000/60000 [==============================] - 4s 70us/sample - loss: 0.2138 -
categorical_accuracy: 0.9188
>
```

In addition to the console output, the preceding code also produces a plot, which is a graphical representation of the same information. In your **Viewer** pane, you will see a plot like this:

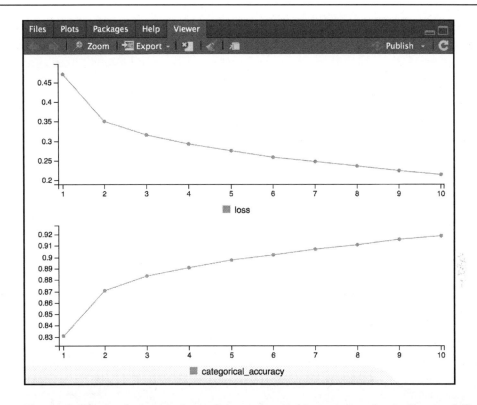

The two pieces of output show that our model improves a lot at first and then improves at a much slower pace after additional iterations of the model.

11. After this, we can run our model on our test dataset and use the test target variables to evaluate our model, as shown in the following screenshot. We can calculate the loss and categorical accuracy metric and print out the categorical accuracy metric by running the following code:

```
score <- model %>% evaluate(test, test_target)

score$categorical_accuracy
```

You should see the following printed out to your console:

```
> score <- model %>% evaluate(test, test_target)
10000/10000 [==============================] - 0s 28us/sample - loss: 0.3220 -
categorical_accuracy: 0.8866
> score$categorical_accuracy
[1] 0.8866
>
```

We have achieved a categorical accuracy of 88.66%. This is a decrease from our previous accuracy; however, keep in mind that the accuracy metric before pertained to a binary response and this describes predictions for all classes.

12. Making predictions using the model is achieved through the `predict()` function. In the following code, `predict_classes` can be used to choose one of the 10 classes that are most likely based on the probability scores, while `preds` will calculate the probabilities:

```
preds <- model %>% predict(test)

predicted_classes <- model %>% predict_classes(test)
```

After running the preceding code, we can see the difference in our **Environment** pane, which contains two new data objects. Your **Environment** pane will look like this:

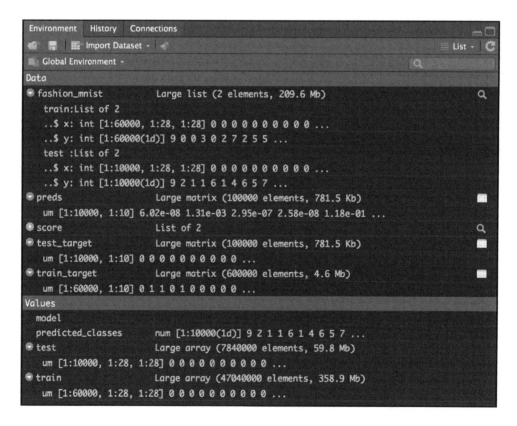

We can see that `preds` is a large matrix with a probability value for each class, while `predicted_classes` is a vector where every value indicates the most probable class for each case.

13. Finally, we can use a confusion matrix to review our results. In order to run this code, we will need our test target labels back in vector format rather than in a matrix. To do this, we will just read in the test target file again, as shown here:

```
test_target_vector <- fashion_mnist$test$y

caret::confusionMatrix(as.factor(predicted_classes),as.factor(test_target_vector))
```

Running the code will produce an evaluation metric output to print to our console. Your console will look like this:

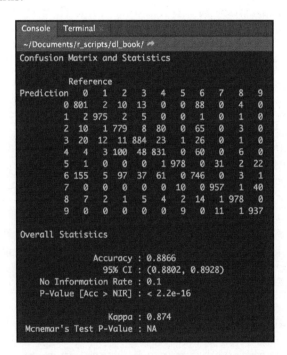

```
Console    Terminal
~/Documents/r_scripts/dl_book/
Confusion Matrix and Statistics

          Reference
Prediction   0   1   2   3   4   5   6   7   8   9
        0 801   2  10  13   0   0  88   0   4   0
        1   2 975   2   5   0   0   1   0   1   0
        2  10   1 779   8  80   0  65   0   3   0
        3  20  12  11 884  23   1  26   0   1   0
        4   4   3 100  48 831   0  60   0   6   0
        5   1   0   0   0   1 978   0  31   2  22
        6 155   5  97  37  61   0 746   0   3   1
        7   0   0   0   0   0  10   0 957   1  40
        8   7   2   1   5   4   2  14   1 978   0
        9   0   0   0   0   0   9   0  11   1 937

Overall Statistics

               Accuracy : 0.8866
                 95% CI : (0.8802, 0.8928)
    No Information Rate : 0.1
    P-Value [Acc > NIR] : < 2.2e-16

                  Kappa : 0.874
 Mcnemar's Test P-Value : NA
```

Our accuracy score has actually decreased from 97.487% to 88.66%. This is in part due to limiting our model to 10 runs and also, again, because we are now building a classifier for 10 categories, whereas the other score was achieved with a binary classifier. At this point, improving the accuracy score is not the priority in any case. The preceding code is here to show how to code a neural network using the `keras` syntax.

In the preceding code, during the compile stage, we chose an optimizer, loss function, and evaluation metric; however, we should note the other options that we could have selected and the difference between the available choices. We'll look at these in the following sections.

Optimizers

Let's look at the following optimizers:

- **Stochastic gradient descent (SGD)**: This is the simplest optimizer. For every weight, the model stores an error rate. Depending on the direction of the error, whether the predicted value is greater than or less than the true value, a small learning rate is applied to the weight to change the next round of results so that the predicted values are incrementally moving in the opposite direction as the error. This process is simple, but for deep neural networks, the fine adjustments at every iteration mean that it can take a long time for the model to converge.

- **Momentum**: Momentum itself is not an optimizer, but is something that can be incorporated with different optimizers. The idea of momentum is that it takes the decaying average of all the corrections that have occurred previously and uses these in combination with the correction calculated for the current move. For this, we can imagine momentum working just like it would if an object was rolled down a hill and then continued to roll up another hill using its own momentum. For every movement that it made, there would be a force pulling it back down the hill; however, for a period of time, the momentum to continue up the hill would be stronger than the force pulling it back down.

- **Adagrad/Adadelta**: Adagrad improves on SGD through the use of a matrix of all previous errors per node rather than one error rate for all nodes; however, the use of this matrix of values means that the learning rate can be canceled out of the model runs for too long. Adadelta is the correction for the limitation of Adagrad. Adadelta uses momentum to solve the growing error rate matrix problem.

- **RMSprop**: This is a separate correction to Adagrad. It is similar to Adadelta, however, with RMSprop, the learning rate is not only divided by a matrix of local per-node decaying average error rates, but also by a global decaying average of all squared error rates.

- **Adam**: This algorithm further corrects and builds upon the algorithms before. Adam includes not only an exponentially decaying average of squared error rates, as seen in RMSprop, but also an exponentially decaying average of error rates (not squared), which is momentum. In this way, Adam is more or less RMSprop with momentum. The combination of the two means that there is a correction to momentum similar to friction, which decreases the effect of momentum and thereby leads to faster convergence, in many cases making Adam a popular optimizer at the time of writing.

Loss functions

With the preceding optimizers, you can select whichever one you like and try different algorithms to see which produces the best results. With the loss function, there are some choices that are more appropriate than others based on the problem being solved:

- `binary_crossentropy`: This loss function is used for classification problems where the requirement is to assign input data to one of two classes. This can also be used when assigning input data to more than one or two classes if it is possible for a given case to belong to more than one class. In this case, each target class is treated as a separate binary class (for each target class the given case belongs to or does not belong to). This can also be used for regression when the target values are between 0 and 1.
- `categorical_crossentropy`: Categorical crossentropy is used with a multinominal classification problem where any given row of input data can only belong to one of the more than two classes. As we noted with binary crossentropy, in order to use categorical crossentropy, the target vector must be converted to a matrix so that there is a value of 1 for the index associated with the target class for every given row. If the target vector contains integers that are meant to be treated as integers and not categorical classes, then `sparse_categorical_crossentropy` can be used without performing the matrix conversion required for categorical crossentropy.
- MSE (**mean squared error**): Mean squared error is an appropriate choice for regression problems since the predicted values and true values can be any number. This loss function takes the square of the difference between the predicted values and the target values.

Evaluation metrics

The evaluation metric is used to measure model performance. While similar to the loss functions, it is not used for making corrections while training the model. It is only used after the model has been trained to evaluate performance:

- **Accuracy**: This metric measures how often the correct class is predicted. By default, 0.5 is used as a threshold, which means that if the predicted probability is below 0.5, then the predicted class is 0; otherwise, it is 1. The total number of cases where the predicted class matches the target class is divided by the total number of target variables.

- **Cosine similarity**: Compares the similarity between two vectors by evaluating the similarity of terms in n-dimensional space. This is used often to evaluate the similarity of text data. For this, we can imagine a piece of text with the word cat four times and the word dog once, and another with the word cat four times and the word dog twice. In this case, with two dimensions, we could envision a line from the origin through the point where $y = 4$ and $x = 1$ for the first piece of text and another line through the point where $y = 4$ and $x = 2$ for the next piece of text. If we evaluate the angle between the two lines, we will arrive at the cosine value used to determine similarity. If the lines overlap, then the documents have a perfect similarity score of 1, and the larger the angle between the lines, the less similar and the lower the similarity score will be.

- **Mean absolute error**: The average value for all absolute errors. The absolute error is the difference between the predicted variable and the target variable.

- **Mean squared error**: The average value for all squared errors. The squared error is the square of the difference between the predicted variable and the target variable. Through squaring the errors, an increased penalty is applied to larger errors relative to mean absolute error.

- **Hinge**: To use the hinge evaluation metric, all target variables should be -1 or 1. From here, the formula is to subtract the product of the predicted value and the target variable from 1 and then to use this value or 0, whichever is greater for evaluation. Results are evaluated as more correct the closer the metric value is to 0.

- **KL divergence**: This metric compares the distribution of true results with the distribution of predicted results and evaluates the similarity of the distribution.

We have, so far, used a tree-based classifier and a traditional neural network to classify our image data. We have also reviewed the `keras` syntax and looked at our options for several functions within the modeling pipeline using this framework. Next, we will add the additional layers before the neural network that we just coded to create a convolutional neural network. For this special type of neural network, we will include a convolution layer and a pooling layer. A dropout layer is often also included; however, we will add this later as it serves a slightly different purpose than the convolution and pooling layers. When used together, these layers find more complex patterns in our data and also reduce the size of our data, which is especially important when working with large image files.

Enhancing the model with additional layers

In this section, we add two important layers: the convolution layer, and pooling layer:

1. Before beginning, we make one small change to the data structure. We will add a fourth dimension that is a constant value. We add the extra dimension using the following code:

```
dim(train) <- c(nrow(train), 28, 28, 1)
dim(test) <- c(nrow(test), 28, 28, 1)
```

When we make this change, we can see the added dimension for these data objects in the **Environment** pane, which will look like the following image:

We make this change to the structure because it is a requirement of modeling a CNN using `keras`.

2. As before, the first step in the modeling process is to establish that we will be building a sequential model by calling the `keras_model_sequential()` function with no arguments using the following code:

```
set.seed(0)

model <- keras_model_sequential()
```

Running the preceding code will place the model object into our **Environment** pane, however, it contains no data at the moment and no output is printed to console.

3. Next, we will add our convolving layer for a two-dimensional object. In the following code, we will decide on the number of filters or subsets of the data and the size of these subsets as well as the activation function used to determine whether the subset contains a certain pattern:

```
model %>%
  layer_conv_2d(filters = 484, kernel_size = c(7,7), activation =
  'relu',
                activation = 'relu', input_shape = c(28,28,1))
```

Let's looks at the preceding code in a little more detail:

- We chose to include 484 filters and a kernel size that is 7 pixels high and wide.
- We applied a filter the size of the kernel on the image and, using the constant values on the filter, the model determined whether it detects a pattern.
- The stride value of 1 that is used in this example means that the kernel slides over the surface of the image by 1 pixel after every filter has been evaluated, though this number can be changed.

4. After this, we will use a max pooling layer in the following code to create a new downsampled version of our data that represents the maximum values within the pool size after the convolving round:

```
model %>% layer_max_pooling_2d(pool_size = c(2, 2))
```

This line of code causes no noticeable changes to the **Environment** pane and prints no output to the console. It adds a layer to our model that will reduce the size of our data to one-quarter of the original size.

5. After this, the steps continue in the same way as we described in the previous example from the *Image recognition with convolutional neural networks* section. Let's have a look at the following code:

```
model %>%
layer_flatten() %>%
    layer_dense(units = 98, activation = 'relu') %>%
    layer_dense(units = 10, activation = 'softmax')

model %>% compile(
    loss = 'categorical_crossentropy',
    optimizer = 'adam',
    metrics = 'accuracy'
)

model %>% fit(
    train, train_target,
    batch_size = 100,
    epochs = 5,
    verbose = 1,
    validation_data = list(test, test_target)
)

scores <- model %>% evaluate(
    test, test_target, verbose = 1
)

preds <- model %>% predict(test)

predicted_classes <- model %>% predict_classes(test)

caret::confusionMatrix(as.factor(predicted_classes),as.factor(test_target_vector))
```

After running the preceding code, we will get model diagnostic data printed to the console, which will look like the following image:

```
Train on 60000 samples, validate on 10000 samples
Epoch 1/5
60000/60000 [==============================] - 120s 2ms/sample - loss: 0.4193
- acc: 0.8480 - val_loss: 0.3424 - val_acc: 0.8733
Epoch 2/5
60000/60000 [==============================] - 128s 2ms/sample - loss: 0.2848
- acc: 0.8951 - val_loss: 0.2945 - val_acc: 0.8915
Epoch 3/5
60000/60000 [==============================] - 125s 2ms/sample - loss: 0.2430
- acc: 0.9092 - val_loss: 0.2804 - val_acc: 0.8998
Epoch 4/5
60000/60000 [==============================] - 122s 2ms/sample - loss: 0.2121
- acc: 0.9200 - val_loss: 0.2766 - val_acc: 0.8995
Epoch 5/5
60000/60000 [==============================] - 125s 2ms/sample - loss: 0.1854
- acc: 0.9300 - val_loss: 0.2779 - val_acc: 0.9026
>
```

You will also get a plot with the same data, which looks like the following image:

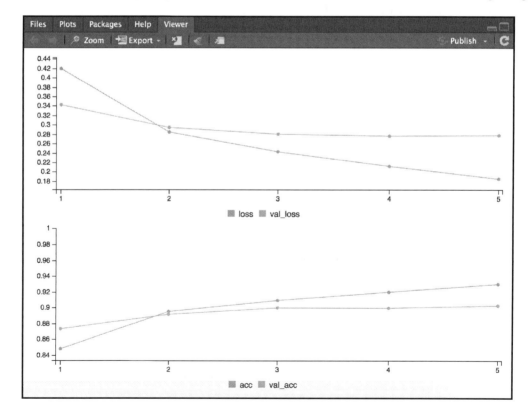

The preceding code also produces performance metrics and prints them to the console. Your console will look like the following image:

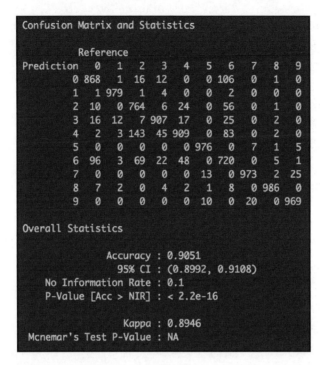

```
Confusion Matrix and Statistics

          Reference
Prediction   0    1    2    3    4    5    6    7    8    9
        0  868    1   16   12    0    0  106    0    1    0
        1    1  979    1    4    0    0    2    0    0    0
        2   10    0  764    6   24    0   56    0    1    0
        3   16   12    7  907   17    0   25    0    2    0
        4    2    3  143   45  909    0   83    0    2    0
        5    0    0    0    0    0  976    0    7    1    5
        6   96    3   69   22   48    0  720    0    5    1
        7    0    0    0    0    0   13    0  973    2   25
        8    7    2    0    4    2    1    8    0  986    0
        9    0    0    0    0    0   10    0   20    0  969

Overall Statistics

               Accuracy : 0.9051
                 95% CI : (0.8992, 0.9108)
    No Information Rate : 0.1
    P-Value [Acc > NIR] : < 2.2e-16

                  Kappa : 0.8946
 Mcnemar's Test P-Value : NA
```

By adding our convolution layer and our pooling layer, we have already increased our accuracy score from 88.66% to 90.51%, and we did so with five fewer rounds to prevent using a long-running model while learning.

As discussed previously, deep learning occurs when there are many layers for the signal to pass through, so in the following method, we will see how we can continue to add more layers. Using this, you can continue to add as many layers as you need as you refine your model:

1. We start by redefining our model. We will state again that it is a sequential model in the following code:

```
set.seed(0)

model <- keras_model_sequential()
```

The preceding code will reset the model object; however, no noticeable changes will occur in the **Environment** pane and nothing will print to the console.

2. In the next step, we will use a convolving layer with 128 filters and then a pooling layer. In this case, we also add `padding = "same"` to prevent dimension reduction after the convolution layer. This is in order to make it possible to add additional layers. If we reduce the dimensionality of our data too quickly, then we will not be able to fit a filter of any kernel size on the data later. We define our first convolving layer and pooling layer using the following code:

```
model %>%
  layer_conv_2d(filters = 128, kernel_size = c(7,7), activation =
'relu',
                input_shape = c(28,28,1), padding = "same") %>%
  layer_max_pooling_2d(pool_size = c(2, 2))
```

The preceding code results in no noticeable changes to the **Environment** pane and nothing will print to the console.

3. As shown in the following code, we will add in another convolving layer with 64 filters and a pooling layer. We add these two additional layers using the following code:

```
model %>%
  layer_conv_2d(filters = 64, kernel_size = c(7,7), activation =
'relu', padding = "same") %>%
  layer_max_pooling_2d(pool_size = c(2, 2))
```

The preceding code results in no noticeable changes to the **Environment** pane and nothing will print to the console.

4. We then add in one more convolving layer. This time, we will use 32 filters and a pooling layer, as shown in the following code. We add these two additional layers using the following code:

```
model %>%
  layer_conv_2d(filters = 32, kernel_size = c(7,7), activation =
'relu', padding = "same") %>%
  layer_max_pooling_2d(pool_size = c(2, 2))
```

The preceding code results in no noticeable changes to the **Environment** pane and nothing will print to the console.

5. Finally, in the following code, we flatten the values and proceed in the same way as we have in the previous examples:

```
model %>%
layer_flatten() %>%
  layer_dense(units = 128, activation = 'relu') %>%
```

```r
  layer_dense(units = 10, activation = 'softmax')

model %>% compile(
  loss = 'categorical_crossentropy',
  optimizer = 'adam',
  metrics = 'accuracy'
)

model %>% fit(
  train, train_target,
  batch_size = 100,
  epochs = 5,
  verbose = 1,
  validation_data = list(test, test_target)
)

score <- model %>% evaluate(
  test, test_target, verbose = 1
)

preds <- model %>% predict(test)

predicted_classes <- model %>% predict_classes(test)

caret::confusionMatrix(as.factor(predicted_classes),as.factor(test_
target_vector))
```

The preceding code produces model diagnostics in our console. Your console will look like the following image:

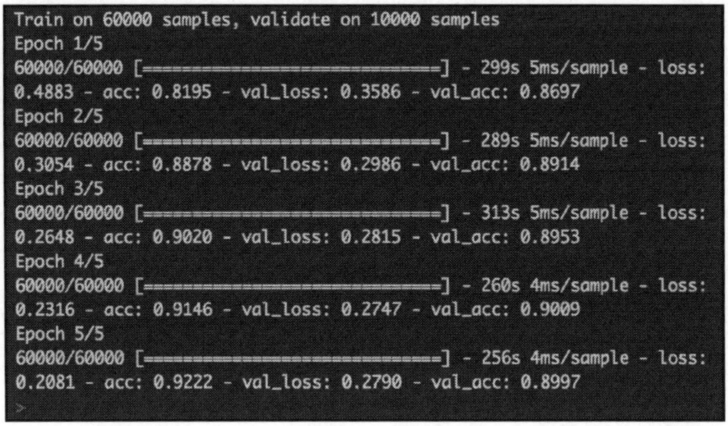

```
Train on 60000 samples, validate on 10000 samples
Epoch 1/5
60000/60000 [==============================] - 299s 5ms/sample - loss:
0.4883 - acc: 0.8195 - val_loss: 0.3586 - val_acc: 0.8697
Epoch 2/5
60000/60000 [==============================] - 289s 5ms/sample - loss:
0.3054 - acc: 0.8878 - val_loss: 0.2986 - val_acc: 0.8914
Epoch 3/5
60000/60000 [==============================] - 313s 5ms/sample - loss:
0.2648 - acc: 0.9020 - val_loss: 0.2815 - val_acc: 0.8953
Epoch 4/5
60000/60000 [==============================] - 260s 4ms/sample - loss:
0.2316 - acc: 0.9146 - val_loss: 0.2747 - val_acc: 0.9009
Epoch 5/5
60000/60000 [==============================] - 256s 4ms/sample - loss:
0.2081 - acc: 0.9222 - val_loss: 0.2790 - val_acc: 0.8997
>
```

The preceding code also produces a plot. You will see a plot in your **Viewer** pane that looks like the following image:

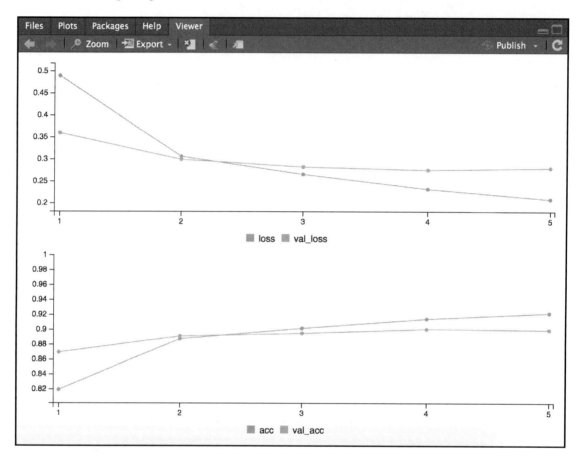

We also produce additional performance metrics and print these to our console. You will see the following output in your console:

```
Confusion Matrix and Statistics

          Reference
Prediction   0    1    2    3    4    5    6    7    8    9
         0 770    0   13    6    0    0   62    0    2    0
         1   1  980    2    4    1    0    3    0    1    0
         2  14    0  750    6   25    0   24    0    2    0
         3  24   13    6  928   22    1   29    0    2    0
         4   1    3   84   27  826    0   41    0    5    0
         5   0    0    0    0    0  975    0    9    1    3
         6 182    3  144   26  126    0  839    0    7    1
         7   0    0    0    0    0   13    0  979    0   25
         8   8    1    1    3    0    1    2    0  979    0
         9   0    0    0    0    0   10    0   12    1  971

Overall Statistics

               Accuracy : 0.8997
                 95% CI : (0.8936, 0.9055)
    No Information Rate : 0.1
    P-Value [Acc > NIR] : < 2.2e-16

                  Kappa : 0.8886
 Mcnemar's Test P-Value : NA
```

Our accuracy score remains almost the same at 89.97%. We could likely get the accuracy to improve with more filters per layer; however, this will significantly increase run time, so that is why we keep the filter count per layer as it is. We have seen here how to write code to create a CNN and a CNN with a deeper layer structure, and we noticed how it improved performance. We have so far used the ReLU activation function, which is a very popular and common activation function; however, we know there are other options, so next, we will write code to select a different activation function.

Choosing the most appropriate activation function

Using `keras`, you can use a number of different activation functions. Some of these have been discussed in previous chapters; however, there are some that have not been previously covered. We can begin by listing the ones we have already covered with a quick note on each function:

- **Linear**: Also known as the identity function. Uses the value of x.
- **Sigmoid**: Uses 1 divided by 1 plus the exponent of negative x.
- **Hyperbolic tangent (tanh)**: Uses the exponent of x minus the exponent of negative x divided by x plus the exponent of negative x. This has the same shape as the sigmoid function; however, the range along the y-axis goes from 1 to -1 instead of from 1 to 0.
- **Rectified Linear Units (ReLU)**: Uses the value of x if x is greater than 0; otherwise, it assigns a value of 0 if x is less than or equal to 0.
- **Leaky ReLU**: Uses the same formula as ReLU; however, it applies a small alpha value when x is less than 0.
- **Softmax**: Provides a probability for each possible target class.

Let's look at all the functions that were not mentioned in previous chapters:

- **Exponential Linear Unit (ELU)**: Uses the exponent of x - 1 multiplied by a constant alpha value if the value for x is less than 0
- **Scaled Exponential Linear Unit (SELU)**: Uses the ELU function and then multiplies the result of the function by a constant scale value
- **Thresholded ReLU**: Uses the same formula as ReLU; however, instead of using 0 as the threshold for whether x is x or 0, it uses a user-defined value of theta to determine this threshold.
- **Parametric Rectified Linear Unit (PReLU)**: The same as the formula for Leaky ReLu; however, it uses an array of values for alpha rather than a single value.
- **Softplus**: Uses the log of the exponent of x plus 1
- **Softsign**: Uses x divided by the absolute value of $x + 1$
- **Exponential**: Uses the exponent of x.
- **Hard Sigmoid**: Uses a modified and faster version of the sigmoid function. If x is less than -2.5, then the value is 0 and if x is greater than 2.5, then the value is 1; otherwise, it uses $0.2 * x + 0.5$.

So far, we have used the ReLU activation function by assigning the `relu` value to the activation argument within our layer function call. For some activation functions, such as the sigmoid function, we can simply swap out the `relu` value with the `sigmoid` value; however, more advanced activation functions require a separate activation function layer. Let's switch the activation function from ReLu to Leaky ReLU in our code by removing the activation argument from the layer function call and adding a Leaky ReLU activation function:

```
model <- keras_model_sequential()
model %>%
  layer_conv_2d(filters = 8, kernel_size = c(3,3), input_shape =
c(28,28,1)) %>%
  layer_activation_leaky_relu() %>%
  layer_max_pooling_2d(pool_size = c(2, 2)) %>%
  layer_conv_2d(filters = 16, kernel_size = c(3,3)) %>%
  layer_activation_leaky_relu() %>%
  layer_max_pooling_2d(pool_size = c(2, 2)) %>%
  layer_conv_2d(filters = 32, kernel_size = c(3,3)) %>%
  layer_activation_leaky_relu() %>%
  layer_max_pooling_2d(pool_size = c(2, 2)) %>%
  layer_flatten() %>%
  layer_dense(units = 128) %>%
  layer_activation_leaky_relu() %>%
  layer_dense(units = 10, activation = 'softmax')

# compile model
model %>% compile(
  loss = loss_categorical_crossentropy,
  optimizer = 'rmsprop',
  metrics = c('accuracy')
)
# train and evaluate
model %>% fit(
  train, train_target,
  batch_size = 100,
  epochs = 5,
  verbose = 1,
  validation_data = list(test, test_target)
)
scores <- model %>% evaluate(
  test, test_target, verbose = 1
)
preds <- model %>% predict(test)
predicted_classes <- model %>% predict_classes(test)
caret::confusionMatrix(as.factor(predicted_classes),as.factor(test_target_v
ector))
```

The preceding code prints model diagnostic data to our console. Your console will look like the following image:

```
Train on 60000 samples, validate on 10000 samples
Epoch 1/5
60000/60000 [==============================] - 255s 4ms/sample - loss:
0.4631 - acc: 0.8278 - val_loss: 0.3447 - val_acc: 0.8724
Epoch 2/5
60000/60000 [==============================] - 258s 4ms/sample - loss:
0.2981 - acc: 0.8893 - val_loss: 0.3185 - val_acc: 0.8828
Epoch 3/5
60000/60000 [==============================] - 264s 4ms/sample - loss:
0.2536 - acc: 0.9058 - val_loss: 0.2711 - val_acc: 0.9014
Epoch 4/5
60000/60000 [==============================] - 266s 4ms/sample - loss:
0.2259 - acc: 0.9151 - val_loss: 0.2541 - val_acc: 0.9081
Epoch 5/5
60000/60000 [==============================] - 264s 4ms/sample - loss:
0.2016 - acc: 0.9242 - val_loss: 0.2529 - val_acc: 0.9095
>
```

The preceding code also produces a plot with model performance data. You will see a plot like the following image in your **Viewer** pane:

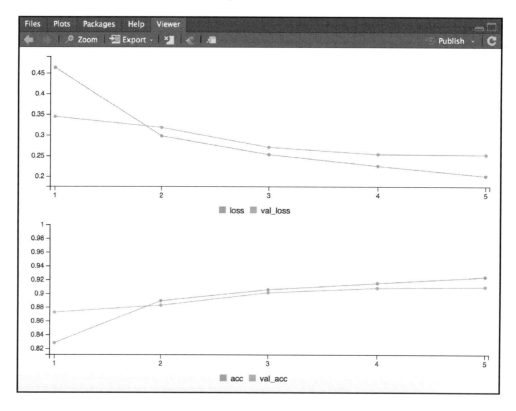

The preceding code also produces performance metrics. These will print to your console and will look like the following image:

```
Confusion Matrix and Statistics

           Reference
Prediction   0    1    2    3    4    5    6    7    8    9
         0 868    3   18   19    2    0  116    0    2    0
         1   2  979    1    4    0    0    1    0    0    0
         2  15    0  844    7   60    0   50    0    1    0
         3   8   15    9  928   45    0   25    0    4    0
         4   0    0   59   14  821    0   50    0    1    0
         5   3    0    0    0    0  980    0    9    3    6
         6  97    1   69   26   71    0  753    0    1    1
         7   0    0    0    0    0    8    0  969    7   21
         8   7    2    0    2    1    0    5    0  981    0
         9   0    0    0    0    0   12    0   22    0  972

Overall Statistics

               Accuracy : 0.9095
                 95% CI : (0.9037, 0.9151)
    No Information Rate : 0.1
    P-Value [Acc > NIR] : < 2.2e-16

                  Kappa : 0.8994
 Mcnemar's Test P-Value : NA
```

After switching our activation function, our accuracy score is 90.95%, which is very similar to the score we have been getting so far. In this case, switching our activation function did not improve performance; however, there will be times when this will be helpful, so it is important to know how to make this modification.

Selecting optimal epochs using dropout and early stopping

To avoid overfitting, we can use two techniques. The first is adding a dropout layer. The dropout layer will remove a subset of the layer output. This makes the data a little different at every iteration so that the model generalizes better and doesn't fit the solution too specifically to the training data. In the preceding code, we add the dropout layer after the pooling layer:

```
model <- keras_model_sequential()
model %>%
   layer_conv_2d(filters = 128, kernel_size = c(7,7), input_shape =
c(28,28,1), padding = "same") %>%
```

```
    layer_activation_leaky_relu() %>%
    layer_max_pooling_2d(pool_size = c(2, 2)) %>%
    layer_dropout(rate = 0.2) %>%
    layer_conv_2d(filters = 64, kernel_size = c(7,7), padding = "same") %>%
    layer_activation_leaky_relu() %>%
    layer_max_pooling_2d(pool_size = c(2, 2)) %>%
    layer_dropout(rate = 0.2) %>%
    layer_conv_2d(filters = 32, kernel_size = c(7,7), padding = "same") %>%
    layer_activation_leaky_relu() %>%
    layer_max_pooling_2d(pool_size = c(2, 2)) %>%
    layer_dropout(rate = 0.2) %>%
    layer_flatten() %>%
    layer_dense(units = 128) %>%
    layer_activation_leaky_relu() %>%
    layer_dropout(rate = 0.2) %>%
    layer_dense(units = 10, activation = 'softmax')

# compile model
model %>% compile(
  loss = 'categorical_crossentropy',
  optimizer = 'adam',
  metrics = 'accuracy'
)
# train and evaluate
model %>% fit(
  train, train_target,
  batch_size = 100,
  epochs = 5,
  verbose = 1,
  validation_data = list(test, test_target)
)
scores <- model %>% evaluate(
  test, test_target, verbose = 1
)
preds <- model %>% predict(test)
predicted_classes <- model %>% predict_classes(test)
caret::confusionMatrix(as.factor(predicted_classes),as.factor(test_target_v
ector))
```

The preceding code prints model diagnostic data to our console. Your console will look like the following image:

```
Train on 60000 samples, validate on 10000 samples
Epoch 1/5
60000/60000 [==============================] - 284s 5ms/sample - loss:
0.5105 - acc: 0.8105 - val_loss: 0.3549 - val_acc: 0.8680
Epoch 2/5
60000/60000 [==============================] - 272s 5ms/sample - loss:
0.3305 - acc: 0.8770 - val_loss: 0.3026 - val_acc: 0.8868
Epoch 3/5
60000/60000 [==============================] - 278s 5ms/sample - loss:
0.2921 - acc: 0.8917 - val_loss: 0.2814 - val_acc: 0.8934
Epoch 4/5
60000/60000 [==============================] - 276s 5ms/sample - loss:
0.2693 - acc: 0.9004 - val_loss: 0.2701 - val_acc: 0.8975
Epoch 5/5
60000/60000 [==============================] - 278s 5ms/sample - loss:
0.2497 - acc: 0.9064 - val_loss: 0.2733 - val_acc: 0.9007
```

The preceding code also produces a plot with model performance data. You will see a plot like the following image in your **Viewer** pane:

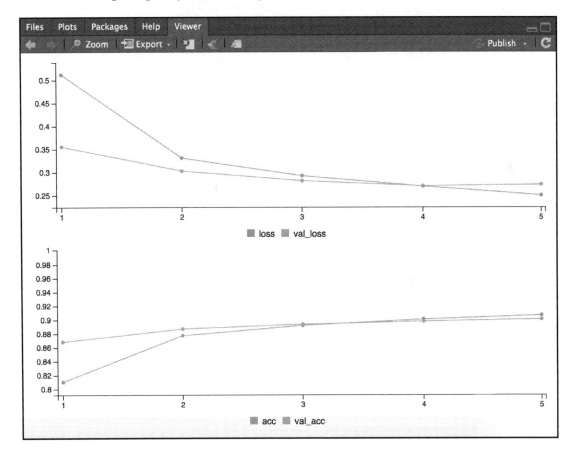

The preceding code also produces some performance metrics. The output printed to your console will look like the following image:

```
Confusion Matrix and Statistics

          Reference
Prediction   0    1    2    3    4    5    6    7    8    9
        0  808    0    8    2    0    0   79    0    2    0
        1    0  970    0    1    1    0    0    0    1    0
        2   10    1  764    6   24    0   41    0    4    0
        3   48   25   14  949   35    0   55    0    3    0
        4    4    1  103   24  865    0   52    0    8    0
        5    1    0    0    0    0  987    0   19    1    8
        6  127    2  111   16   74    0  770    0    5    1
        7    0    0    0    0    0   10    0  947    2   18
        8    2    1    0    1    1    0    3    0  974    0
        9    0    0    0    1    0    3    0   34    0  973

Overall Statistics

               Accuracy : 0.9007
                 95% CI : (0.8947, 0.9065)
    No Information Rate : 0.1
    P-Value [Acc > NIR] : < 2.2e-16

                  Kappa : 0.8897
 Mcnemar's Test P-Value : NA
```

In this case, using this tactic caused our accuracy score to decrease slightly to 90.07%. This could be due to working with a dataset of such small images that the model suffered from the removal of data at every step. With larger datasets, this will likely help make models more efficient and generalize better.

The other tactic for preventing overfitting is using early stopping. Early stopping will monitor progress and stop the model from continuing to train on the data when the model no longer improves. In the following code, we have set the patience argument to 2, which means that the evaluation metric must fail to improve for two epochs in a row.

In the following code, with epochs kept at 5, the model will complete all five rounds; however, if you have time, feel free to run all the preceding code and then, when it is time to fit the model, increase the number of epochs to see when the early stopping function stops the model. We add early stopping functionality to our model using the following code:

```
model %>% fit(
   train, train_target,
   batch_size = 100,
   epochs = 5,
   verbose = 1,
   validation_data = list(test, test_target),
   callbacks = list(
      callback_early_stopping(patience = 2)
   )
)
```

From the preceding code, we can deduce the following:

- Using dropout and early stopping, we demonstrated methods for discovering the optimal number of epochs or rounds for our model.
- When thinking of the number of epochs we should use, the goal is twofold.
- We want our model to run efficiently so that we are not waiting for our model to finish running, even though the additional rounds are not improving performance. We also want to avoid overfitting where a model is trained too specifically on the training data and is unable to generalize to new data.
    - Dropout helps with the second issue by arbitrarily removing some data on each round. It also introduces randomness that prevents the model from learning too much about the whole dataset.
    - Early stopping helps with the first problem by monitoring performance and stopping the model when the model is no longer producing better results for a given length of time.
    - Using these two techniques together will allow you to find the epoch number that allows the model to run efficiently and also generalize well.

Summary

In this chapter, we started by showing how image classification models can be created using standard machine-learning techniques; however, this has limitations as the images get larger and more complex. We can use convolutional neural networks to combat this issue. Using this approach, we demonstrated how we could perform dimensionality reduction and make it more computationally efficient to train a classification model on image data. We built a model with one convolution and pooling layer and then showed how we could make the model even deeper by adding further layers. Lastly, we used dropout layers and early stopping to avoid overfitting our model. Using all of these tactics in concert, we are now able to build models for classifying any type of image data.

In the next chapter, we will learn how to code a multilayer perceptron. The multilayer perceptron is a feedforward neural network that includes only dense, fully connected hidden layers. With fewer options to adjust, we will take a deeper dive into what is available for us to tune. In addition, we will use the MXNet package for the first time, aside from the brief introduction in Chapter 2, *CNNs for Image Recognition*.

Multilayer Perceptron for Signal Detection

5

This chapter will show you how to build a multilayer perceptron neural network for signal detection. We will first discuss the architecture of multilayer perceptron neural networks. Then we will cover how to prepare the data, how to decide on hidden layers and neurons, and how to train and evaluate the model.

The section on preparing the data will be important going forward as these deep learning models require data to be in particular formats in order to pass the data to the models. The hidden layer is the part of the neural network that separates it from other machine learning algorithms, and in this chapter, we will show you how to search for the optimal number of nodes in a hidden layer. In addition, over the course of this chapter, you will become much more familiar with the MXNet syntax, including the model training and evaluation steps.

This chapter will cover the following topics:

- Understanding multilayer perceptrons
- Preparing and processing the data
- Deciding on the hidden layers and neurons
- Training and evaluating the model

Technical requirements

You can find the code files of this chapter at the corresponding GitHub link at https://github.com/PacktPublishing/Hands-on-Deep-Learning-with-R.

Understanding multilayer perceptrons

A multilayer perceptron is an instance of a feedforward neural network that only uses fully connected layers consisting of perceptrons. A perceptron is a node that takes input values and multiplies them by weights, and then passes this aggregate value to an activation function that returns a value that indicates how much this set of inputs and weights matches the pattern we are trying to find.

The multilayer perceptron can be thought of as the most basic neural network implementation. As we mentioned, all layers are fully connected, which means that there are no convolution or pooling layers. It is also a feedforward model, which means that information from backpropagation is not looped back at every step, as it is in a recurrent neural network.

Simplicity can be an asset in terms of the ease of the interpretability of the network and its initial setup; however, the main drawback is that with so many fully connected layers, the count of weights will grow to such a level that the model will take a long time to train for large datasets. It also has a vanishing gradient problem, which means that the model will reach a point where the value that is passed back to correct the model is so small that it no longer significantly impacts the results.

Preparing and preprocessing data

For this example, we will use the Adult dataset. We will walk through the steps to get this dataset in the proper form so that we can train a multilayer perceptron on it:

1. We will first load the libraries that we need. We will use the mxnet package to train the MLP model, the tidyverse family of packages for our data cleaning and manipulation, and caret to evaluate our model. We load the libraries using the following code:

```
library(mxnet)
library(tidyverse)
library(caret)
```

This code will not produce any output to the console; however, you will see a checkmark next to these libraries in the **Packages** pane, indicating that the packages are now ready to use. Your **Packages** pane should look like the following screenshot:

	Name	Description	Version	
☐	mlbench	Machine Learning Benchmark Problems	2.1-1	⊗
☐	mnormt	The Multivariate Normal and t Distributions	1.5-5	⊗
☐	ModelMetrics	Rapid Calculation of Model Metrics	1.2.2	⊗
☐	modelr	Modelling Functions that Work with the Pipe	0.1.2	⊗
☐	munsell	Utilities for Using Munsell Colours	0.4.3	⊗
☑	mxnet	MXNet: A Flexible and Efficient Machine Learning Library for Heterogeneous Distributed Systems	1.4.0	⊗
☐	numDeriv	Accurate Numerical Derivatives	2016.8-1.1	⊗
☐	openssl	Toolkit for Encryption, Signatures and Certificates Based on OpenSSL	1.0.1	⊗
☐	pacman	Package Management Tool	0.4.6	⊗
☐	pander	An R 'Pandoc' Writer	0.6.1	⊗
☐	pillar	Coloured Formatting for Columns	1.4.2	⊗
☐	pkgconfig	Private Configuration for 'R' Packages	2.0.1	⊗
☐	plogr	The 'plog' C++ Logging Library	1.2.0	⊗
☐	plyr	Tools for Splitting, Applying and Combining Data	1.8.4	⊗

2. Next, we will load our training and test data. In addition, we will add a column called `dataset` that we will populate with the `train` and `test` values to label our data. We will do this so that we can combine our data and perform some manipulation on the full data to save ourselves from repeating steps, and then be able to split the data again afterward. We then load the data and add the label with the following code:

```
train <- read.csv("adult_processed_train.csv")
train <- train %>% mutate(dataset = "train")
test <- read.csv("adult_processed_test.csv")
test <- test %>% mutate(dataset = "test")
```

The preceding code will place two data objects in your **Environment** pane. This will be the train and test data that we will use for this modeling exercise. Your **Environment** pane will look like the following screenshot:

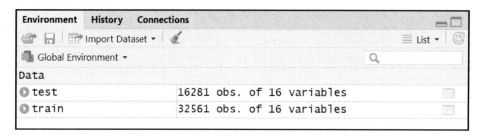

3. In this step, we will combine our data with a row bind and then remove any rows with NA values. Removing rows with missing values is not always the most appropriate course of action; at times, other tactics should be used to handle missing values. These tactics include **imputation** and **replacement**. In this case, we would just like to remove these rows for ease of use, since we are just using this data for example purposes. We combine the data and remove rows with missing values using the following code:

```
all <- rbind(train,test)

all <- all[complete.cases(all),]
```

The preceding code will add one more data object to our **Environment** pane. Your **Environment** pane will now look like the following screenshot:

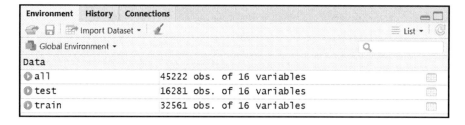

You can see that the data object `all` contains rows from `test` and `train`. We can now modify both `train` and `test` at the same time.

4. In the next step, we take any factor value and trim the whitespace. We do this because there are multiple values that should mean the same thing but are showing up as distinct values because of whitespace, such as `Male` and `Male`. We will demonstrate that whitespace is causing an issue when accurately defining categories and then correct the issue with the following code:

```
unique(all$sex)

all <- all %>%
    mutate_if(~is.factor(.),~trimws(.))
```

When we run the first line of the preceding code, we will print the distinct factor levels to the console. Your console will look similar to the following screenshot:

```
> unique(all$sex)
[1] Male     Female   Male     Female
Levels: Female Male  Female  Male
>
```

However, after running the second line and removing the whitespace, we will see that this has been corrected, and the output will look different. If you run the `unique()` function again, the output in your console will look like the following screenshot:

```
> unique(all$sex)
[1] "Male"    "Female"
>
```

Correcting this issue will help the algorithm to use the proper number of categories when creating the model.

5. Next, we filter just our training data. We will extract the target variable to a vector and convert the values to numeric. Afterward, we can remove the target variable from the dataset, as well as the dataset variable. We extract the train data, create the target variable vector, and remove the unneeded columns using the following code:

```
train <- all %>% filter(dataset == "train")
train_target <- as.numeric(factor(train$target))
train <- train %>% select(-target, -dataset)
```

After we run this code, we will see that the `train` data has been updated in our Environment pane and the `train_target` vector has been added. Your Environment pane will look like the following screenshot:

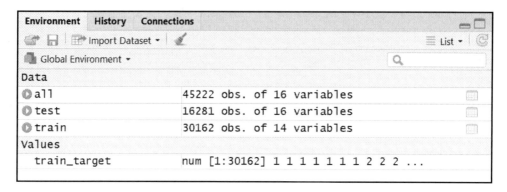

We can see that the train data has two fewer variables now that we have removed the target and the dataset. The `target` column is now extracted to its own vector and we have the dependent variable and independent variables in separate data objects so that they are in the proper format and ready to be passed to the modeling function.

6. The next step is to separate the data column-wise so that one subset contains only columns containing numeric values while the other contains only columns containing string values. As stated earlier, all values will need to be numeric, so we will be using one-hot encoding on the string values, which is also known as creating dummy variables. This will create a column for every possible field name–value pair and populate this column with either a 1 or 0, representing whether the value is present for the given field name per row. We split our data column-wise in the way described here using the following code:

```
train_chars <- train %>%
  select_if(is.character)

train_ints <- train %>%
  select_if(is.integer)
```

After we run the preceding code, we will see two new data objects—one with the 6 numeric columns among the 14 total and the other with the remaining 8 columns, which contain string values. Your **Environment** pane will now look as follows:

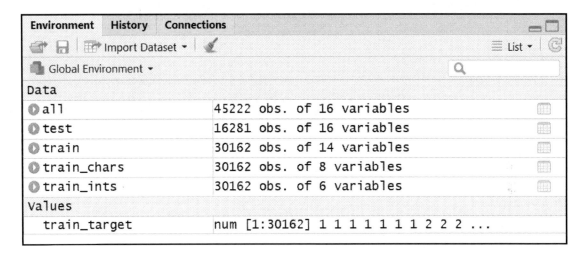

Now that our data is in this format, we can one-hot encode the columns that contain only strings.

7. In this step, we will actually create our dummy variables. We use the dummyVars() function from the caret package. This takes two steps. In the first, we define the columns that we would like converted to dummy variables. Since we would like all columns to be converted, we just include a dot after the tilde. Next, we use the predict() function to actually create the new variables using the formula. We create our new dummy variable columns using the following code:

```
ohe <- caret::dummyVars(" ~ .", data = train_chars)
train_ohe <- data.frame(predict(ohe, newdata = train_chars))
```

After running the preceding code, we will have two new data objects in our **Environment** pane. One is the `ohe` object, which is a list with all the details that we need to convert our string columns to dummy variables, and the other is the `train_ohe` object, which contains the dummy variables. Your **Environment** pane will now look as follows:

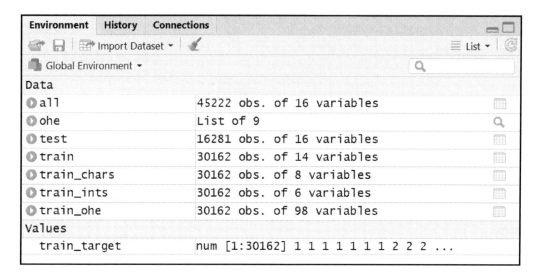

We can see that creating dummy variables results in a dataset with many more columns than our original data. As stated, we take every column name and value pair and create a new column, which results in the growth of columns.

8. After the columns containing string values have been converted to columns with numeric values, then we can column-bind both subsets back together again. We combine the data that was already numeric and the data that was converted to a numeric format using the following line of code:

```
train <- cbind(train_ints,train_ohe)
```

We can see that the `train` object in our **Environment** pane has changed. Your **Environment** pane will now look as follows:

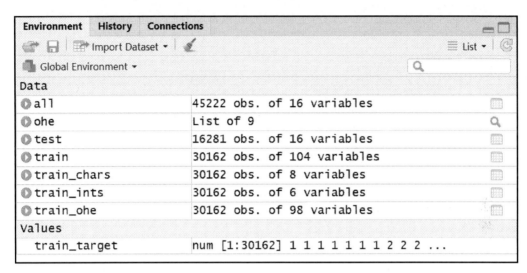

The train data now contains all numeric columns and is in the proper format to be used with a neural network.

9. Lastly, for the columns that originally held numeric values, we will rescale the values so that all values are in a range between 0 and 1, and as such are on the same scale as our one-hot encoded columns. We get all of our data on the same scale using the following code:

```
train <- train %>% mutate_all(funs(scales::rescale(.) %>%
as.vector))
```

Before we run the preceding code, let's first see what the train data columns look like in our **Environment** pane. Yours will look like the following screenshot before running the code:

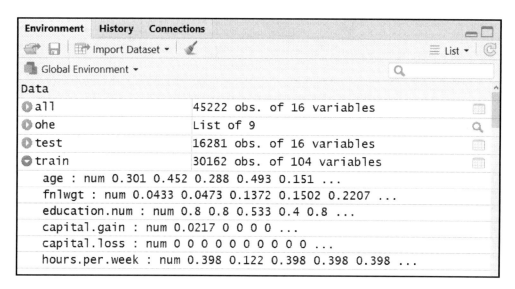

Your **Environment** pane will look like the following screenshot after running the code:

We can see that all the values that were on different scales in the first image are now all rescaled so that all values are between 0 and 1. Having all values on the same scale will help to make training the model more efficient.

10. We can now repeat the same steps for the test dataset. We prepare our test data for modeling using the same steps as the training data by running the following lines of code:

```
test <- all %>% filter(dataset == "test")
test_target <- as.numeric(factor(test$target))
test <- test %>% select(-target, -dataset)

test_chars <- test %>%
  select_if(is.character)

test_ints <- test %>%
  select_if(is.integer)

ohe <- caret::dummyVars(" ~ .", data = test_chars)
test_ohe <- data.frame(predict(ohe, newdata = test_chars))

test <- cbind(test_ints,test_ohe)

test <- test %>% mutate_all(funs(scales::rescale(.) %>% as.vector))
```

As a result of running this code, you will see test data objects that have been modified in the same way as the training data objects. Your **Environment** pane will now look like the following screenshot:

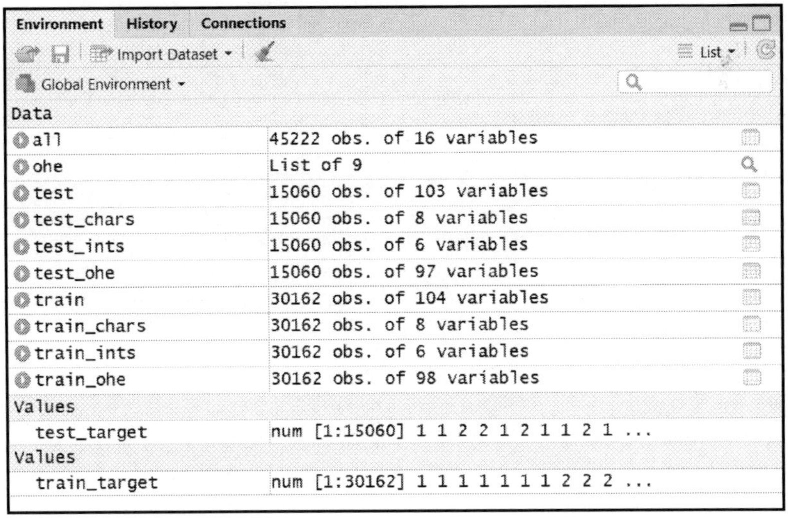

All of our data is now in the proper format and ready to be used for training our neural network model.

11. There is one last cleanup step. If we look at our column count, we can see that the train dataframe has one more column than the test dataframe. We can use the `setdiff` function to see which column exists in the `train` and not in the `test` set. Once that has been identified, we can just remove that column from the `train` set. We need our data to have the same number of columns for modeling. We find the column that doesn't exist in both datasets and remove it using the following two lines of code:

```
setdiff(names(train), names(test))

train <- train %>% select(-native.countryHoland.Netherlands)
```

When we run the first line of code, we will print the value of the output to our console. Your console output will look like the following screenshot:

```
> setdiff(names(train), names(test))
[1] "native.countryHoland.Netherlands"
>
```

We now know that the `train` has the column `native.countryHoland.Netherlands` while `test` does not. We use the second line of code to remove this column from the `train`. After we run the second line of code, we will notice a difference in our **Environment** pane. Your **Environment** pane will now look like the following screenshot:

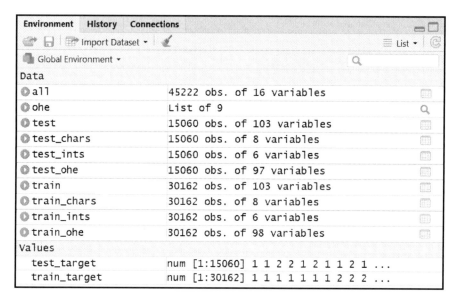

When we look at `train` and `test` now, we can see that both data objects have the same number of columns, which is required for using the two data objects to train and test our model.

12. The last data preparation step is to take our target variable vectors and subtract 1 from all values. When we first cast these to numeric format, we took their factor level values so that we got vectors coded with values of either 1 or 2; however, we want these to be coded as either 0 or 1 so that they are at the same scale as our independent variables. We get our target variables on the same scale as our independent variables by running the following code:

```
train_target <- train_target-1
test_target <- test_target-1
```

After running the following code, you will notice one last change to your **Environment** pane. Your **Environment** pane will now look like the following screenshot:

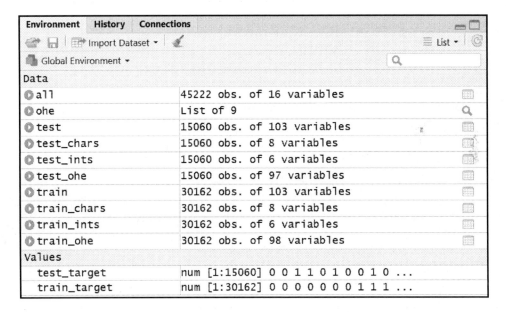

All of our data is now numeric and on the same scale, so the data is completely prepared for modeling at this point.

We started with data in the state that it was originally stored in and took some steps to get the data into the proper format so that we could use it to train a neural network. Neural networks, especially deep-learning implementations, offer the convenience of not needing to perform feature engineering like you might have to do with other machine-learning techniques. That being the case, some data preparation is still often required as neural networks require all data to be stored as numeric values, and your model will perform better if all numeric value data is on the same scale. The data manipulation and transformation steps that we just performed are representative of the type of data preparation work that will need to be completed for other data that you will use for training neural networks. With our data in the proper format, we can now devise a system to search for the optimal number of nodes for the hidden layer in our model.

Deciding on the hidden layers and neurons

Multilayer perceptrons provide only a few choices during the model design process: the activation function used in the hidden layers, the number of hidden layers, and the number of nodes or artificial neurons in each layer. The topic of selecting the optimal number of layers and nodes will be covered in this section. We can begin with a single layer and use a set of heuristics to guide our starting point for selecting the number of nodes to include in this hidden layer.

When beginning this process, a good starting point is 66% of the length of the input or the number of independent variable columns. This value, in general, will fall within a range between the size of the output to two times the size of the input; however, 66% of the length of the input is a good starting point within this range.

This does not mean that this starting point will always be the optimal number of nodes to use. To discover the optimal number, we can write a function that will train our model using a different number of nodes right around our starting point in order to see trends and attempt to find the optimal value. In this case, we will train with a larger learning rate using only a few rounds for fast run-time. If you are working with a large dataset, then it may be necessary to use a subset of the data when using this strategy so that long run times per iteration do not create an issue.

We will now walk through the creation of a function to test the performance of the model given a number of different nodes in the hidden layer:

1. To start, let's look at the number of independent variable columns and then get 66% of this value to arrive at our starting point. We decide on the starting point for the number of nodes to include in our hidden layer by running the following code:

    ```
    length(train)*.66
    ```

    The preceding code will print the following output to your console:

    ```
    > length(train)*.66
    [1]  67.98
    >
    ```

    The precise value is 67.98, but we will round this up to 70 as our starting value. Keep in mind that you can use any value you like, as this is just a heuristic—working with round numbers is convenient, and you can always drill down to the exact optimal number of neurons at a later time—however, the performance difference when making small changes will be minimal and may not be present when generalizing with this model later.

2. Next, let's choose two values that are larger than this starting point as well as two that are smaller and store these in a vector. These will be the options that we will pass through as arguments to our function. In this case, we started with 70, so we will also include 50, 60, 80, and 90. We create the vector of possible nodes for our hidden layer by running the following code:

    ```
    possible_node_values <- c(50,60,70,80,90)
    ```

After running the preceding code, we will see that this data object is now in our **Environment** pane. Your **Environment** pane will now look like the following screenshot:

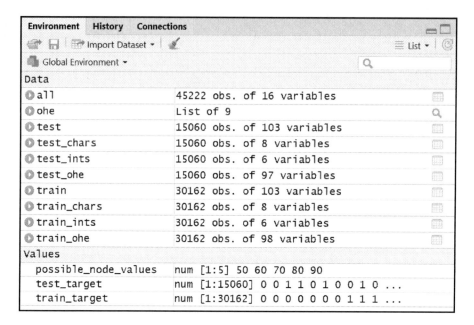

We will use the values from this vector later to loop through these choices and see which performs best.

3. We will set our seed at this point to ensure reproducibility. This is always important, and should always be done when working with any type of model that introduces quasirandom numbers. In our case, it is important for this demonstration to show that the function we create produces the same result as running the code alone. We set the seed specifically for use with our MXNet model by running the following line of code:

```
mx.set.seed(0)
```

After running this code, no output is printed to the console and there are no noticeable changes in RStudio; however, using this method, we ensure consistent model results.

4. Before writing our function, we will first define and run our model and look at the syntax and options for training a multilayer perceptron using the `mxnet` package. We define and run our multilayer perceptron model using the following code:

```
model <- mx.mlp(data.matrix(train), train_target,
hidden_node=70,out_node=2, out_activation="softmax",num.round=10,
array.batch.size=32, learning.rate=0.1, momentum=0.8,
eval.metric=mx.metric.accuracy)
```

After running the preceding code, we will see model details printed to our console for every run. The output to your console will look like the following screenshot:

```
Start training with 1 devices
[1] Train-accuracy=0.819658006362672
[2] Train-accuracy=0.82986479321315
[3] Train-accuracy=0.83225079533404
[4] Train-accuracy=0.833344379639449
[5] Train-accuracy=0.835531548250265
[6] Train-accuracy=0.836691410392365
[7] Train-accuracy=0.837354188759279
[8] Train-accuracy=0.837718716861082
[9] Train-accuracy=0.83858032873807
[10] Train-accuracy=0.839243107104984
```

The output to the console lists all the accuracy values using a holdout set from the `train` data. We will cover all the options for modeling with MXNet after this code to cover each argument in more detail. Simply put, we are using values to make the model run quickly at this point, while we are preparing to test for the optimal number of nodes to include.

5. In addition to training this model, we would also like a data object to hold performance results so that we can compare the performance after trying the different hidden layer sizes. Here, we can make a prediction using our model and then select the class with the highest likelihood. Lastly, we calculate the accuracy by summing up the cases where the prediction is correct over the length of the test target variables. We can also see how we can now store these two values in a table. We do this here to demonstrate the entire inside of our function, which will hold all the different node size choices along with the accuracy of using that given number of nodes. We make predictions and calculate the accuracy using the following code:

```
preds = predict(model, data.matrix(test))

pred.label = max.col(t(preds))-1
```

```
acc = sum(pred.label == test_target)/length(test_target)

vals <- tibble(
nodes = 70,
accuracy = acc
)

vals
```

After running the preceding code, we will have four new data objects in our **Environment** pane. Your **Environment** pane will look like the following screenshot:

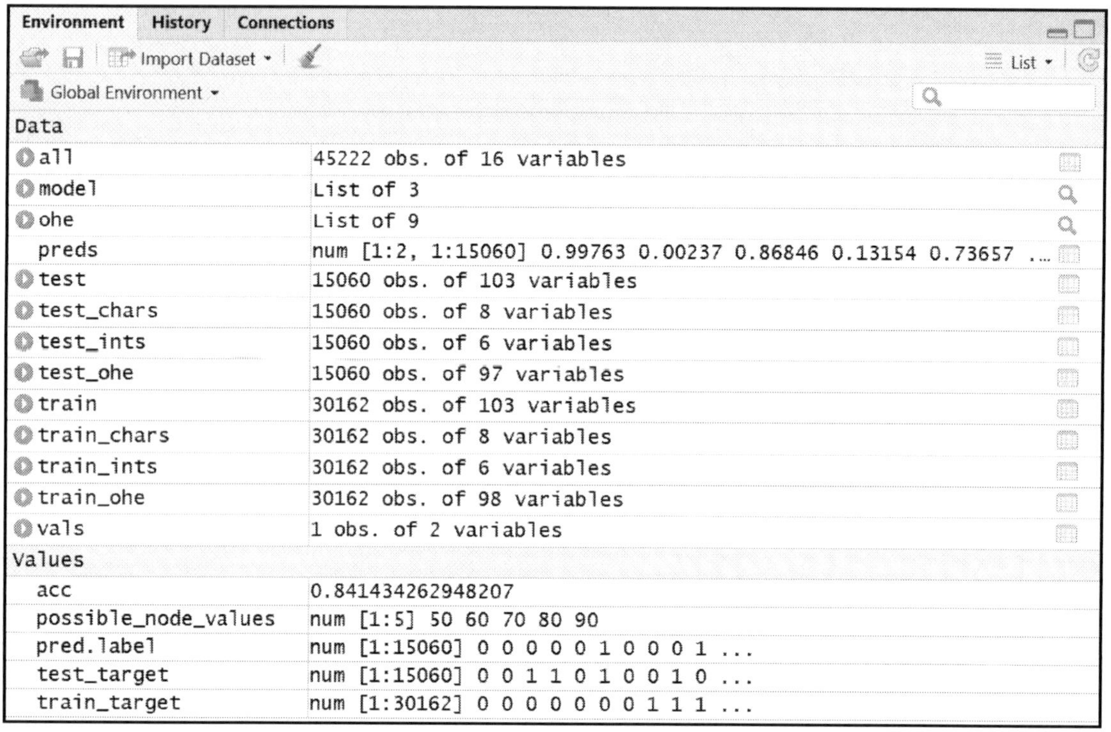

The `preds` object holds the results from making predictions with our model. MXNet stores these prediction results in a matrix with the probabilities for each class. If we transpose this matrix or rotate it 90 degrees and select the maximum value for every column, then we will get the highest row number that corresponds with the most likely class; however, this will be using values 1 and 2 for the rows, so we subtract 1 from all values to get our prediction values on the same scale as our true test classes, which are 0 or 1. For the accuracy value, we sum all the cases where the predicted values and true values are the same over the total number of true cases. Finally, we can put the node count and accuracy score in a table. This will be useful for comparing results when we try different node counts.

6. Now that we have everything coded for an individual case, we can create our function by replacing the value assigned to the argument that we would like to test with a variable. We then move that variable to be the argument for our new function. We can see that everything in the code is the exact same as it was previously, except that the 70 that we had as a value for the `hidden_node` argument, and that we had later as a value to add under the `nodes` column in the new table we will create, are now replaced with x. The x is then moved outside and added as an argument for our new function. In this way, we can now pass any value to our new `mlp_loop()` function and have it replace the two instances of x in our code. We write our custom function to try different values for the `hidden_node` argument using the following code:

```
mlp_loop <- function(x) {
  model <- mx.mlp(data.matrix(train), train_target, hidden_node=x,
out_node=2, out_activation="softmax",
num.round=10, array.batch.size=32, learning.rate=0.1,
momentum=0.8,eval.metric=mx.metric.accuracy)
  preds = predict(model, data.matrix(test))
  pred.label = max.col(t(preds))-1
  acc = sum(pred.label == test_target)/length(test_target)
  vals <- tibble(
    nodes = x,
    accuracy = acc
  )
}
```

After we run the preceding code, we will see the change in our **Environment** pane. Your **Environment** pane will now look like the following screenshot:

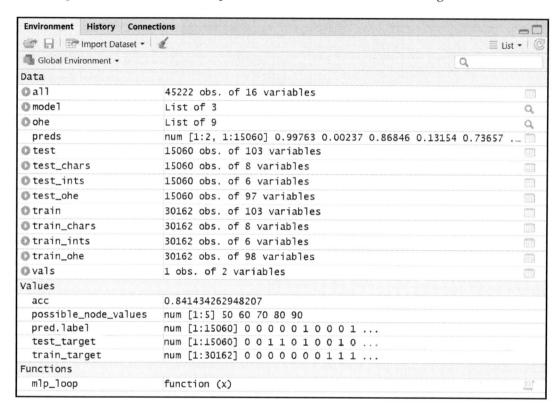

We can see that we now have a custom function defined and stored in our environment.

7. Now we can first test our function with the value from the previous run. We test our function by supplying the value 70 to the function that we just made using the following lines of code:

```
results <- mlp_loop(70)

results

all.equal(results$accuracy, acc)
```

After we run the following code, we will get a printout on our console with the accuracy value and the number of nodes that we included in the hidden layer, as well as the results of testing for equality. Your console will look like the following screenshot:

```
>
> results
# A tibble: 1 x 2
  nodes accuracy
  <dbl>    <dbl>
1    70    0.841
>
> all.equal(results$accuracy,acc)
[1] TRUE
>
```

Based on the results of the code that we just ran, we can see that our function produces the same results that it would produce by just passing the values to the modeling code directly. This makes sense, as we are just swapping in 70 for all places where x is in the model function.

8. Now that it is confirmed that our new function is working (as we get the same result when passing the value 70 through the function that we get by just having it in the code), we can now pass our entire vector of values through the function. In order to do so, we will use the map() function from the purrr package, which makes iterating very simple and straightforward. In this case, we will use the map_df() function in order to get a dataframe, after looping all values through the function call. We loop through our function, passing in all values from the vector we created earlier by using the following code:

```
results <- map_df(possible_node_values, mlp_loop)

results
```

When we run the preceding code, we will see a printout to the console just like in *step 4* for all five model runs. After this, we will get the `results` dataframe, which now has all the accuracy scores for all the node count attempts. In your console, you may notice some rounding, which prevents an immediate determination of which model performed best. Let's click on the results from our **Environment** pane instead and view the data that way. After clicking on `results`, you should see a table similar to the following screenshot:

	nodes	accuracy
1	50	0.8426295
2	60	0.8356574
3	70	0.8369190
4	80	0.8365870
5	90	0.8428287

9. While we were able to create a loop to pass different node count values to the `mlp()` function to determine the optimal count, we will see in the next step that using a similar loop technique for finding the optimal layers is not as straightforward. To add layers, we must abandon the convenience of the `mlp()` function and create our multilayer perceptron one layer at a time. We can create an MLP one layer at a time using the following code:

```
data <- mx.symbol.Variable("data")
fc1 <- mx.symbol.FullyConnected(data, num_hidden=90)
fc2 <- mx.symbol.FullyConnected(fc1, num_hidden=50)
smx <- mx.symbol.SoftmaxOutput(fc2)

model <- mx.model.FeedForward.create(smx, data.matrix(train),
train_target,num.round=10, array.batch.size=32,
learning.rate=0.1, momentum=0.8, eval.metric=mx.metric.accuracy)


preds = predict(model, data.matrix(test))

pred.label = max.col(t(preds))-1

acc = sum(pred.label == test_target)/length(test_target)

acc
```

After running the preceding code, we will have a number of new data objects in our **Environment** pane and an accuracy score printed to our console. Your console will look like the following screenshot:

```
> acc
[1] 0.8406375
>
```

From this output, we can see that using the two highest-scoring values from our test of node counts in two separate layers did not improve our score. Adding more layers will not always lead to a better performing model, though you can continue to experiment with different layers using the preceding code as a guide to try to see if you can improve the score. Let's review what the preceding code is doing and how it differs from the model we created using the `mlp()` function.

In this case, we initiate our model by creating a symbolic variable. We then create two fully connected layers with 90 and 50 nodes respectively. We then define an output layer using the softmax activation function. We then use the `FeedForward()` function to define the other options that we used previously. In doing this, we can see that most of the arguments can be passed to `FeedForward` while the `hidden_node` argument moves to the `FullyConnected()` function for as many layers as you want and the `out_node` and `out_activation` arguments move to an output function, which in this case is `SoftmaxOutput`.

Using our prepared data, we looked at how to test for the optimal number of nodes for a hidden layer. We also looked at how we need to change our code to add additional layers. With MLPs, there are fewer options than other neural network implementations, so we have focused on making changes to the hidden layers to try to optimize our model using the main strength of neural network models. In the next step, we will take everything we have learned while tuning parameters to run a model that will maximize performance while giving a more in-depth explanation of our model options using MXNet.

Training and evaluating the model

After parameter tuning, we can now run the model for maximum performance. In order to do so, we will make a few important changes to the model options. Ahead of making the changes, let's have a more in-depth review of the model options:

- `hidden_node`: These are the number of nodes in the hidden layer. We used a looping function to find the optimal number of nodes.

- `out_node`: These are the number of nodes in the output layer and must be set equal to the number of target classes. In this case, that number is 2.

- `out_activation`: This is the activation function to use for the output layer.

- `num.round`: This is the number of iterations we take to train our model. In the parameter tuning stage, we set this number low so that we could quickly loop through a number of options; to get maximum accuracy, we would allow the model to run for more rounds while at the same time dropping the learning rate, which we will cover soon.

- `array.batch.size`: This sets the batch size, which is the number of rows that are trained at the same time during each round. The higher this is set, the more memory will be required.

- `learning.rate`: This is the constant value applied to the gradient from the loss function that is used to adjust weights. For parameter tuning, we set this to a large number to move quickly along the cost surface in a small number of rounds. To achieve the best performance, we will set this to a lower number to make more subtle adjustments while learning new weights so we don't constantly overadjust the values.

- `momentum`: This uses the decaying values from previous gradients to avoid sudden shifts in movement along the cost surface. As a heuristic, a good starting value for `momentum` is between 0.5 and 0.8.

- `eval.metric`: This is the metric that you will use to evaluate performance. In our case, we are using `accuracy`.

Now, that we have covered the options included in our model using the `mlp()` function, we will make adjustments to improve accuracy. In order to improve accuracy, we will increase the number of rounds while simultaneously dropping the learning rate. We will keep the other values constant and use the node count that led to the best performance from our loop earlier. You can set the model for better performance using what we learned when parameter tuning using the following code:

```
model <- mx.mlp(data.matrix(train), train_target, hidden_node=90,
out_node=2, out_activation="softmax",num.round=200, array.batch.size=32,
learning.rate=0.005, momentum=0.8,eval.metric=mx.metric.accuracy)

preds = predict(model, data.matrix(test))

pred.label = max.col(t(preds))-1

acc = sum(pred.label == test_target)/length(test_target)

acc
```

After running this code, you will see a printout in your console with the accuracy score after running the model with the adjustments to the parameters. Your console output will look like this:

```
>
> acc
[1] 0.8501328
>
```

We can see that our accuracy has improved from our adjustments. Before, when we were testing parameters, the best accuracy we could achieve was 84.28%, and we can see that we now have an accuracy score of 85.01%.

After preparing our data so that it is in the proper format to model with MXNet, and then parameter tuning to find the best values for our model, we then made adjustments to further improve performance using what we learned earlier. All of these steps together describe a complete cycle of manipulating and transforming data, optimizing parameters, and then running our final model. We saw how to use MXNet, which offers a convenience function for simple MLPs and also offers the functionality to build MLPs with additional hidden layers using the activation, output, and feedforward functions.

Summary

Multilayer perceptrons are the simplest form of neural networks. They are feedforward without the feedback loops of recurrent neural networks, and all hidden layers are dense, fully connected layers, unlike convolutional neural networks, which feature convolutional layers and pooling layers. Given their simplicity, there are fewer options to adjust; however, in this chapter, we focused on adjusting the nodes in the hidden layer and looked at adding additional layers, as this aspect is the main element that separates neural network models, and as such, all deep learning methods from other machine learning algorithms. Using all the code in this chapter, you have learned how to process data so that it was ready to model, how to select the optimal number of nodes and layers, and how to train and evaluate a model using the `mxnet` library for R.

In the next chapter, you will learn how to code deep autoencoders. This model is a form of unsupervised learning that is used to automatically categorize our input data. We will use this clustering process to code a recommender system using collaborative filtering.

6
Neural Collaborative Filtering Using Embeddings

In the previous chapter, you learned how to implement a **multilayer perceptron** (MLP) neural network for signal detection.

In this chapter, you will explore how to build a recommender system using collaborative filtering with neural network-based embeddings. We will briefly introduce recommender systems and then proceed from concept to implementation. Specifically, you will learn how to use the custom Keras API to construct a neural network-based recommender system with embedded layers to predict user ratings.

This chapter covers the following topics:

- Introducing recommender systems
- Collaborative filtering with neural networks
- Preparing, preprocessing, and exploring data
- Performing exploratory data analysis
- Creating user and item embeddings
- Building and training a neural recommender system
- Evaluating results and tuning hyperparameters

Technical requirements

We will use the Keras (TensorFlow API) library in this chapter.

We will be using the `steam200k.csv` dataset. This dataset was generated from publicly available Steam data, which is one of the world's most popular gaming hubs. This data contains a list of items (`game-title`), users (`user-id`), and two user behaviors (`own` and `value`), where `value` represents the number of hours played for each game. You can find the dataset at: `https://www.kaggle.com/tamber/steam-video-games/version/1#steam-200k.csv`.

You can find the code files of this chapter on GitHub: `https://github.com/PacktPublishing/Hands-on-Deep-Learning-with-R`.

Introducing recommender systems

Recommender systems are information filtering systems designed to generate accurate and relevant item suggestions for users based on available data. Netflix, Amazon, YouTube, and Spotify are some popular services with recommender systems in commercial use today.

There are three primary types of recommender systems:

- **Collaborative filtering**: Item recommendations reflect personalized preferences based on similarity to other users. Preferences can be **explicit** (item ratings) or **implicit** (item ratings per user-item interactions such as views, purchases, and so on).
- **Content-based filtering**: Item recommendations reflect contextual factors such as item attributes or user demographics; item suggestions can also use temporal factors such as location, date, and time where applicable.
- **Hybrid**: Item recommendations combine a variety (ensemble) of collaborative and content-based filtering methods, which have been used in notable competitions such as the Netflix Prize (2009).

See `https://www.netflixprize.com` for historical details about the Netflix Prize (2009) and various recommender system approaches.

Recommender systems often use data in the form of a sparse matrix of users and the items you wish to recommend to them. As its name suggests, a sparse matrix is a matrix whose data elements primarily comprise zero values.

Many recommender system algorithms seek to fill in a user-item interaction matrix with item suggestions based on various types of interactions between users and items. If there is no item preference or user interaction data available, this is frequently referred to as a **cold start problem**, which can be addressed with hybrid methods (collaborative and content-based filtering), contextual models (temporal, demographic, and metadata), as well as random item and feedback sampling strategies, among others. While these interventions are beyond the scope of this chapter, it is important to be aware of the diverse, experimental, and rapidly evolving types of techniques available.

For purposes of illustration, we will focus our attention on collaborative filtering, which is a popular technique that generates recommendations based on user-item interactions. Moreover, collaborative filtering is particularly suitable for our user-item dataset. In the absence of explicit ratings such as user-item preferences (for example, 1 to 5, and like or dislike), we will create implicit preferences of user-item ratings based on the hours of gameplay, which is available in our dataset.

Collaborative filtering with neural networks

Collaborative filtering (**CF**) is a core method used by recommender systems to filter suggestions by collecting and analyzing preferences about other similar users. CF techniques use available information and preference pattern data to make predictions (filters) about a particular user's interests.

The collaborative aspect of CF is associated with the notion that relevant recommendations are derived from other user preferences. CF also assumes that two individuals with similar preferences are more likely to share preferences for a particular item than two other individuals selected at random. Accordingly, the primary task of CF is to generate item suggestions (predictions) based on other (collaborative) similar users within the system.

To identify similar users and find ratings (preferences) of unrated items, recommender systems *typically* need an index of similarity between users and user-item preferences based on available input data. Traditional memory-based approaches include calculating similarity using distance metrics (cosine similarity, Jaccard), correlations (Pearson), or taking a weighted average of user preferences. Other machine learning approaches to determine user-item preferences of unrated items include generalized matrix factorization methods such as **Principal Component Analysis** (**PCA**), **Singular Value Decomposition** (**SVD**), and deep learning matrix factorization, among others.

Exploring embeddings

Broadly speaking, deep neural networks seek to minimize the loss (error) associated with non-linear data representations used for learning important features from input data.

In addition to traditional dimensionality reduction methods such as clustering and KNN or matrix factorization (PCA, clustering, and other probabilistic techniques), recommender systems can use neural network embeddings to support dimensionality reduction and distributed, non-linear data representations in scalable and efficient ways.

Embeddings are low-dimensional representations (vectors) of continuous numbers learned from representations (vectors) of discrete input variables in neural networks.

Neural network embeddings offer several advantages such as the following:

- Reduced computational time and costs (scalability)
- Decreased amount of input data required for some learning activation functions (sparsity)
- Representations of complex, non-linear relationships (flexibility)
- Automated feature importance and selection (efficiency)

Let's take a look at an introductory example of how to prepare data in order to implement collaborative filtering using neural networks with embeddings.

Preparing, preprocessing, and exploring data

Before we build a model, we need to first explore the input data to understand what is available for user-item recommendations. In this section, we will prepare, process, and explore the data, which includes users, items (games), and interactions (hours of gameplay), using the following steps:

1. First, let's load some R packages for preparing and processing our input data:

```
library(keras)
library(tidyverse)
library(knitr)
```

2. Next, let's load the data into R:

```
steamdata <- read_csv("data/steam-200k.csv", col_names=FALSE)
```

3. Let's inspect the input data using `glimpse()`:

```
glimpse(steamdata)
```

This results in the following output:

```
Observations: 200,000
Variables: 5
$ X1 <dbl> 151603712, 151603712, 151603712, 151603712, 151603712, 15...
$ X2 <chr> "The Elder Scrolls V Skyrim", "The Elder Scrolls V Skyrim...
$ X3 <chr> "purchase", "play", "purchase", "play", "purchase", "play...
$ X4 <dbl> 1.0, 273.0, 1.0, 87.0, 1.0, 14.9, 1.0, 12.1, 1.0, 8.9, 1...
$ X5 <dbl> 0, 0, 0, 0, 0, 0, 0, 0, 0, 0, 0, 0, 0, 0, 0, 0, 0, 0, 0, ...
```

4. Let's manually add column labels to organize this data:

```
colnames(steamdata) <- c("user", "item", "interaction", "value",
"blank")
```

5. Let's remove any blank columns or extraneous whitespace characters:

```
steamdata <- steamdata %>%
  filter(interaction == "play") %>%
  select(-blank) %>%
  select(-interaction) %>%
  mutate(item = str_replace_all(item,'[ [:blank:][:space:] ]',""))
```

6. Now, we need to create sequential user and item IDs so we can later specify an appropriate size for our lookup matrix via the following code:

```
users <- steamdata %>% select(user) %>% distinct() %>%
rowid_to_column()
steamdata <- steamdata %>% inner_join(users) %>%
rename(userid=rowid)

items <- steamdata %>% select(item) %>% distinct() %>%
rowid_to_column()
steamdata <- steamdata %>% inner_join(items) %>%
rename(itemid=rowid)
```

7. Let's rename the `item` and `value` fields to clarify we are exploring user-item interaction data and implicitly defining user ratings based on the `value` field, which represents the total number of hours played for a particular game:

```
steamdata <- steamdata %>% rename(title=item, rating=value)
```

8. This dataset contains user, item, and interaction data. Let's use the following code to identify the number of users and items available for analysis:

```
n_users <- steamdata %>% select(userid) %>% distinct() %>% nrow()
n_items <- steamdata %>% select(itemid) %>% distinct() %>% nrow()
```

We identified there are 11,350 users (players) and 3,598 items (games) to explore for analysis and recommendations. Since we don't have explicit item ratings (yes/no, 1-5, for example), we will generate item (game) recommendations based on implicit feedback (hours of gameplay) for illustration purposes. Alternatively, we could seek to acquire additional user-item data (such as contextual, temporal, or content), but we have enough baseline item-interaction data to build our preliminary CF-based recommender system with neural network embeddings.

9. Before proceeding, we need to normalize our rating (user-item interaction) data, which can be implemented using standard techniques such as min-max normalization:

```
# normalize data with min-max function
minmax <- function(x) {
  return ((x - min(x)) / (max(x) - min(x)))
}

# add scaled rating value
steamdata <- steamdata %>% mutate(rating_scaled = minmax(rating))
```

10. Next, we will split the data into training and test data:

```
# split into training and test
index <- sample(1:nrow(steamdata), 0.8* nrow(steamdata))
train <- steamdata[index,]
test <- steamdata[-index,]
```

11. Now we will create matrices of users, items, and ratings for the training and test data:

```
# create matrices of user, items, and ratings for training and test
x_train <- train %>% select(c(userid, itemid)) %>% as.matrix()
y_train <- train %>% select(rating_scaled) %>% as.matrix()
x_test <- test %>% select(c(userid, itemid)) %>% as.matrix()
y_test <- test %>% select(rating_scaled) %>% as.matrix()
```

Prior to building our neural network models, we will first conduct **Exploratory data analysis (EDA)** to better understand the scope, type, and characteristics of the underlying data.

Performing exploratory data analysis

Recommender systems seek to use available information and preference pattern data to generate predictions about a particular user's interests.

As a starting point, we can use EDA to identify important patterns and trends in the underlying data to inform our understanding and subsequent analysis:

1. Let's identify the top 10 items based on implicit ratings constructed from user-item interaction data using the following code:

```
# user-item interaction exploratory data analysis (EDA)
item_interactions <- aggregate(
    rating ~ title, data = steamdata, FUN = 'sum')
item_interactions <- item_interactions[
    order(item_interactions$rating, decreasing = TRUE),]
item_top10 <- head(item_interactions, 10)
kable(item_top10)
```

Dota 2 is the most popular item (game) by collective hours played:

	item	value
920	Dota2	981684.6
674	Counter-StrikeGlobalOffensive	322771.6
3005	TeamFortress2	173673.3
671	Counter-Strike	134261.1
2700	SidMeier'sCivilizationV	99821.3
676	Counter-StrikeSource	96075.5
3083	TheElderScrollsVSkyrim	70889.3
1307	Garry'sMod	49725.3
490	CallofDutyModernWarfare2-Multiplayer	42009.9
1730	Left4Dead2	33596.7

2. Let's produce some summary statistics of user-item interactions to identify insights with the following code:

```
# average gamplay
steamdata %>% summarise(avg_gameplay = mean(rating))

# median gameplay
steamdata %>% summarise(median_gameplay = median(rating))
```

```
# top game by individual hours played
topgame <- steamdata %>% arrange(desc(rating)) %>% top_n(1,rating)

# show top game by individual hours played
kable(topgame)
```

According to this exploratory analysis, Sid Meier's *Civilization V* is the most popular game by individual hours played:

user	title	rating	userid	itemid	rating_scaled
73017395	SidMeier'sCivilizationV	11754	6941	29	1

3. Now, let's identify and visualize the top 10 games by hours played:

```
# top 10 games by hours played
mostplayed <-
   steamdata %>%
   group_by(item) %>%
   summarise(hours=sum(rating)) %>%
   arrange(desc(hours)) %>%
   top_n(10, hours) %>%
   ungroup

# show top 10 games by hours played
kable(mostplayed)

# reset factor levels for items
mostplayed$item <- droplevels(mostplayed$item)

# top 10 games by collective hours played
ggplot(mostplayed, aes(x=item, y=hours, fill = hours)) +
   aes(x = fct_inorder(item)) +
   geom_bar(stat = "identity") +
   theme(axis.text.x = element_text(size=8, face="bold", angle=90))
+
   theme(axis.ticks = element_blank()) +
   scale_y_continuous(expand = c(0,0), limits = c(0,1000000)) +
   labs(title="Top 10 games by collective hours played") +
   xlab("game") +
   ylab("hours")
```

This results in the following output:

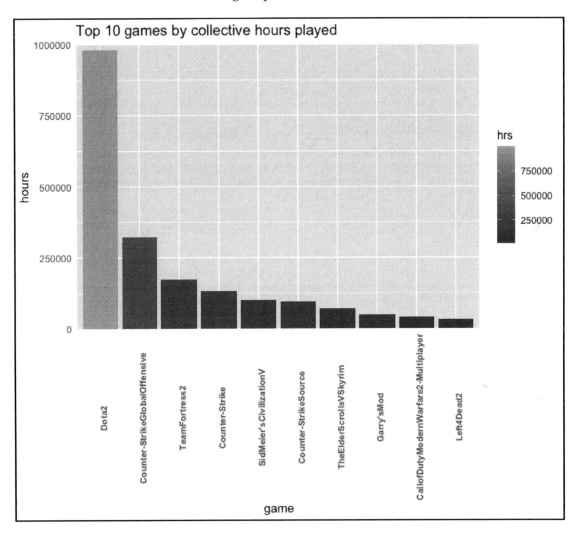

4. Next, let's identify the most popular games by total users:

```
# most popular games by total users
mostusers <-
  steamdata %>%
  group_by(item) %>%
  summarise(users=n()) %>%
  arrange(desc(users)) %>%
  top_n(10, users) %>%
  ungroup

# reset factor levels for items
mostusers$item <- droplevels(mostusers$item)

# top 10 popular games by total users
ggplot(mostusers, aes(x=item, y=users, fill = users)) +
  aes(x = fct_inorder(item)) +
  geom_bar(stat = "identity") +
  theme(axis.text.x = element_text(size=8, face="bold", angle=90))
+
  theme(axis.ticks = element_blank()) +
  scale_y_continuous(expand = c(0,0), limits = c(0,5000)) +
  labs(title="Top 10 popular games by total users") +
  xlab("game") +
  ylab("users")
```

This results in the following output:

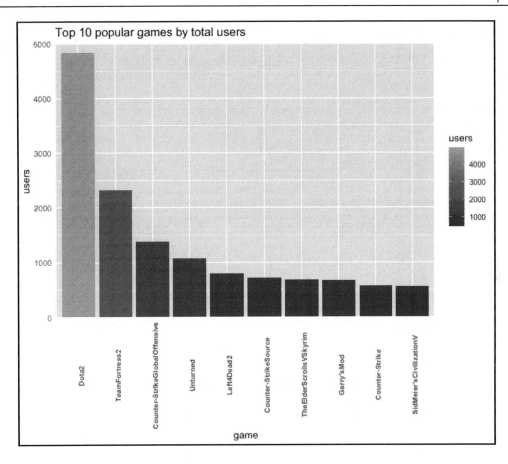

5. Now, let's calculate summary statistics of user-item interaction with the following code:

```
summary(steamdata$value)
```

This results in the following output:

```
> summary(steamdata$value)
   Min. 1st Qu.  Median    Mean 3rd Qu.     Max.
   0.10    1.00    4.50   48.88   19.10 11754.00
```

The summary statistics for overall user-item interaction show average (median) interaction is 4.5 hours and average (mean) interaction is 48.88 hours, which makes sense when you take into consideration the max (outlier) interaction value: 11,754 hours of Sid Meier's *Civilization V*!

6. Next, let's take a look at the distribution of items by individual hours played:

```
# plot item iteraction
ggplot(steamdata, aes(x=steamdata$value)) +
  geom_histogram(stat = "bin", binwidth=50, fill="steelblue") +
  theme(axis.ticks = element_blank()) +
  scale_x_continuous(expand = c(0,0)) +
  scale_y_continuous(expand = c(0,0), limits = c(0,60000)) +
  labs(title="Item interaction distribution") +
  xlab("Hours played") +
  ylab("Count")
```

Here is the resultant output of items by hours played:

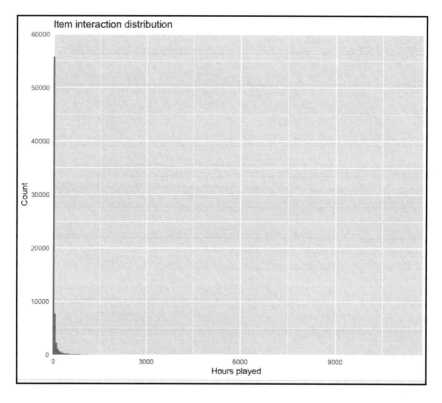

7. Since it's difficult to determine any clear user-item interaction patterns with this approach, let's re-examine items by hours played with a log transformation of hours to reveal any other distributional patterns:

```
# plot item iteraction with log transformation
ggplot(steamdata, aes(x=steamdata$value)) +
  geom_histogram(stat = "bin", binwidth=0.25, fill="steelblue") +
```

```
theme(axis.ticks = element_blank()) +
scale_x_log10() +
labs(title="Item interaction distribution with log
transformation") +
xlab("log(Hours played)") +
ylab("Count")
```

This results in the following output:

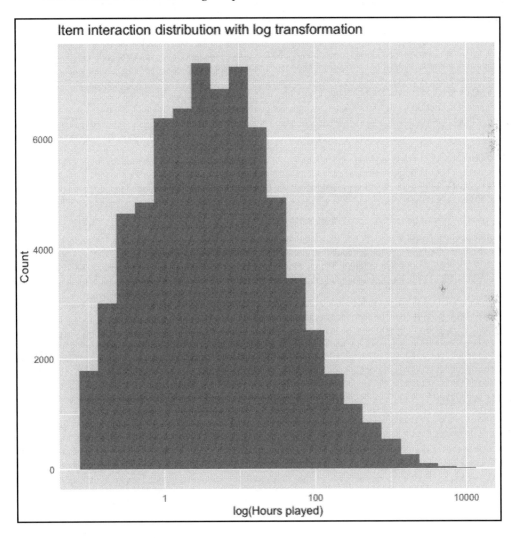

By applying a simple log transformation of hours played, we can clearly see the majority of games in this dataset are associated with 1,000 hours of gameplay or less.

Now that we have a better sense of the underlying data, let's focus our attention on building a neural network with embeddings to predict user ratings.

Creating user and item embeddings

Recommender systems can use deep neural networks to support complex, non-linear data representations in flexible, scalable, and efficient ways.

Embeddings are low-dimensional representations (vectors) of continuous numbers learned from representations (vectors) of discrete input variables in neural networks. As previously noted in this chapter, recommender systems *typically* need an index of similarity between users and user-item preferences to identify similar users and find ratings (preferences) of unrated items.

However, unlike traditional collaborative filtering approaches that use generalized matrix factorization methods to produce user-item affinity vectors, neural networks can store important information about user-item affinity in a latent (hidden) space using distributed, low-dimensional representational (embeddings).

Accordingly, as long as we have representations (embeddings) of users and items (games) accessible within the same latent space, we can determine the mutual importance of the relationship between users and items (games) using a dot product function. Presuming user and item vectors have already been normalized, this is effectively the same as using **cosine similarity**, $\cos(\Theta)$, as a distance metric, where A_i and B_i are components of vector A and B, respectively:

$$\cos(\theta) = \frac{\mathbf{A}\mathbf{B}}{\|\mathbf{A}\|\|\mathbf{B}\|} = \frac{\sum_{i=1}^{n} \mathbf{A}_i \mathbf{B}_i}{\sqrt{\sum_{i=1}^{n} (\mathbf{A}_i)^2} \sqrt{\sum_{i=1}^{n} (\mathbf{B}_i)^2}}$$

By creating neural network embeddings for users and items, we can decrease the amount of input data required for some learning activation functions, which is especially helpful with the data sparsity conditions typically encountered with user-item data in CF systems. In the next section, we will outline how to build, compile, and train a neural recommender system.

Building and training a neural recommender system

We are now going to build, compile, and train our model using our user-item ratings data. Specifically, we will use Keras to construct a customized neural network with embedded layers (one for users and one for items) and a lambda function that computes the dot product to build a working prototype of a neural network-based recommender system:

1. Let's get started using the following code:

```
# create custom model with user and item embeddings
dot <- function(
  embedding_dim,
  n_users,
  n_items,
  name = "dot"
) {
  keras_model_custom(name = name, function(self) {
    self$user_embedding <- layer_embedding(
        input_dim = n_users+1,
        output_dim = embedding_dim,
        name = "user_embedding")
    self$item_embedding <- layer_embedding(
        input_dim = n_items+1,
        output_dim = embedding_dim,
        name = "item_embedding")
    self$dot <- layer_lambda(
        f = function(x)
        k_batch_dot(x[[1]],x[[2]],axes=2),
        name = "dot"
    )
    function(x, mask=NULL, training=FALSE) {
      users <- x[,1]
      items <- x[,2]
      user_embedding <- self$user_embedding(users)
      item_embedding <- self$item_embedding(items)
      dot <- self$dot(list(user_embedding, item_embedding))
    }
  })
}
```

In the preceding code, we defined a custom model with user and item embeddings using the `keras_model_custom` function. You will notice that the input size of each embedding layer is initialized to the size of the input data (`n_users` and `n_items`, respectively).

2. In the following code, we define the size of the embedding parameter (embedding_dim) and define the architecture of our neural collaborative filtering model and vector representations (embeddings) to predict user ratings:

```
# initialize embedding parameter
embedding_dim <- 50

# define model
model <- dot(
  embedding_dim,
  n_users,
  n_items
)
```

3. Now, let's compile our model:

```
# compile model
model %>% compile(
  loss = "mse",
  optimizer = "adam"
)
```

4. Next, let's train our model with the following code:

```
# train model
history <- model %>% fit(
  x_train,
  y_train,
  epochs = 10,
  batch_size = 500,
  validation_data = list(x_test,y_test),
  verbose = 1
)
```

This results in the following output:

```
Train on 56391 samples, validate on 14098 samples
Epoch 1/10
56391/56391 [==============================] - 1s 22us/sample - loss: 4.3163e-04 - val_loss: 3.9349e-04
Epoch 2/10
56391/56391 [==============================] - 1s 13us/sample - loss: 3.6810e-04 - val_loss: 3.9461e-04
Epoch 3/10
56391/56391 [==============================] - 1s 14us/sample - loss: 2.5844e-04 - val_loss: 4.1381e-04
Epoch 4/10
56391/56391 [==============================] - 1s 14us/sample - loss: 1.5304e-04 - val_loss: 4.2834e-04
Epoch 5/10
56391/56391 [==============================] - 1s 14us/sample - loss: 1.5096e-04 - val_loss: 4.2402e-04
Epoch 6/10
56391/56391 [==============================] - 1s 13us/sample - loss: 1.2473e-04 - val_loss: 4.2150e-04
Epoch 7/10
56391/56391 [==============================] - 1s 13us/sample - loss: 8.3409e-05 - val_loss: 4.2922e-04
Epoch 8/10
56391/56391 [==============================] - 1s 13us/sample - loss: 6.7453e-05 - val_loss: 4.2921e-04
Epoch 9/10
56391/56391 [==============================] - 1s 13us/sample - loss: 5.1228e-05 - val_loss: 4.3472e-04
Epoch 10/10
56391/56391 [==============================] - 1s 13us/sample - loss: 4.6724e-05 - val_loss: 4.3407e-04
```

5. Now, let's inspect the baseline architecture of our model for reference:

```
summary(model)
```

Here is a printout of our model's architecture:

```
Model: "dot"
_____
Layer (type)                    Output Shape             Param #
=================================================================
user_embedding (Embedding)      multiple                 567550
_____
item_embedding (Embedding)      multiple                 179950
_____
dot (Lambda)                    multiple                 0
=================================================================
Total params: 747,500
Trainable params: 747,500
Non-trainable params: 0
_____
```

In the following section, we will evaluate the model results, tune parameters, and make some iterative adjustments to improve performance in terms of loss metrics.

Evaluating results and tuning hyperparameters

Building a recommender system, evaluating its performance, and tuning the hyperparameters is a highly iterative process. Ultimately, the goal is to maximize the model's performance and results. Now that we have built and trained our baseline model, we can monitor and evaluate its performance during the training process using the following code:

```
# evaluate model results
plot(history)
```

This results in the following model performance output:

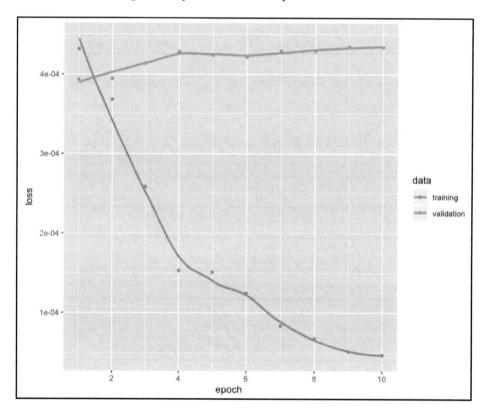

In the following sections, we will experiment with tuning model parameters to improve its performance.

Hyperparameter tuning

Let's try changing the `embedding_dim` hyperparameter to 32 and the `batch_size` hyperparameter to 50 to see if we get improved results:

```
# initialize embedding parameter
embedding_dim <- 32

# train model
history <- model %>% fit(
  x_train,
  y_train,
  epochs = 10,
  batch_size = 50,
  validation_data = list(x_test,y_test),
  verbose = 1)

# show model
summary(model)
```

Here is a printout of the model's architecture:

```
Model: "dot"
_____
Layer (type)                        Output Shape                 Param #
========================================================================
user_embedding (Embedding)          multiple                     363232
_____
item_embedding (Embedding)          multiple                     115168
_____
dot (Lambda)                        multiple                     0
========================================================================
Total params: 478,400
Trainable params: 478,400
Non-trainable params: 0
_____
```

Now, we will plot the results as follows:

```
# evaluate results
plot(history)
```

This results in the following output:

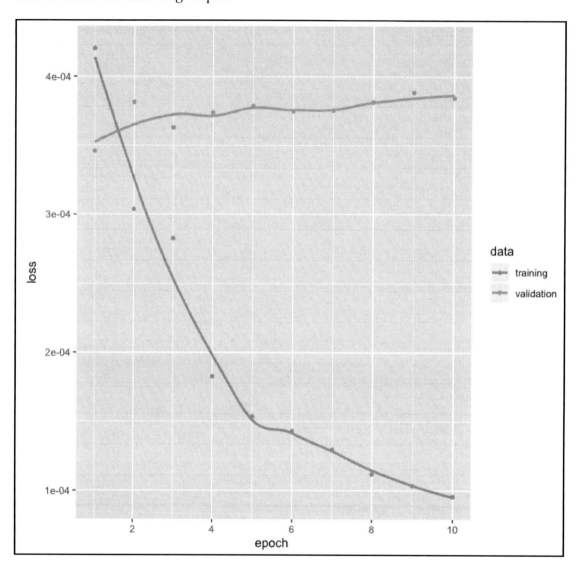

Unfortunately, these model performance results do not look significantly different than our baseline model, so let's explore some additional model configurations.

Adding dropout layers

In the following code, we will add dropout layers and encourage you to experiment with different dropout rates to see what empirically leads to optimal results:

```
# initialize embedding parameter
embedding_dim <- 64

# create custom model with dropout layers
dot_with_dropout <- function(
  embedding_dim,
  n_users,
  n_items,
  name = "dot_with_dropout"
) {
  keras_model_custom(name = name, function(self) {
    self$user_embedding <- layer_embedding(
      input_dim = n_users+1,
      output_dim = embedding_dim,
      name = "user_embedding")
    self$item_embedding <- layer_embedding(
      input_dim = n_items+1,
      output_dim = embedding_dim,
      name = "item_embedding")
    self$user_dropout <- layer_dropout(
        rate = 0.2)
    self$item_dropout <- layer_dropout(
        rate = 0.4)
    self$dot <-
      layer_lambda(
        f = function(x)
        k_batch_dot(x[[1]],x[[2]],axes=2),
        name = "dot"
      )
    function(x, mask=NULL, training=FALSE) {
      users <- x[,1]
      items <- x[,2]
      user_embedding <- self$user_embedding(users) %>%
          self$user_dropout()
      item_embedding <- self$item_embedding(items) %>%
          self$item_dropout()
      dot <- self$dot(list(user_embedding,item_embedding))
    }
  })
}
```

In the preceding code, we added dropout layers using `layer_dropout()`, which adds some complexity to our preliminary model. In the following code, we define, compile, and train our custom model with dropout layers:

```
# define model
model <- dot_with_dropout(
  embedding_dim,
  n_users,
  n_items)

# compile model
model %>% compile(
  loss = "mse",
  optimizer = "adam"
)

# train model
history <- model %>% fit(
  x_train,
  y_train,
  epochs = 10,
  batch_size = 50,
  validation_data = list(x_test,y_test),
  verbose = 1
)
```

This results in the following output:

```
Epoch 1/10
56391/56391 [==============================] - 10s 175us/sample - loss: 4.6713e-04 - val_loss: 3.6753e-04
Epoch 2/10
56391/56391 [==============================] - 9s 158us/sample - loss: 4.0496e-04 - val_loss: 3.6545e-04
Epoch 3/10
56391/56391 [==============================] - 10s 169us/sample - loss: 3.6718e-04 - val_loss: 3.7142e-04
Epoch 4/10
56391/56391 [==============================] - 10s 170us/sample - loss: 3.2149e-04 - val_loss: 3.7354e-04
Epoch 5/10
56391/56391 [==============================] - 10s 169us/sample - loss: 3.0240e-04 - val_loss: 3.7747e-04
Epoch 6/10
56391/56391 [==============================] - 10s 171us/sample - loss: 2.8544e-04 - val_loss: 3.7531e-04
Epoch 7/10
56391/56391 [==============================] - 10s 169us/sample - loss: 2.7523e-04 - val_loss: 3.8042e-04
Epoch 8/10
56391/56391 [==============================] - 10s 171us/sample - loss: 2.5837e-04 - val_loss: 3.8178e-04
Epoch 9/10
56391/56391 [==============================] - 10s 172us/sample - loss: 2.5977e-04 - val_loss: 3.8619e-04
Epoch 10/10
56391/56391 [==============================] - 10s 171us/sample - loss: 2.4823e-04 - val_loss: 3.9079e-04
```

Now, we print out a summary of our model, as follows:

```
summary(model)
```

Here's a summary of the model architecture:

```
Model: "dot_with_dropout"

Layer (type)                      Output Shape              Param #
=================================================================
user_embedding (Embedding)        multiple                 726464
_____
item_embedding (Embedding)        multiple                 230336
_____
dropout_10 (Dropout)              multiple                 0
_____
dropout_11 (Dropout)              multiple                 0
_____
dot (Lambda)                      multiple                 0
=================================================================
Total params: 956,800
Trainable params: 956,800
Non-trainable params: 0
_____
```

Now, we will plot the results, as follows:

```
# evaluate results
plot(history)
```

This results in the following model performance output:

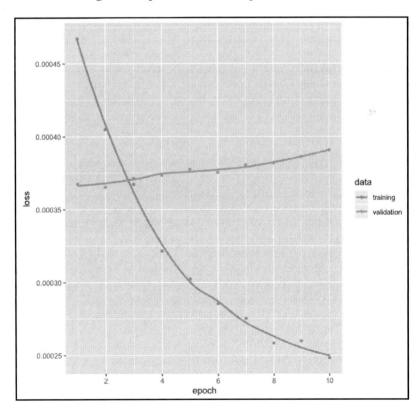

While we added dropout layers, the observed model improvements are minimal.

Let's revisit our underlying assumptions and try another approach.

Adjusting for user-item bias

It is important to recognize that some users, in reality, may interact with items (games) differently than other users in terms of gaming frequency and affinity by proxy. This discrepancy, in turn, could potentially translate to different implicit ratings based on the user-item interaction (hours of gameplay) data available for this particular analysis.

Based on our previous findings, we will now modify the model to account for user and item biases by including embeddings for average users and items (games) using the following code:

```
# caculate minimum and max rating
min_rating <- steamdata %>% summarise(min_rating = min(rating_scaled)) %>%
pull()
max_rating <- steamdata %>% summarise(max_rating = max(rating_scaled)) %>%
pull()

# create custom model with user, item, and bias embeddings
dot_with_bias <- function(
  embedding_dim,
  n_users,
  n_items,
  min_rating,
  max_rating,
  name = "dot_with_bias"
) {
keras_model_custom(name = name, function(self) {
  self$user_embedding <- layer_embedding(
    input_dim = n_users+1,
    output_dim = embedding_dim,
    name = "user_embedding")
  self$item_embedding <- layer_embedding(
    input_dim = n_items+1,
    output_dim = embedding_dim,
    name = "item_embedding")
  self$user_bias <- layer_embedding(
    input_dim = n_users+1,
    output_dim = 1,
    name = "user_bias")
  self$item_bias <- layer_embedding(
    input_dim = n_items+1,
```

```
        output_dim = 1,
        name = "item_bias")
```

In the preceding code, we create a custom model with user and item embeddings
(`user_embedding` and `item_embedding`) and embeddings for user bias and item bias
(`user_bias` and `item_bias`). In the following code, we add dropout layers for both users
and items and encourage you to experiment with different dropout rates for optimal
results:

```
self$user_dropout <- layer_dropout(
    rate = 0.3)
self$item_dropout <- layer_dropout(
    rate = 0.5)
self$dot <- layer_lambda(
    f = function(x)
    k_batch_dot(x[[1]],x[[2]],axes=2),
    name = "dot")
self$dot_bias <- layer_lambda(
    f = function(x)
    k_sigmoid(x[[1]]+x[[2]]+x[[3]]),
    name = "dot_bias")
self$min_rating <- min_rating
self$max_rating <- max_rating
self$pred <- layer_lambda(
    f = function(x)
    x * (self$max_rating - self$min_rating) + self$min_rating,
    name = "pred")
function(x,mask=NULL,training=FALSE) {
    users <- x[,1]
    items <- x[,2]
    user_embedding <- self$user_embedding(users) %>% self$user_dropout()
    item_embedding <- self$item_embedding(items) %>% self$item_dropout()
    dot <- self$dot(list(user_embedding,item_embedding))
    dot_bias <- self$dot_bias(list(dot, self$user_bias(users),
self$item_bias(items)))
    self$pred(dot_bias)
    }
  })
}
```

Next, let's define, compile, and train our modified neural network model:

```
# define model
model <- dot_with_bias(
  embedding_dim,
  n_users,
  n_items,
  min_rating,
```

```
    max_rating)

# compile model
model %>% compile(
  loss = "mse",
  optimizer = "adam"
)

# train model
history <- model %>% fit(
  x_train,
  y_train,
  epochs = 10,
  batch_size = 50,
  validation_data = list(x_test,y_test),
  verbose = 1)
)
```

This results in the following output:

```
Train on 56391 samples, validate on 14098 samples
Epoch 1/10
56391/56391 [==============================] - 11s 190us/sample - loss: 0.1912 - val_loss: 0.1437
Epoch 2/10
56391/56391 [==============================] - 9s 167us/sample - loss: 0.0994 - val_loss: 0.0652
Epoch 3/10
56391/56391 [==============================] - 10s 170us/sample - loss: 0.0404 - val_loss: 0.0316
Epoch 4/10
56391/56391 [==============================] - 9s 167us/sample - loss: 0.0185 - val_loss: 0.0196
Epoch 5/10
56391/56391 [==============================] - 9s 168us/sample - loss: 0.0099 - val_loss: 0.0141
Epoch 6/10
56391/56391 [==============================] - 9s 167us/sample - loss: 0.0057 - val_loss: 0.0111
Epoch 7/10
56391/56391 [==============================] - 10s 171us/sample - loss: 0.0035 - val_loss: 0.0093
Epoch 8/10
56391/56391 [==============================] - 10s 179us/sample - loss: 0.0022 - val_loss: 0.0082
Epoch 9/10
56391/56391 [==============================] - 10s 177us/sample - loss: 0.0014 - val_loss: 0.0074
Epoch 10/10
56391/56391 [==============================] - 10s 170us/sample - loss: 9.9242e-04 - val_loss: 0.0067
```

Now, we will print out the summary:

```
# summary model
summary(model)
```

By adding these additional layers of embeddings and tuning the hyperparameters, we have nearly doubled the total number of trainable parameters from our original baseline neural network, as reflected in the following model summary:

```
Model: "dot_with_bias"
_____
Layer (type)                    Output Shape            Param #
========================================================================
user_embedding (Embedding)      multiple                726464
_____
item_embedding (Embedding)      multiple                230336
_____
user_bias (Embedding)           multiple                11351
_____
item_bias (Embedding)           multiple                3599
_____
dropout_12 (Dropout)            multiple                0
_____
dropout_13 (Dropout)            multiple                0
_____
dot (Lambda)                    multiple                0
_____
dot_bias (Lambda)               multiple                0
_____
pred (Lambda)                   multiple                0
========================================================================
Total params: 971,750
Trainable params: 971,750
Non-trainable params: 0
_____
```

Finally, we plot the results of the model as follows:

```
# evaluate results
plot(history)
```

This results in the following output:

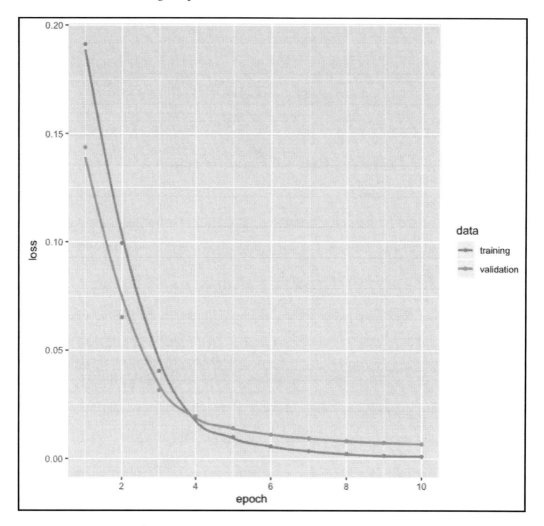

Through a succession of iterative configurations and empirically guided adjustments, we have improved overfitting relative to our previous models and achieved a notable RMSE below 0.1 on our validation dataset. With additional hyperparameter tuning and dropout layer rate configurations, we might be able to further improve the performance of this model. Future recommendations to build on this model would be to acquire and implement explicit rating data, as well as to experiment with additional contextual information and user demographic data to better understand the relationships and factors associated with user-item interactions.

Summary

In this chapter, you learned how to use the custom Keras API and embeddings to construct a deep neural network recommender system. We briefly introduced collaborative filtering concepts and saw how to prepare data for building a custom neural network. During this iterative process, we created user and item embeddings, trained a deep neural network using embedded layers, tuned hyperparameters, and evaluated results using common performance metrics. In the next chapter, you will continue applying neural network approaches to other domains, such as natural language processing.

7
Deep Learning for Natural Language Processing

In this chapter, you will learn how to create document summaries. We will begin by removing parts of documents that should not be considered and tokenizing the remaining text. Next, we will apply embeddings and create clusters. These clusters will then be used to make document summaries. Also, we will learn how to use **restricted Boltzmann machines (RBMs)** as building blocks to create deep belief networks for topic modeling. We will begin with coding the RBM and defining the Gibbs sampling rate, contrastive divergence, and free energy for the algorithm. We will conclude by compiling multiple RBMs to create a deep belief network.

This chapter covers the following topics:

- Formatting data using tokenization
- Cleaning text to remove noise
- Applying word embeddings to increase usable data
- Clustering data into topic groups
- Summarizing documents using model results
- Creating an RBM
- Defining the Gibbs sampling rate
- Speeding up sampling with contrastive divergence
- Computing free energy for model evaluation
- Stacking RBMs to create a deep belief network

Formatting data using tokenization

The first step we will take to begin analyzing text is loading text files and then tokenizing our data by transforming the text from sentences into smaller pieces, such as words or terms. A text object can be tokenized in a number of ways. In this chapter, we will tokenize text into words, although other sized terms could also be tokenized. These are referred to as n-grams, so we can get two-word terms (2-grams), three-word terms, or a term of any arbitrary size.

To get started with the process of creating one-word tokens from our text objects, we will use the following steps:

1. Let's load the libraries that we will need. For this project, we will use `tidyverse` for data manipulation, `tidytext` for special functions to manipulate text data, `spacyr` for extracting text metadata, and `textmineR` for word embeddings. To load these libraries, we run the following code:

   ```
   library(tidyverse)
   library(tidytext)
   library(spacyr)
   library(textmineR)
   ```

   In this chapter, the data that we will use will be the 20 Newsgroups dataset. This consists of pieces of text that come from one of 20 Newsgroups. The format of the data that we will pull in has a unique ID, the group the text belongs to, and the group.

2. Let's read in the data using the following code:

   ```
   twenty_newsgroups <-
   read_csv("http://ssc.wisc.edu/~ahanna/20_newsgroups.csv")
   ```

   After running this code, you should see the `twenty_newsgroups` object appear in your `Environment` window. The object has 11,314 rows and 3 columns.

3. Let's take a look at a sample of the data. In this case, let's print the first row of data to our console. We look at the first row of data by running the following code:

   ```
   twenty_newsgroups[1,]
   ```

After running this code, you will see the following printed to your console:

```
> twenty_newsgroups[1,]
  X target
1 0      9
```

```
                                                                      text
1 From: cubbie@garnet.berkeley.edu (                 ) Subject: Re: Cubs b
ehind Marlins? How? Article-I.D.: agate.1pt592$f9a Organization: University of Californi
a, Berkeley Lines: 12 NNTP-Posting-Host: garnet.berkeley.edu   gajarsky@pilot.njin.net w
rites:  morgan and guzman will have era's 1 run higher than last year, and  the cubs wil
l be idiots and not pitch harkey as much as hibbard.  castillo won't be good (i think h
e's a stud pitcher)          This season so far, Morgan and Guzman helped to lead the Cub
s         at top in ERA, even better than THE rotation at Atlanta.       Cubs ERA at 0.0
56 while Braves at 0.059. We know it is early      in the season, we Cubs fans have le
arned how to enjoy the       short triumph while it is still there.
```

4. Now, let's break this text into tokens. Tokens are some atomic portion of the text character string that we see in the preceding screenshot. In this case, we will break this string into word tokens. The final result will be a row for each word listed, alongside the ID and newsgroup ID. We tokenize the text data using the following code:

```
word_tokens <- twenty_newsgroups %>%
  unnest_tokens(word, text)
```

After running this code, we can see that our data object has grown substantially. We now have 3.5 million rows when we previously only had 11,000, since each word now gets its own row.

5. Let's take a quick look at term frequency, now that we have each word separated out into its own line. In this step, we can begin to see whether certain terms are used more than others with the text included in this dataset. To plot the frequency of each term in the data, we will use the following code:

```
word_tokens %>%
  group_by(word) %>%
  summarize(word_count = n()) %>%
  top_n(20) %>%
  ggplot(aes(x=reorder(word, word_count), word_count)) +
  xlab("word") +
geom_col() +
  coord_flip()
```

After running this code, we will see the following plot generated:

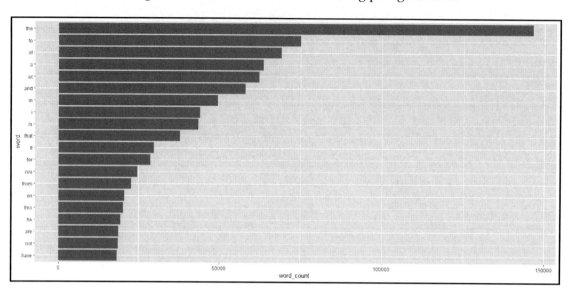

We have successfully taken some text and divided it into tokens. However, we can see from the plot that terms such as **the**, **to**, **of**, and **a** are most frequent. These types of words are often bundled into a collection of terms referred to as **stop words**. Next, we will learn how to remove these types of terms that have no information value.

Cleaning text to remove noise

The next step we will take to prepare for text analysis is doing some preliminary cleaning. This is a common way to get started, regardless of what machine learning method will be applied later. When working with text, there are several terms and patterns that will not provide meaningful information. Some of these terms are generally not useful and steps to remove these pieces of text data can be used every time, while others will be more context-dependent.

As previously noted, there are collections of terms referred to as stop words. These terms have no information value and can usually be removed. To remove stop words from our data, we use the following code:

```
word_tokens <- word_tokens %>%
    filter(!word %in% stop_words$word)
```

After running the preceding code, our row count goes down from 3.5 million to 1.7 million. In effect, our data (`word_tokens`) has almost been cut in half by removing all the stop words. Let's run the plot we ran earlier to see which terms are most frequent now. We can identify the term frequency as we did before with the following lines of code:

```
word_tokens %>%
   group_by(word) %>%
   summarize(word_count = n()) %>%
   top_n(20) %>%
   ggplot(aes(x=reorder(word, word_count), word_count)) +
   xlab("word") +
   geom_col() +
   coord_flip()
```

After running this chunk of code, the following plot is generated:

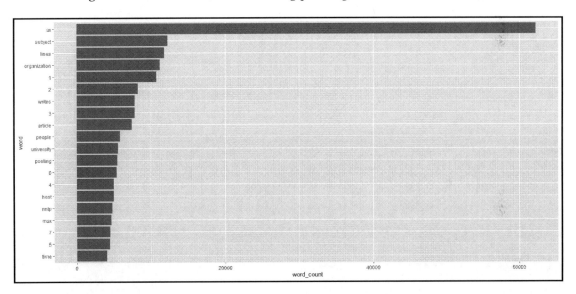

In this plot, we can see that terms such as **the, to, of,** and **a** are now removed. However, we also now see that there are some numbers showing up as frequent terms. This could be context-dependent and there may be cases where pulling numbers from text is very important for a project. However, here we will focus on actual words and will remove all terms that contain non-alphabetic characters. We can accomplish this by using some regular expressions, also known as **regex**. We can remove the terms that do not contain any characters from the alphabet by using the following code:

```
word_tokens <- word_tokens %>%
   filter(str_detect(word, "^[a-z]+[a-z]$"))
```

After running this regex code, we can run the same plot code again, as we did previously. When we do, we generate a plot that looks like the following:

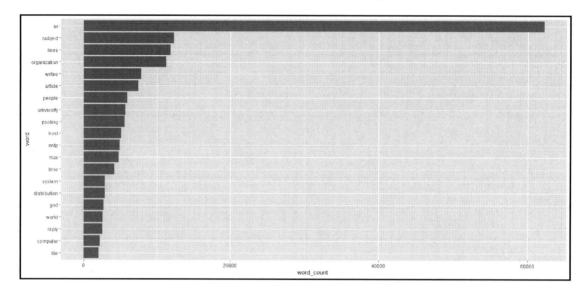

Based on this plot, we see our top twenty terms are all words, including one possible acronym (**nntp**). With our data object now reduced to 1.4 million rows, which includes only terms that start and end with characters from the alphabet, we are ready to move on to the next step where we will use embeddings to add extra context to each term.

Applying word embeddings to increase usable data

Extracting terms from text is a good starting point for text analysis. With the text tokens we have created so far, we can compare term frequency for different categories, which begins to tell us a story about the content that dominates a particular newsgroup. However, the term alone is just one part of the overall information we can glean from a given term. The previous plot contained `people` and, of course, we know what this word means, although there are multiple nuanced details connected to this term. For instance, `people` is a noun. It is similar to terms such as *person* and *human* and is also related to a term such as *household*. All of these details for `people` could be important but, by just extracting the term, we cannot directly derive these other details. This is where embeddings are especially helpful.

Embeddings, in the context of natural language processing, are pre-trained neural networks that perform the type of mapping just described. We can use these embeddings to match parts of speech to terms, as well as to find the lexical distance between words. Let's get started by looking at the parts-of-speech embeddings. To examine the parts of speech for every term in our text dataset, we run the following code:

```
spacy_install()

spacy_initialize(model = "en_core_web_sm")

spacy_parse(twenty_newsgroups$text[1], entity = TRUE, lemma = TRUE)
```

Using the preceding code, we first install `spacy` on our machine. Next, we initialize `spacy` using a small (sm) English (en) model that is trained on web text (web) for the core `spacy` elements: named entities, part-of-speech tags, and syntactic dependencies. Afterward, we apply the model to the first piece of text in our dataset. Once we do this, we will see the following results printed to the console:

```
> spacy_parse(twenty_newsgroups$text[1], entity = TRUE, lemma = TRUE)
   doc_id sentence_id token_id                    token                    lemma    pos  entity
1   text1           1        1                     From                     from    ADP
2   text1           1        2                        :                        :  PUNCT
3   text1           1        3  cubbie@garnet.berkeley.edu  cubbie@garnet.berkeley.edu  PUNCT
4   text1           1        4                        (                        (  PUNCT
5   text1           1        5                                                   SPACE
6   text1           1        6                        )                        )  PUNCT
7   text1           1        7                  Subject                  subject   NOUN
8   text1           1        8                        :                        :  PUNCT
9   text1           1        9                       Re                       re    ADP
10  text1           1       10                        :                        :  PUNCT
11  text1           1       11                     Cubs                     Cubs  PROPN   ORG_B
12  text1           1       12                   behind                   behind    ADP
13  text1           1       13                   Marlins                   marlin   NOUN
14  text1           1       14                        ?                        ?  PUNCT
15  text1           2        1                      How                      how    ADV
16  text1           2        2                        ?                        ?  PUNCT
17  text1           3        1                  Article                  Article  PROPN
18  text1           4        1                        -                        -  PUNCT
19  text1           4        2                     I.D.                     I.D.  PROPN
20  text1           4        3                        :                        :  PUNCT
```

In the preceding example, we see that `spacy` stores each token separately with a token ID and a sentence ID. The three additional pieces of data supplied are listed next to each token. Let's look at the example for the `11` token ID. In this case, `Cubs`, which the model has identified as a part of speech, is a proper noun and the named entity type is **organization**. We see the `ORG_B` code, which means this token begins with the name of an organization. In this case, the one-term begins and ends with the name of the organization.

Let's look at a few other examples. If you scroll down the results in your console, you should find a section that looks like the following output:

75	text1	8	1	castillo	castillo	PROPN	
76	text1	8	2	wo	will	VERB	
77	text1	8	3	n't	not	PART	
78	text1	8	4	be	be	AUX	
79	text1	8	5	good	good	ADJ	
80	text1	9	1	(	(	PUNCT	
81	text1	9	2	i	i	PRON	
82	text1	9	3	think	think	VERB	
83	text1	9	4	he	-PRON-	PRON	
84	text1	9	5	's	be	AUX	
85	text1	9	6	a	a	DET	
86	text1	9	7	stud	stud	ADJ	
87	text1	9	8	pitcher	pitcher	NOUN	
88	text1	9	9	)	)	PUNCT	
89	text1	9	10			SPACE	
90	text1	10	1	This	this	DET	DATE_B
91	text1	10	2	season	season	NOUN	DATE_I
92	text1	10	3	so	so	ADV	
93	text1	10	4	far	far	ADV	
94	text1	10	5	,	,	PUNCT	
95	text1	10	6	Morgan	Morgan	PROPN	PERSON_B
96	text1	10	7	and	and	CCONJ	
97	text1	10	8	Guzman	Guzman	PROPN	PERSON_B

In the preceding screenshot, we see additional information that spacy can identify. Let's look at lines 76 and 77. We see that the term used in the text is won't. However, the spacy model used lemmatization to break up this contraction. Of course, won't is just a contracted form of will not and the model has split out the two terms that are part of the contracted term. In addition, the part of the speech for each term is included. Another example is lines 90 and 91. Here, the terms this and season are adjacent and the model correctly identifies these two terms together to refer to a particular date part of the speech, which means that it is not last season or next season, but this season. In the named entities column, this has a DATE_B tag, which means the term refers to a date and this term is the beginning of this particular date-type. Similarly, season has a tag of DATE_I, which means that it refers to a date-type piece of data and the token is inside the entity. We know from these two tags that this and season are related and together refer to a specific point in time.

Another way we can use word embedding is to cluster our text data into topic groups. Topic grouping will result in a data object with lists of terms that co-occur near each other in the text. Through this process, we can see which topics are being discussed the most in the text data that we are analyzing. We will create topic group clusters next.

Clustering data into topic groups

Let's use word embeddings to find all semantically similar words. To do this, we will use the textmineR package to create a skip-gram model. The objective of the skip-gram model is to look for terms that occur often within a given window of another term. Since these terms are so frequently close to each other within sentences in our text, we can conclude they have some connection to each other. We will start by using the following steps:

1. To begin building our skip-gram model, we first create a term co-occurrence matrix by running the following code:

```
tcm <- CreateTcm(doc_vec = twenty_newsgroups$text,
                 skipgram_window = 10,
                 verbose = FALSE,
                 cpus = 2)
```

After running the code, you will have a sparse matrix in your environment window. The matrix has every possible term along both dimensions, as well as a value at the intersection of the terms if they occur together within the skip-gram window, which in this case is 10. An example of what a portion of this matrix looks like can be seen here:

```
> tcm[1148:1151,60002:60005]
4 x 4 sparse Matrix of class "dgCMatrix"
             traslation traumatic traversal travesty
anolog           .          .          .         .
anology          .          .          .         .
anomality        .          .          .         .
anomalous        .          .          .         .
>
```

2. Next, we will fit a **Latent Dirichlet allocation (LDA)** model on the text co-occurrence matrix that we just made. For our model, we will choose to create 20 topics and will have the model perform 500 Gibbs iterations, setting the burning value to 200, which is the number of samples we will discard first. We will set calc_coherence to TRUE to include this metric. coherence is the relative distance between terms for a topic and we will use this distance value to rank the strength of the topics we have found. We define our LDA model by running the following code:

```
embeddings <- FitLdaModel(dtm = tcm,
                          k = 20,
                          iterations = 500,
                          burnin = 200,
                          calc_coherence = TRUE)
```

3. Our next step will be to get the top terms for each topic. We will use `phi`, which represents a distribution of words over topics as the topics and the argument, M, to choose how many terms to include in each topic cluster. We can retrieve our top terms per topic by running the following code:

```
embeddings$top_terms <- GetTopTerms(phi = embeddings$phi,
                                    M = 5)
```

4. We will take our topics and top terms and add in the `coherence` score along with a `prevalence` score, which shows how often the terms occur in the entire text corpus we are analyzing. We can assemble this summary data object by running the following code:

```
embeddings$summary <- data.frame(topic = rownames(embeddings$phi),
                                 coherence =
round(embeddings$coherence, 3),
                                 prevalence =
round(colSums(embeddings$theta), 2),
                                 top_terms =
apply(embeddings$top_terms, 2, function(x){
                                     paste(x, collapse = ", ")
                                 }),
                                 stringsAsFactors = FALSE)
```

5. Now that we have created this summary data object, we can look at the top five topics by the `coherence` value. We can identify which topics have the most terms that are relatively close to each other by running the following code:

```
embeddings$summary[order(embeddings$summary$coherence, decreasing =
TRUE),][1:5,]
```

When we run the preceding code, we see the top five topics that we have identified in the text object. You will see the following topics printed to your console:

```
> embeddings$summary[ order(embeddings$summary$coherence, decreasing = TRUE) , ][ 1:5 , ]
      topic coherence prevalence                                      top_terms
t_32   t_32     0.523    1554.72         posting, lines, host, organization, nntp
t_38   t_38     0.426    2135.63 subject, lines, writes, organization, article
t_21   t_21     0.390    1929.54          law, gun, government, people, rights
t_7     t_7     0.381    1649.87       ca, stanford, james, writes, subject
t_40   t_40     0.374    2034.05               team, game, year, games, play
>
```

We have loaded in text data, extracted terms from the text, used a model to identify associated information for the terms—such as named entity details and part of speech—and organized terms according to topics discovered in the text. Next, we will reduce our text objects by using modeling to summarize documents in our text.

Summarizing documents using model results

In this last step, before moving on to building our own model, we will use the `textrank` package to summarize the text. The approach this algorithm uses to summarize text is to look for a sentence with the most words that are also used in other sentences in the text data. We can see how this type of sentence would be a good candidate for summarizing the text since it contains many words found elsewhere. To get started, let's select a piece of text from our data:

1. Let's view the text in row `400` by running the following code:

    ```
    twenty_newsgroups$text[400]
    ```

    When we run this line of code, we will see the following piece of text printed to the console:

    ```
    > twenty_newsgroups$text[400]
    [1] "From: rschnapp@metaflow.com (Russ Schnapp) Subject: Re: Once tapped, your code is no good any more. Nntp-Posting-Host: habu Organization: Metaflow
    Technologies Inc. Lines: 19  It might be nice to:  1. cut out the ad hominem attacks on Prof. Denning, Mr. Sternlight, etc.  If you have something obj
    ective to say about their views, go ahead and say it (subject to point 2.).  Personal attacks reflect more on the attacker more than on the attackee.
    Throw light, not heat!  2. restrict the discussion to appropriate newsgroups. I submit that comp.org.acm and comp.org.ieee are not appropriate for thi
    s discussion.  You have now made subscribers to these newsgroups aware of the issue.  If they want to know more or participate in the discussion, they
    can easily join sci.crypt, comp.security.misc, alt.security, or comp.org.eff.talk. --    ...Russ Schnapp Email: netcom!metaflow!rschnapp or rschnapp@Me
    taflow.com or rschnapp@BIX.com Metaflow Technologies   Voice: 619/452-6608x230;  FAX: 619/452-0401 La Jolla, California   Unless otw specified, I'm sp
    eaking only for myself! "
    ```

    In this email, we can see that the subject matter regards objecting to someone else's email because it is off-topic.

2. Let's see which sentence the `textrank` algorithm will extract to summarize the text. To get started, we will first perform tokenization on the text. However, unlike earlier where we created word tokens, this time we will create sentence tokens. In addition, we will use the row numbers for each sentence extracted as the sentence ID. To create sentence tokens from our text, we run the following code:

    ```
    sentences <- tibble(text = twenty_newsgroups$text[400]) %>%
        unnest_tokens(sentence, text, token = "sentences") %>%
    ```

```
mutate(id = row_number()) %>%
select(id, sentence)
```

3. Next, we will create word tokens as we did previously. Remember that the reason we create sentence and word tokens is because we need to see which words occur in the most sentences and, of those words, which sentence contains the most frequently occurring words. To create the data object with one word per row, we run the following code:

```
words <- sentences %>%
unnest_tokens(word, sentence)
```

4. Next, we run the `textrank_sentences` function, which calculates the best summary sentences in the way previously described. We calculate the `textrank` score, which measures which sentences best summarize the text, by running the following code:

```
article_summary <- textrank_sentences(data = sentences, terminology
= words)
```

We have now ranked the sentences. If we view the summary, we can see the top five sentences by default. However, in this case, let's start by looking at the very top-ranked sentence and see how well that does at summarizing the overall text.

5. To look at just the top-ranked sentence, we first have to look at the first object in the returned list, which is a data frame of the sentences with their corresponding `textrank` score. Next, we arrange them by descending `textrank` score to select the highest-rated sentence. Afterward, we select the top row and extract just the sentence data. To print the top-ranked sentence based on the `textrank` algorithm, we run the following code:

```
article_summary[["sentences"]] %>%
arrange(desc(textrank)) %>%
top_n(1) %>%
pull(sentence)
```

After running this code, you will see the following console output:

```
> article_summary[["sentences"]] %>%
+    arrange(desc(textrank)) %>%
+    top_n(1) %>%
+    pull(sentence)
Selecting by textrank
[1] "2. restrict the discussion to appropriate newsgroups."
>
```

The sentence selected is **restrict the discussion to appropriate newsgroups**. If we read the entire text again, we can see that this sentence does capture the essence of what the writer is communicating. In fact, if the email only had this line it would convey almost the same information. In this way, we can confirm that the `textrank` algorithm performed well and that the selected sentence is a good summary of the entire text.

Now that we have covered some of the essential text analytics tools offered by various R packages, we will proceed with creating our own deep learning text model.

Creating an RBM

So far, we have extracted elements from text, added metadata, and created term clusters to discover latent topics. We will now identify latent features by using a deep learning model known as an RBM. As you may recall, we have discovered latent topics in the text by looking for term co-occurrence within a given window size. In this case, we will go back to using a neural network approach. The RBM is half the typical neural network. Instead of taking data through hidden layers to an output layer, the RBM model just takes the data to the hidden layers and this is the output. The end result is similar to factor analysis or principal component analysis. Here, we will begin the process of finding each of the 20 Newsgroups in the dataset and throughout the rest of this chapter, we will make modifications to the model to improve its performance.

To get started with building our RBM, we will need to load two libraries. The first library will be `tm`, which is used for text mining in R, and has functions for creating a document-term matrix and performing text cleanup. The other library that we will need is `deepnet`, which has a function for the RBM. To load these two libraries, we run the following code:

```
library(tm)
library(deepnet)
```

Next, we will take our text data and create a corpus, which in this case will place the contents from each newsgroup email into a separate list element. From there, we will remove some non-informative elements. We will also cast all text to lowercase to decrease the unique term count, as well as group like terms together regardless of their letter case. Afterward, we will cast the remaining terms to a document-term matrix, where all the terms make up one dimension of the matrix and all the documents make up the other dimension and the represented value in the matrix if the term is present in the document. We will also use **term frequency-inverse document frequency (tf-idf)** weighting.

In this case, the value in the matrix will not be binary but rather a float representing the uniqueness of the term within the document, down-weighting terms that occur frequently in all documents and giving more weight to terms that are only present in one or some documents but not all. To perform these steps and prepare our text data to be inputted into an RBM model, we run the following code:

```
corpus <- Corpus(VectorSource(twenty_newsgroups$text))

corpus <- tm_map(corpus, content_transformer(tolower))
corpus <- tm_map(corpus, removeNumbers)
corpus <- tm_map(corpus, removePunctuation)
corpus <- tm_map(corpus, removeWords, c("the", "and",
stopwords("english")))
corpus <- tm_map(corpus, stripWhitespace)

news_dtm <- DocumentTermMatrix(corpus, control = list(weighting =
weightTfIdf))
news_dtm <- removeSparseTerms(news_dtm, 0.95)
```

We will now split our data into `train` and `test` sets as with any modeling exercise. In this case, we will create our `train` and `test` sets by running the following code:

```
split_ratio <- floor(0.75 * nrow(twenty_newsgroups))

set.seed(614)
train_index <- sample(seq_len(nrow(twenty_newsgroups)), size = split_ratio)

train_x <- news_dtm[train_index,]
train_y <- twenty_newsgroups$target[train_index]
test_x <- news_dtm[-train_index,]
test_y <- twenty_newsgroups$target[-train_index]
```

With the data in the proper format and split into `train` and `test` sets, we can now train our RBM model. Training the model is quite straightforward and there are not too many parameters to configure. For now, we will modify a few arguments and make changes to others as we progress through the chapter. To start, we will train a starter RBM model by running the following code:

```
rbm <- rbm.train(x = as.matrix(train_x), hidden = 20, numepochs = 100)
```

In the preceding code, we set the `hidden` layers to the number of newsgroups to see if there is enough latent information to map the text to the newsgroups. We start with `100` rounds and leave everything else as a default.

We can now explore the latent features found in the text. We use our trained model to perform this task by passing in data as input, which results in inferred hidden units being produced as output. We infer the hidden units for the `test` data by running the following code:

```
test_latent_features <- rbm.up(rbm, as.matrix(test_x))
```

After running this code, we have defined the latent feature space for the `test` data.

Defining the Gibbs sampling rate

Gibbs sampling plays a key role in constructing an RBM, so we will take a moment here to define this sampling type. We will briefly walk through a couple of quick concepts that lead to how to perform Gibbs sampling and why it matters for this type of modeling. With RBM models, we are first using a neural network to map our input or visible units to hidden units, which can be thought of as latent features. After training our model, we want to either take a new visible unit and define the probability that it belongs to the hidden units in the model, or do the reverse. We also want this to be computationally efficient, so we use a Monte Carlo approach.

Monte Carlo methods involve sampling random points to approximate an area or distribution. A classic example involves drawing a 10-by-10 inch square and inside this square draw a circle. We know that a circle with a 10-inch diameter has an area of 78.5 inches. Now, if we use a random number generator to choose float pairs between 0 and 10 and do this 20 times and plot the points, we will likely end up with around 15 points in the circle and 5 outside the circle. If we use just these points, then we would approximate the area is 75 inches. Now, if we try this again with a less conventional shape but something with many curves and angles, then it would be much more difficult to calculate the area. However, we could use the same approach to approximate the area. In this way, Monte Carlo approaches work well when a distribution is difficult or computational costly to define precisely, which is the case with our RBM model.

Next, a Markov Chain is a technique in defining conditional probability that only takes into account the event that just preceded the event probability we are trying to predict, rather than events that happened two or more steps back. This is a very simple form of conditional probability. A classic example for explaining this concept is the game Chutes and Ladders. In this game, there are 100 squares and a player rolls a six-sided die to determine the number of spaces to move, with the object being to get to square 100. Along the way, a square may contain a slide that will move the player backward a certain number of squares, or a ladder that will move the player forward a certain number of squares.

When determining the likelihood of landing on a given square, the only thing that matters is the previous roll that resulted in the player landing on a certain square. Whichever combination of rolls got the player to that point does not have any impact on the probability of reaching a certain square based on the square the player is currently on.

For context, we will discuss these two concepts briefly because they are both involved in Gibbs sampling. This type of sampling is a Monte Carlo Markov Chain method, which means that we start from an initial state and afterward we predict the likelihood that a certain event, x, happens given another event, y, and vice versa. By calculating this type of back-and-forth conditional probability over a certain number of samples, we efficiently approximate the probability that a given `visible` unit belongs to a given `hidden` unit. We can perform a few very simple examples of sampling from a Gibbs distribution. In this example, we will create a function with an argument, `rho`, as a coefficient value to modify the given term when calculating the value for the other variable, while in our RBM model the learned weights and the bias term perform this function. Let's create a sampler using the following steps:

1. Let's first define a very simple Gibbs sampler to understand the concept by running the following code:

```
gibbs<-function (n, rho)
{
  mat <- matrix(ncol = 2, nrow = n)
  x <- 0
  y <- 0
  mat[1, ] <- c(x, y)
  for (i in 2:n) {
    x <- rnorm(1, rho * y, sqrt(1 - rho^2))
    y <- rnorm(1, rho * x, sqrt(1 - rho^2))
    mat[i, ] <- c(x, y)
  }
  mat
}
```

Now that we have defined the function, let's calculate two separate 10 x 2 matrices by choosing two different values for `rho`.

2. We calculate our first 10 x 2 matrix by running the following code using a value of `0.75` for `rho`:

```
gibbs(10,0.75)
```

3. Next, we calculate a 10 x 2 matrix using a value of `0.03` for `rho`, using the following line of code:

```
gibbs(10,0.03)
```

After running each of these, you should see a 10 x 2 matrix printed to your console. This function involves drawing random values from a normal distribution, so the matrix printed to your console will be slightly different. However, you will see the way the values are generated iteratively using the values from the previous iteration to determine the value in the current iteration. We see here how the Monte Carlo randomness is employed in calculating our value along with the Markov Chain conditional probability. Now, with an understanding of Gibbs sampling, we will explore contrastive divergence, which is a way we can use what we learned about Gibbs sampling to modify our model.

Speeding up sampling with contrastive divergence

Before proceeding, we need to change up the dataset being used. While the 20 Newsgroups dataset has worked well up until this point for all the concepts on text analysis, it becomes less usable as we try to really tune our model to predict latent features. All the additional changes that we will do next actually have minimal impact on the model when using the 20 Newsgroups, so we will switch to the spam versus ham dataset, which is similar. However, instead of involving emails to a newsgroup, these are SMS text messages. In addition, instead of the target variable being a given newsgroup, the target is either that the message is spam or a legitimate text message.

Contrastive divergence is the argument that allows us to leverage what we learned about Gibbs sampling. The value that we pass to this argument in the model will adjust how many times the Gibbs sampling is performed. In other words, this controls the length of the Markov Chain. The lower the value, the faster each round of the model will be. If the value is higher, then each round is computationally more costly, although the model may converge more quickly. In the following steps, we can train a model with three different values for contrastive divergence to see how adjusting this argument affects the model:

1. To begin, we will load in the spam versus ham dataset using the following code:

```
spam_vs_ham <- read.csv("spam.csv")
```

2. Next, we will move our target variables to a vector, y, and the predictor text data to a variable, x. Afterward, we will perform some basic text preprocessing by removing special characters and one- and two-character words, as well as removing any white space. We define our target variable and predictor variables, along with cleaning the text, by running the following code:

```
y <- if_else(spam_vs_ham$v1 == "spam", 1, 0)
x <- spam_vs_ham$v2 %>%
  str_replace_all("[^a-zA-Z0-9/:-_]|\r|\n|\t", " ") %>%
  str_replace_all("\b[a-zA-Z0-9/:-]{1,2}\b", " ") %>%
  str_trim("both") %>%
  str_squish()
```

3. Next, we convert this cleaned up text into a `corpus` data object and then into a document-term matrix. We convert our text data into a suitable format for modeling by running the following code:

```
corpus <- Corpus(VectorSource(x))
dtm <- DocumentTermMatrix(corpus)
```

4. Next, let's divide our data into `train` and `test` sets, exactly as we did with the 20 Newsgroups dataset. We get our data divided and ready for modeling using the following code:

```
split_ratio <- floor(0.75 * nrow(dtm))

set.seed(614)
train_index <- sample(seq_len(nrow(dtm)), size = split_ratio)

train_x <- dtm[train_index,]
train_y <- y[train_index]
test_x <- dtm[-train_index,]
test_y <- y[-train_index]
```

5. Now that all of our data is prepared, let's run our three models and see how they compare. We run a quick version of the three RBM models to evaluate the impact of adjusting the contrastive divergence value by running the following code:

```
rbm3 <- rbm.train(x = as.matrix(train_x),hidden = 100,cd = 3,numepochs = 5)
rbm5 <- rbm.train(x = as.matrix(train_x),hidden = 100,cd = 5,numepochs = 5)
rbm1 <- rbm.train(x = as.matrix(train_x),hidden = 100,cd = 1,numepochs = 5)
```

To measure how much change this argument has had on the model, we will use the free energy values in the model object.

Computing free energy for model evaluation

RBMs belong to a class of energy-based models. These use a free energy equation that is analogous to the cost function in other machine learning algorithms. Just like a cost function, the objective is to minimize the free energy values. A lower free energy value equates to a higher probability that the visible unit variables are being described by the hidden units and a higher value equates to a lower likelihood.

Let's now look at the three models we just created and compare free energy values for these models. We compare the free energy to identify which model is performing better by running the following code:

```
rbm5$e[1:10]
rbm3$e[1:10]
rbm1$e[1:10]
```

After running this code, an output similar to the following will be printed to your console:

```
> rbm3$e[1:10]
 [1] 2509.51004 1417.24109  742.68367  376.16692  189.77672  110.74476   77.41884   54.53539   42.77029   31.34814
> rbm5$e[1:10]
 [1] 2509.73975 1417.21736  768.38120  379.36603  204.05841  113.36577   77.43481   56.32113   47.16665   39.14905
> rbm1$e[1:10]
 [1] 2419.40759  482.54272  306.78399  165.75944  113.83501   84.49505   61.42198   44.18864   28.68965   22.52887
>
```

In this case, using just one round of Gibbs sampling produces the best performing model in terms of reducing free energy in the quickest way.

Stacking RBMs to create a deep belief network

RBM models are a neural network with just two layers: the input, that is, the visible layer, and the hidden layer with latent features. However, it is possible to add additional hidden layers and an output layer. When this is done within the context of an RBM, it is referred to as a **deep belief network**. In this way, deep belief networks are like other deep learning architectures. For a deep belief network, each hidden layer is fully connected meaning that it learns the entire input.

The first layer is the typical RBM, where latent features are calculated from the input units. In the next layer, the new hidden layer learns the latent features from the previous hidden layer. This, in turn, can lead to an output layer for classification tasks.

Implementing a deep belief network uses a similar syntax to what was used to train the RBM. To get started, let's first perform a quick check of the latent feature space from the RBM we just trained. To print a sample of the latent feature space from the model, we use the following code:

```
train_latent_features <- rbm.up(rbm1, as.matrix(train_x))
test_latent_features <- rbm.up(rbm1, as.matrix(test_x))
```

In the preceding code, we use the `up` function to generate a matrix of latent features using the model that we just fit. The `up` function takes as input an RBM model and a matrix of visible units and outputs a matrix of hidden units. The reverse is also possible. The `down` function takes a matrix of hidden units as input and outputs visible units. Using the preceding code, we will see an output like the following printed to the console:

```
> train_latent_features[1:10,1:10]
Docs       [,1]       [,2]       [,3]       [,4]       [,5]       [,6]       [,7]       [,8]       [,9]       [,10]
  1125 0.9995219 3.498864e-02 0.9999849 1.974980e-02 0.0713228507 0.0419965645 2.580451e-02 0.0804697882 1.589923e-02 1.708103e-02
   333 0.9979948 1.381208e-03 0.9999962 1.615541e-04 0.0015373632 0.0013940013 5.747632e-04 0.0027432697 1.365966e-04 3.463469e-04
  1715 0.9996641 4.128829e-02 0.9999847 2.568044e-02 0.0611993728 0.0478576967 2.756783e-02 0.0112565075 1.975733e-02 3.152628e-02
   189 0.9999658 5.606589e-03 0.3791738 3.384625e-03 0.0099489304 0.0089141830 4.005954e-03 0.0187326589 3.033027e-03 4.812017e-03
  4381 0.9992794 3.522254e-02 0.9999668 2.011267e-02 0.0561978252 0.0401003866 2.409929e-02 0.0784871891 1.640035e-02 2.082187e-02
  2669 0.9981014 1.933048e-04 0.9999761 2.020750e-05 0.0005525759 0.0002296240 3.963189e-05 0.0007125059 1.060147e-05 3.600504e-05
  3318 0.9994751 3.388523e-02 0.9999846 2.395679e-02 0.0530874673 0.0330113552 2.941328e-02 0.0728463075 1.722368e-02 1.913727e-02
  4385 0.9999553 8.878147e-05 0.9896087 3.107481e-05 0.0002576984 0.0003048883 6.000928e-05 0.0004189729 1.142492e-05 5.776982e-05
  4604 0.9995033 3.610973e-02 0.9999799 2.663464e-02 0.0686185078 0.0506779933 3.059856e-02 0.0887321096 2.495606e-02 2.786809e-02
  2982 0.9997332 3.530154e-02 0.9999937 2.011169e-02 0.0617361486 0.0329333307 2.679921e-02 0.0802057132 2.113651e-02 1.886073e-02
> test_latent_features[1:10,1:10]
Docs       [,1]       [,2]       [,3]       [,4]       [,5]       [,6]       [,7]       [,8]       [,9]       [,10]
   1 0.9986300 0.0024654624 9.999546e-01 1.203269e-03 0.0061731030 0.0040925062 1.071672e-03 0.0081400659 4.413182e-04 0.0013184575
   5 0.9991490 0.0161457284 9.999284e-01 5.590435e-03 0.0197498050 0.0128317824 6.517652e-03 0.0246660936 3.595630e-03 0.0089861349
   9 0.9997876 0.0002590099 6.205917e-02 9.449147e-05 0.0006795492 0.0004980877 1.456341e-04 0.0005515220 4.888717e-05 0.0001577932
  21 0.9999598 0.0129352162 2.649340e-01 1.015972e-02 0.0198527023 0.0189956030 1.058271e-02 0.0320306516 7.609615e-03 0.0121016466
  24 0.9974138 0.0066556035 9.999903e-01 6.236626e-04 0.0098731340 0.0054002557 1.575756e-03 0.0161411576 1.208833e-03 0.0012210601
  25 0.9999441 0.0077977057 5.291170e-01 8.468595e-03 0.0168932628 0.0214328038 9.159199e-03 0.0238278523 6.279842e-03 0.0103134302
  29 0.9999742 0.0042721571 5.447453e-01 3.842273e-03 0.0074185090 0.0099070512 3.351298e-03 0.0133319284 1.914261e-03 0.0035735858
  31 0.9999651 0.0009533030 8.464429e-02 1.416167e-04 0.0015204274 0.0007032235 1.177667e-04 0.0036041608 1.268889e-04 0.0002641598
  42 1.0000000 0.0000709821 9.469889e-21 1.500244e-04 0.0000421829 0.0004666625 8.719796e-05 0.0001845007 1.050034e-04 0.0003664744
  48 0.9993911 0.0356110207 9.999695e-01 2.262362e-02 0.0499151872 0.0350992069 2.455113e-02 0.0819124742 1.357471e-02 0.0186628721
>
```

We can see variance in the feature space of this first layer. To prepare for the next step, we imagine using this matrix now as input to another RBM that will further learn features. In this way, we can code our deep belief network using an almost identical syntax to the syntax used for training the RBM. The exception will be that for the hidden layer argument, rather than a single value representing the number of units in a single hidden layer, we can now use a vector of values that represent the number of units in each successive hidden layer. For our deep belief network, we will start with `100` units, just like in our RBM.

We will then reduce this to 50 units in the next layer and 10 units in the layer after that. The other difference is that we now have a target variable. While an RBM is an unsupervised, generative model, we can use our deep belief network to perform a classification task. We train our deep belief network using the following code:

```
dbn <- dbn.dnn.train(x = as.matrix(train_x), y = train_y, hidden =
c(100,50,10), cd = 1, numepochs = 5)
```

With the deep belief network trained, we can now make predictions using our model. We perform this prediction task in a similar way to how we generate predictions for most machine learning tasks. However, in this case, we will use the nn.predict function to use our trained neural network to predict whether the new test input should be classified as spam or a legitimate text. We make a prediction on the test data using the following code:

```
predictions <- nn.predict(dbn, as.matrix(test_x))
```

We now have the probability values that tell us whether a given message is or is not spam. The probabilities are currently within a constrained range; however, we can still use it. Let's make a cut in the probabilities and assign 1 for those above the threshold signifying that the message is predicted to be spam, and everything under the cut point will receive a value of 0. After making this dividing line and creating a vector of binary values, we can create a confusion matrix to see how well our model performed. We create our binary variables and then see how well our model performed by running the following code:

```
pred_class <- if_else(predictions > 0.3, 1, 0)
table(test_y,pred_class)
```

After running the preceding code, we will see the following output to our console:

```
> pred_class <- if_else(predictions > 0.3, 1, 0)
>
> table(test_y,pred_class)
        pred_class
test_y    0    1
      0 1146   54
      1   89  104
>
```

As we can see, even this very simple implementation of a deep belief network has performed fairly well. From here, additional modification can be made to the number of hidden layers, units in these layers, the output activation function, learning rate, momentum, and dropout, along with the contrastive divergence and the number of epochs or rounds.

Summary

In this chapter, we covered a number of methods for analyzing text data. We started with techniques for extracting elements from text data, such as taking a sentence and breaking it into tokens and comparing term frequency, along with collecting topics and identifying the best summary sentence and extracting these from the text. Next, we used some embedding techniques to add additional details to our data, such as parts of speech and named entity recognition. Lastly, we used an RBM model to find latent features in the input data and stacked these RBM models to perform a classification task. In the next chapter, we will look at using deep learning for time series tasks, such as predicting stock prices, in particular.

8
Long Short-Term Memory Networks for Stock Forecasting

This chapter will show you how to use **long short-term memory** (**LSTM**) models to forecast stock prices. This type of model is particularly useful for time series-based forecasting tasks. An LSTM model is a special type of **recurrent neural network** (**RNN**). These models contain special characteristics that allow you to reuse recent output as input. In this way, these types of models are often described as having memory. We will begin by creating a simple baseline model for predicting stock prices. From there, we will create a minimal LSTM model and we will dive deeper into the advantages of this model type over our baseline model, as well as explore how this model type is an improvement over a more traditional RNN. Lastly, we will look at some ways to tune our model to further improve its performance.

In this chapter, we will cover the following topics:

- Understanding common methods for stock market prediction
- Preparing and preprocessing data
- Configuring a data generator
- Training and evaluating the model
- Tuning hyperparameters to improve performance

Technical requirements

You can find the code files used in this chapter at https://github.com/PacktPublishing/Hands-on-Deep-Learning-with-R.

Understanding common methods for stock market prediction

In this chapter, we will learn about a different type of neural network called an RNN. In particular, we will apply a type of RNN known as an LSTM model to predict stock prices. Before we begin, let's first look at some common methods of predicting stock prices to better understand the problem.

Predicting stock prices is a time-series problem. With most other machine learning problems, variables can be split at random and used in training and test datasets, but this is not possible when solving a time-series problem. The variables must remain in order. The features to solve the problem can be found in the sequence of events and, consequently, the chronology of how events occurred must be maintained to generate meaningful predictions of what will happen next. While this places a constraint on which methods can be used, it also provides an opportunity to use some specific models that are well suited for these types of tasks.

Let's start with some approaches that are relatively straightforward to create a baseline model before creating our deep learning solution, which we can use to compare results later. The first model that we will construct is an **Auto-Regressive Integrated Moving Average (ARIMA)** model. Actually, the concepts from the name of this model explain a lot about the particular challenges of modeling on time-series data.

The **AR** in ARIMA stands for **auto-regressive** and refers to the fact that the model inputs will be for a given observation and set number of lagged observations. The **MA** in ARIMA stands for **moving average** and refers to the autoregressive nature of the model, which states that the variables will include an observation at a given point in time and a set of lagged variables. The moving average component takes into account the mean value between a set of variables over time to capture a more generalized value explaining a trend over time.

The **I** in ARIMA stands for **integrated**, which in this context means that the entire time-series is considered as a whole. More specifically, it refers to the idea that the solutions must be generalizable across the entire series just as we strive for with other machine learning solutions. To aid with this, with time-series problems we transform the data so that it is said to be stationary. With ARIMA, we look at the differences between an observation and the observation preceding it and then use these relative differences. By using the relative differences, we can maintain a more generalized shape over the series, which helps to control the mean and variance, which are important elements in forecasting predicted future states.

With this context, let's now create an ARIMA model. To get started, we will use the `quantmod` package to load stock information. The `getSymbols` function from this package is a very convenient way to pull in stock price information for any company within a set time frame from a number of sources. We set `auto.assign` to `FALSE` since we will assign this ourselves. For our example, we will load 5 years of Facebook stock:

1. In the following code, we will read in the data as well as load all the libraries we will be using:

```
library(quantmod)
library(tseries)
library(ggplot2)
library(timeSeries)
library(forecast)
library(xts)
library(keras)
library(tensorflow)

FB <- getSymbols('FB', from='2014-01-01', to='2018-12-31', source = 'google', auto.assign=FALSE)
```

After running this code, we will see that we have an `FB` object in our environment with an `xts` class type. This object class type is similar to a standard data frame, but the row names are dates. Let's inspect a few rows of `xts` data.

2. We can view the first five rows from the `FB` object by using the following line of code:

```
FB[1:5,]
```

After running this code, you will see the following output printed to your console:

```
> FB[1:5,]
           FB.Open FB.High FB.Low FB.Close FB.Volume FB.Adjusted
2014-01-02   54.83   55.22  54.19    54.71  43195500       54.71
2014-01-03   55.02   55.65  54.53    54.56  38246200       54.56
2014-01-06   54.42   57.26  54.05    57.20  68852600       57.20
2014-01-07   57.70   58.55  57.22    57.92  77207400       57.92
2014-01-08   57.60   58.41  57.23    58.23  56682400       58.23
>
```

We can see from these selected rows that we have a number of stock price points taken from the day, including the opening and closing price, as well as the highest and lowest price for the stock during the day. The volume of stock traded is also included. For our purposes, we will use the price at the close of trading.

3. We select just the closing prices from the data and store them in a new object by running the following code:

```
closing_prices <- FB$FB.Close
```

4. We can now use the `plot.xts` function to plot the stock data. Usually, plotting this data would require the dates to be held in a column, but this plotting function is a convenient way of plotting a time series without needing the dates present within a column in the data frame. We can plot the full 5 years of Facebook closing stock prices by running the following line of code:

```
plot.xts(closing_prices,main="Facebook Closing Stock Prices")
```

After we run this line of code, we will see the following plot generated in our **Plots** tab:

5. Now that we can see how stock prices for Facebook have changed over this time frame, let's build an ARIMA model. Afterward, we will create a forecast using the ARIMA model and then plot these forecast values. We create our model, forecast, and plot by running the following code:

```
arima_mod <- auto.arima(closing_prices)

forecasted_prices <- forecast(arima_mod,h=365)

autoplot(forecasted_prices)
```

After running the preceding code, we will see the following plot in the **Plots** tab:

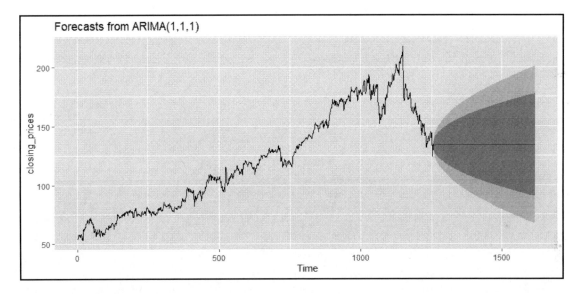

The ARIMA model did not find a pattern and instead offers an upper and lower bound, within which prices are predicted, which is not very helpful. ARIMA is a popular baseline model for forecasting time-series data that often performs well. However, in this case, we can see that our ARIMA model doesn't appear to provide much useful information.

6. Before continuing, we can add in the actual stock price values from this frame to see whether the prices did fall within the bounds predicted by the ARIMA model. To pull in the data and add it to our plot, we run the following code:

```
fb_future <- getSymbols('FB', from='2019-01-01', to='2019-12-31',
source = 'google', auto.assign=FALSE)

future_values <- ts(data = fb_future$FB.Close, start = 1258, end =
1509)

autoplot(forecasted_prices) + autolayer(future_values,
series="Actual Closing Prices")
```

After we run the preceding code, we will see the following plot in the **Plots** tab:

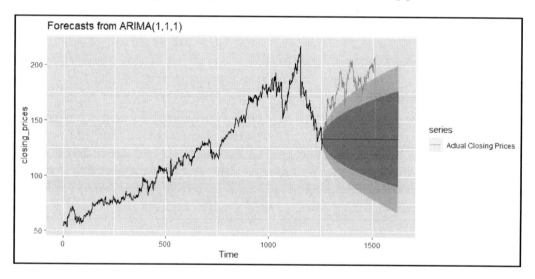

As noted, the values for these dates are outside the bounds of the ARIMA model. We can see that we chose a difficult time-series dataset to model since the stock price is on a downward trend and then begins to rise again. With this being said, over the 5-year period, there is a general upward trend. Can we build a model that learns this upward trend and reflects it properly in the predicted results? Let's take what we have learned about the particular challenges of modeling time-series data and see whether we can improve upon our baseline results using a deep learning approach.

Preparing and preprocessing data

When working with time-series data, there are a number of data type formats to choose from and use for conversion. We have already used two of these formats, of which there are three that are most widely used. Let's briefly review these data types before moving on to our deep learning model.

When we wanted to add actual data as an overlay to our ARIMA model plot, we used the `ts` function to create a time-series data object. For this object, the index values must be integers. In the case of using the `autolayer` function with the `arima` plot, a time-series data object is required. This is one of the more simple time-series data types and it will look like a vector in your **Environment** tab. However, this only works with regular time series.

Another data type is `zoo`. The `zoo` data type will work with regular and irregular time series, and zoo objects can also contain a number of different data types as index values. The drawback of the `zoo` objects is that there is not much information available in the **Environment** pane. The only detail provided is the date range. At times, the `zoo` data works better for plotting, especially when overlaying multiple time-series objects, which is what we will use it for later in this chapter.

The last time-series data type is `xts`. This data type is an extension of `zoo`. Like `zoo`, the index values are dates. However, in addition, the data is stored in a matrix and numerous attributes are present in the **Environment** pane, making it easier to inspect the size and contents of the data object. This is generally a good choice for working with time-series data, unless there are particular reasons to use one of the other types that we have, and will, cover. Another benefit of `xts` is that the default plot function uses different formatting to the base plot.

When we are working with time-series data, there is another part of preprocessing in addition to data type conversion that is often useful for modeling: converting our data to delta values rather than absolute values in order to make the data stationary. In this case, we will also log transform the price values to further control the outliers. When we are done with this process, we will need to remove the missing value that we introduced as well. Let's convert our combined stock price data from the closing price to the daily change in the log value of the closing price by running the following code:

```
future_prices <- fb_future$FB.Close

closing_deltas <- diff(log(rbind(closing_prices,future_prices)),lag=1)
closing_deltas <- closing_deltas[!is.na(closing_deltas)]
```

After running this code, we have data that should be more stationary than the data we were working with before. Let's view what our data looks like now by running the following code:

```
plot(closing_deltas,type='l', main='Facebook Daily Log Returns')
```

When we run the preceding code, we will see the following plot generated in the **Plots** pane:

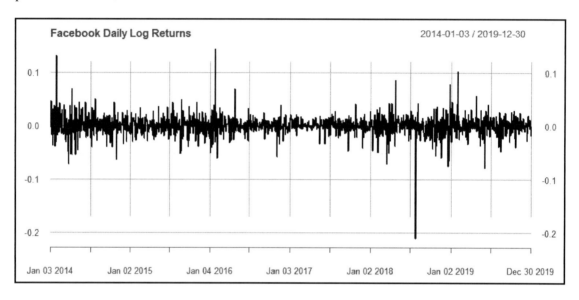

The values we are working with are far more constrained and the patterns from one section appear as if they will generalize better to explain movement in a different section. Even though we can see that the values are better scaled here, we can also run a quick test to prove that the data is now stationary. To check for stationarity, we can use the **Augmented Dickey-Fuller test**, which we can run on our data using this line of code:

```
adf.test(closing_deltas)
```

After running this code, we will see the following output printed to the console:

```
> adf.test(closing_deltas)

        Augmented Dickey-Fuller Test

data:  closing_deltas
Dickey-Fuller = -13.114, Lag order = 11, p-value = 0.01
alternative hypothesis: stationary

Warning message:
In adf.test(closing_deltas) : p-value smaller than printed p-value
>
```

Although the actual p-value isn't reported as output when running this function, we can see that the p-value is small enough that we can accept the alternate hypothesis that the data is stationary. With this preprocessing complete, we can now move on to setting up our `train` and `test` sets for our deep learning model.

Configuring a data generator

Similar to ARIMA, for our LSTM model, we would like the model to use lagging historical data to predict actual data at a given point in time. However, in order to feed this data forward to an LSTM model, we must format the data so that a given number of columns contain all the lagging values and one column contains the target value. In the past, this was a slightly tedious process, but now we can use a data generator to make this task much simpler. In our case, we will use a time-series generator that produces a tensor that we can use for our LSTM model.

The arguments we will include when generating our data are the data objects we will use along with the target. In this case, we can use the same data object as values for both arguments. The reason this is possible has to do with the next argument, called `length`, which configures the time steps to look back in order to populate the lagging price values. Afterward, we define the sampling rate and the stride, which determine the number of time steps between consecutive values for the target values per row and the lagging values per sequence, respectively. We also define the starting index value and the ending index value. We also need to determine whether data should be shuffled or kept in chronological order and whether the data should be in reverse chronological order or maintain its current sort order. Finally, we select a batch size, which specifies how many time series samples should be in each batch of the model.

For this model, we will create our generated time-series data with a `length` value of 3, meaning that we will look back 3 days to predict a given day. We will keep the sampling rate and stride at 1 to include all data. Next, we will split the `train` and `test` sets with an index point of `1258`. We will not shuffle or reverse the data, but rather maintain its chronological order and set the batch size to 1 so that we model one price at a time. We create our `train` and `test` sets using these values for our parameters via the following code:

```
train_gen <- timeseries_generator(
    closing_deltas,
    closing_deltas,
    length = 3,
    sampling_rate = 1,
    stride = 1,
    start_index = 1,
    end_index = 1258,
    shuffle = FALSE,
    reverse = FALSE,
    batch_size = 1
)

test_gen <- timeseries_generator(
    closing_deltas,
    closing_deltas,
    length = 3,
    sampling_rate = 1,
    stride = 1,
    start_index = 1259,
    end_index = 1507,
    shuffle = FALSE,
    reverse = FALSE,
    batch_size = 1
)
```

After running this code, you will see two tensor objects in your **Environment** pane. Now that we have configured our data generator and used it to create two sequence tensors, we are ready to model our data using LSTM.

Training and evaluating the model

Our data is properly formatted and we can now train our model. For this task, we are using LSTM. This is a particular type of RNN. These types of neural networks are a good choice for time-series data because they are able to take time into account during the modeling process.

Most neural networks are classified as **feedforward networks**. In these model architectures, the signals start at the input node and are passed forward to any number of hidden layers until they reach an output node. There is some variation in feedforward networks. A multilayer perceptron model is composed of all dense, fully connected layers while a convolutional neural network includes layers that operate on particular parts of the input data before arriving at a dense layer and subsequent output layer. In these types of models, the backpropagation step passes back derivatives from the cost function, but this happens after the entire feedforward pass is complete. RNNs differ in a very important way. Rather than waiting until the entire forward pass is complete, a certain data point that represents a point in time is fed forward and evaluated by the activation function in a hidden layer unit. The output from this activation function is then fed back into the node and calculated with the next time-based data element. In this way, RNNs can use what they just learned to inform how to process the next data point. We can see now why these work so well when we are considering data that includes a time component.

While RNNs are designed to work well for time-series data, they do have one important limitation. The recurrent element of the model only takes into account the time period that just preceded it and, during backpropagation, the signal being passed back can decay when there are a large number of hidden layers. These two model characteristics mean that a given node cannot use the information it has learned on a distant time horizon, even though it may be useful. The LSTM model solves this problem.

In the LSTM model, there are two paths for data entering a node. One is the same as in an RNN and contains the given time-based data point as well as the output from the time point preceding it. However, if the output from the activation function of this vector is greater than 0, then it is passed forward. In the next node, it goes on a separate path towards an activation function known as the **forget gate**. If the data passes through this function with a positive value, then it is combined with the output from the activation function that takes the current state and immediate past output as input. In this way, we can see how data from many time periods in the past can continue to be included as input to nodes much further forward. Using this model design, we can overcome the limitations of a traditional RNN. Let's get started with training our model:

1. First, we run the following line of code to initiate a Keras sequential model:

```
model <- keras_model_sequential()
```

2. After running this line of code, we will now add our LSTM layer. In our LSTM layer, we will choose the number of units for our hidden layer and also define our input shape, which is the length of the look-back defined earlier as one dimension and 1 as the other. We will then add a dense layer with one unit, which will be assigned our predicted price. To define our LSTM model, we use the following code:

```
model %>%
  layer_lstm(units = 4,
             input_shape = c(3, 1)) %>%
  layer_dense(units = 1)
```

3. After defining our model, we next include the compile step. In this case, we will use mean squared error (mse) as our loss function, since this is a regression task, and we will use adam as our optimizer. We define the compile step and view our model using the following code:

```
model %>%
  compile(loss = 'mse', optimizer = 'adam')

model
```

After running this block of code, you will see the following printed to your console:

```
> model
Model
Model: "sequential_10"

Layer (type)                  Output Shape              Param #
=================================================================
lstm_8 (LSTM)                 (None, 4)                 96

dense_8 (Dense)               (None, 1)                 5
=================================================================
Total params: 101
Trainable params: 101
Non-trainable params: 0


>
```

4. We can now train our model. To train our model, we use the generated `train` dataset. We will run our model for `100` rounds initially and just take one time step every round. We will set the verbose argument to print the results of every round. We train our LSTM model using the following code:

```
history <- model %>% fit_generator(
    train_gen,
    epochs = 100,
    steps_per_epoch=1,
    verbose=2
)
```

5. Now that the model has been trained, we can make our predictions. In the `predict` step, we choose a given number of time steps for both the `train` and `test` data. Afterward, we can compare these predictions with the actual values. We use our LSTM model to predict stock prices by running the following code:

```
testpredict <- predict_generator(model, test_gen, steps = 200)
trainpredict <- predict_generator(model, train_gen, steps = 1200)
```

After running the preceding code, we now have our predictions.

6. Our next step will be to plot these together with the actual values to see how well our model worked. This step will require converting our data between a number of formats. Our first step will be to convert our vector of prediction to an `xts` object. In order to do this, we need to define the index values. We will use the `4` through `1203` index values for our `trainpredict` data. The reason that we start at four is because we have three lagging values being used to predict the value at the fourth index point. We will do the same for the test, but we start at the `1263` index point. We create our `xts` data objects from our predictions by running the following code:

```
trainpredict <- data.frame(pred = trainpredict)
rownames(trainpredict) <- index(closing_deltas)[4:1203]
trainpredict <- as.xts(trainpredict)

testpredict <- data.frame(pred = testpredict)
rownames(testpredict) <- index(closing_deltas)[1262:1461]
testpredict <- as.xts(testpredict)
```

7. Now, we add the values from these `xts` objects to our `closing_deltas` object. Next, we plot our actual values, along with overlaying our predicted values. In order to do this, we first add columns for all the NAs and then populate just the rows that match the index points reflected in the prediction objects. We add additional columns to our `closing_delta` and `xts` objects, reflecting the predictions on the `train` and `test` sets by running the following code:

```
closing_deltas$trainpred <- rep(NA,1507)
closing_deltas$trainpred[4:1203] <- trainpredict$pred

closing_deltas$testpred <- rep(NA,1507)
closing_deltas$testpred[1262:1461] <- testpredict$pred
```

8. Now that we have the predictions merged together with the actual data, we can plot the results. We plot predictions as solid dark lines over the actual values represented by light gray, dotted lines using the following code:

```
plot(as.zoo(closing_deltas), las=1, plot.type = "single", col =
c("light gray","black","black"), lty = c(3,1,1))
```

After running this code, you will see the following plot in your **Plots** tab:

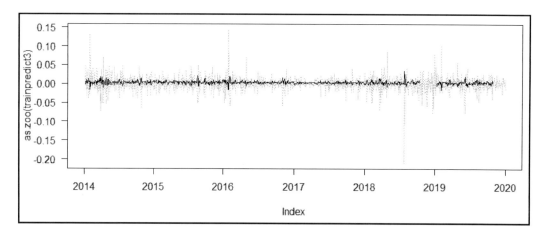

While the predicted results are a little conservative, note how the model is detecting the nuance at various time points. This model is finding more patterns and resulting in output with more movement than our ARIMA model.

9. In addition to plotting our data, we can also print the results of calling the `evaluate_generator` function to calculate the error rate. To print the error rate for our model, we run the following code:

```
evaluate_generator(model, test_gen, steps = 200)
evaluate_generator(model, train_gen, steps = 1200)
```

After running the preceding code, we see the following error rate values:

```
> evaluate_generator(model, test_gen, steps = 200)
WARNING:tensorflow:sample_weight modes were coerced from
  ...
    to
  ['...']
2020-04-01 15:33:35.841414: W tensorflow/core/kernels/data/generat
led: Operation was cancelled
        loss
0.0003431274
> evaluate_generator(model, train_gen, steps = 1200)
WARNING:tensorflow:sample_weight modes were coerced from
  ...
    to
  ['...']
2020-04-01 15:33:38.135730: W tensorflow/core/kernels/data/generat
led: Operation was cancelled
        loss
0.0003528563
>
```

The warnings printed in the console can be ignored. At the time of writing, this is a known issue with TensorFlow through Keras. Our LSTM model so far is fairly minimal. Let's take a look at tuning some hyperparameters next. We will see what we can tune to try to achieve better performance.

Tuning hyperparameters to improve performance

To improve our model, we will now tune our hyperparameters. There are a number of options for tuning our LSTM model. We will focus on adjusting the length value when creating the time-series data with our data generator. In addition, we will add additional layers, adjust the number of units in the layer, and modify our optimizer.

We will do so using the following steps:

1. To get started, let's switch the value that we pass to the `length` argument in the `timeseries_generator` function from 3 to 10 so that our model has a longer window of prices to use for forecasting calculations. To make this change, we run the following code:

```
train_gen <- timeseries_generator(
    closing_deltas,
    closing_deltas,
    length = 10,
    sampling_rate = 1,
    stride = 1,
    start_index = 1,
    end_index = 1258,
    shuffle = FALSE,
    reverse = FALSE,
    batch_size = 1
)

test_gen <- timeseries_generator(
    closing_deltas,
    closing_deltas,
    length = 10,
    sampling_rate = 1,
    stride = 1,
    start_index = 1259,
    end_index = 1507,
    shuffle = FALSE,
    reverse = FALSE,
    batch_size = 1
)
```

We have kept this code the same as we did earlier with just the one change to `length`.

2. Next, we will make our LSTM model deeper by adding an additional LSTM layer, dropout layer, and one additional dense layer. We will also change the input shape to reflect the next `length` parameter in the generator. Lastly, we set `return_sequences` to `True` in the first layer so that the signal can flow through to the additional layers. Without setting this to `True`, you will get an error related to the expected and actual dimensions of the data entering the second LSTM layer. We add additional layers to our LSTM model by running the following code:

```
model <- keras_model_sequential()
```

```
model %>%
  layer_lstm(units = 256,input_shape = c(10,
1),return_sequences="True") %>%
  layer_dropout(rate = 0.3) %>%
  layer_lstm(units = 256,input_shape = c(10,
1),return_sequences="False") %>%
  layer_dropout(rate = 0.3) %>%
  layer_dense(units = 32, activation = "relu") %>%
  layer_dense(units = 1, activation = "linear")
```

3. Our last modification will be to make a change to the optimizer. In this case, we will lower the learning rate for our optimizer. We do this to avoid any major spikes in our predicted values. We can adjust our optimizer by running the following code:

```
model %>%
  compile(
    optimizer = optimizer_adam(lr = 0.001),
    loss = 'mse',
    metrics = 'accuracy')

model
```

After running the preceding code, the following will be printed to your console:

```
> model
Model
Model: "sequential_22"

Layer (type)                  Output Shape              Param #
========================================================================
lstm_37 (LSTM)                (None, 10, 256)           264192

dropout_24 (Dropout)          (None, 10, 256)           0

lstm_38 (LSTM)                (None, 10, 256)           525312

dropout_25 (Dropout)          (None, 10, 256)           0

dense_15 (Dense)              (None, 10, 32)            8224

dense_16 (Dense)              (None, 10, 1)             33
========================================================================
Total params: 797,761
Trainable params: 797,761
Non-trainable params: 0
```

4. Next, we can train our model as before using the following code:

```
history <- model %>% fit_generator(
  train_gen,
  epochs = 100,
  steps_per_epoch=1,
  verbose=2
)
```

5. After training our model, we can evaluate how well it performed and compare this with our first model. We evaluate our model and print the results to our console using the following code:

```
evaluate_generator(model, train_gen, steps = 1200)
evaluate_generator(model, test_gen, steps = 200)
```

When we run this code, we see the following results:

```
> evaluate_generator(model, train_gen, steps = 1200)
WARNING:tensorflow:sample_weight modes were coerced from
  ...
    to
  ['...']
2020-04-01 15:50:49.509367: W tensorflow/core/kernels/data/ge
led: Operation was cancelled
$loss
[1] 0.0003483897

$accuracy
[1] 0.005

> evaluate_generator(model, test_gen, steps = 200)
WARNING:tensorflow:sample_weight modes were coerced from
  ...
    to
  ['...']
2020-04-01 15:50:55.725244: W tensorflow/core/kernels/data/ge
led: Operation was cancelled
$loss
[1] 0.0003377702

$accuracy
[1] 0.005
```

Our modifications have produced mixed results. While the loss value for the train data is slightly worse, the error rate for the test data is improved.

At this point, we have walked through all the steps necessary to create an LSTM model and have taken one pass at adjusting parameters to improve performance. Creating deep learning models is often as much an art as it is a science, so we encourage you to continue making adjustments and seeing whether you can further improve on the model. You may want to try different optimizers other than `adam` or experiment with including additional hidden layers. With these foundations in place, you are ready to make additional changes or apply this approach to a different dataset.

Summary

In this chapter, we started by creating a baseline model to predict stock prices. To do this, we used an ARIMA model. Based on this model, we explored some important components of machine learning with time-series data, including using lagging variable values to predict a current variable value and the importance of stationarity. From there, we built a deep learning solution using Keras to assemble LSTM and then tuned this model further. In the process, we observed that this deep learning approach has some marked advantages compared to other traditional models, such as ARIMA. In the next chapter, we will use a generative adversarial network to create a synthetic face image.

9
Generative Adversarial Networks for Faces

In the last chapter, we used a **long short-term memory (LSTM)** model on a time-series forecasting task. In this chapter, we will create a generator model, which means the model will not output predictions but rather files (in this case, images). We created a generator model in `Chapter 7`, *Deep Learning for Natural Language Processing*; however, in that case, we just generated latent features. Here, we will describe the main components and applications of **generative adversarial networks (GANs)**. You will learn about the common applications of GANs and how to build a face generation model using a GAN.

Over the course of this chapter, we will investigate the architecture of a GAN. A GAN is composed of two competing neural networks, one of which is known as the **generator model**. It takes random data and creates synthetic target data. The other part of a GAN is the **discriminator model**. This model takes two pieces of input—the synthetic target data and the real target data—and it determines which is the real target data. After understanding this process, we will code our own GAN model for face recognition and generation using the Keras package and images from the *labeled faces in the wild* dataset.

In this chapter, we will cover the following topics:

- An overview of GANs
- Defining the generator model
- Defining the discriminator model
- Preparing and preprocessing a dataset
- Training and evaluating a model

Technical requirements

You can find the code files used in this chapter at the following GitHub link:

`https://github.com/PacktPublishing/Hands-on-Deep-Learning-with-R`

An overview of GANs

A GAN is a modeling algorithm that pits two neural networks against each other. One of them uses random data to create output. The other evaluates the real target data and the generated output and determines which is real. Over time, the first neural network creates better fake target data and the second neural network continues to try and determine which is the real target data. The two neural networks continue to compete and the models both improve to create increasingly realistic synthetic data.

Breaking down the term, we can see how this modeling technique differs from others. First, it is generative, which means that the goal is to generate data. This is in contrast to other models, such as classification or regression, that predict probabilities or values. Next, it is adversarial. That is, there are two models that are set to compete against each other. Generally, we have one model and it trains on data that can be evaluated and improved using a variety of metrics. However, in this case, we have one model that seeks to improve prediction performance and that is the discriminator model. In addition, we have another model that creates fake images to try to reduce the performance of the discriminator model.

We generally think of two main categories for machine learning:

- **Supervised learning**: Where the model uses labeled target data to make predictions
- **Unsupervised learning**: Where the model identifies patterns without any labeled target data

However, we can get even more granular with unsupervised learning. GANs belong to a special subset of unsupervised learning that uses learned patterns from unlabeled data to generate synthetic data, rather than just classifying the data. However, this introduces a problem for us. Since the goal is to generate data, there are no direct metrics we can use to evaluate the performance. The relative success or failure of a GAN model is based largely on the subjective interpretation of the output.

For this GAN, we will use images as our input. All images can be represented as a matrix of values for grayscale images, or three matrices of values for color images. The values of the matrix range from 0 to 255 and correspond with the intensity of the pixel value at that location. For example, a pixel value of 255 means high intensity or black for a grayscale image and a value of 0 means low intensity or white. The dimensions of the matrix correspond with the pixel width and height of the image. Color images are represented as a three-dimensional array. This can be thought of as three matrices overlapping, with each corresponding to the intensity of the red, green, and blue pixel values for the image. Let's take a look at a sample image and see how it is represented as a matrix of values. To do this, we will read in the following shape:

To read in this shape, we will use the OpenImageR package. This package reads the file in as a four-dimensional array. In this case, we only want the fourth dimension, which contains the grayscale values. To read in this file and then look at a small segment, we run the following code:

```
library(OpenImageR)

clock <- readImage("Alarms_&_Clock_icon.png")

clock[1:10,46:56,4]
```

After running this code, we will see the following printed to the console:

```
> clock[1:10,46:56,4]
         [,1]      [,2]      [,3] [,4]      [,5]      [,6]      [,7]      [,8] [,9] [,10] [,11]
 [1,] 0.0000000 0.0000000 0.0000000    0 0.2509804 0.5019608 0.5019608 0.7490196    1     1     1
 [2,] 0.2509804 0.5019608 0.7490196    1 1.0000000 1.0000000 1.0000000 1.0000000    1     1     1
 [3,] 1.0000000 1.0000000 1.0000000    1 1.0000000 1.0000000 1.0000000 1.0000000    1     1     1
 [4,] 1.0000000 1.0000000 1.0000000    1 1.0000000 1.0000000 1.0000000 1.0000000    1     1     1
 [5,] 1.0000000 1.0000000 1.0000000    1 1.0000000 1.0000000 1.0000000 1.0000000    1     1     1
 [6,] 1.0000000 1.0000000 1.0000000    1 1.0000000 1.0000000 1.0000000 1.0000000    1     1     1
 [7,] 1.0000000 1.0000000 1.0000000    1 1.0000000 1.0000000 1.0000000 1.0000000    1     1     1
 [8,] 1.0000000 1.0000000 1.0000000    1 1.0000000 1.0000000 1.0000000 1.0000000    1     1     1
 [9,] 1.0000000 1.0000000 1.0000000    1 1.0000000 1.0000000 1.0000000 1.0000000    1     1     1
[10,] 1.0000000 1.0000000 1.0000000    1 1.0000000 1.0000000 1.0000000 1.0000000    1     1     1
>
```

We can see how these values represent the top of the left bell on the alarm clock. The zeroes are the white space and we see a gradient in the second rows and the top rows, showing the curve. In this way, we can see how images can be expressed as a matrix of values between 0 and 1.

Defining the generator model

The generator model is the neural network that creates synthetic target data out of random inputs. In this case, we will use a **convolutional neural network (CNN)** in reverse. What this means is that we will start with a vector of data points and create a fully connected layer, then reshape the data into the size that we want it to be. As a middle step, we will make the target shape only half the size and then we will upsample using a transposed convolution layer. In the end, we have an array of normalized pixel values that is the same shape as our target array. This then becomes the data object that will be used to try to fool the discriminator model. This array of synthetic values will, over time, be trained to resemble the values in the target data object so that the discriminator model cannot predict, with a high probability, which is the true data image. We will define the discriminator model using the following steps:

1. First, we will define that our entry point will be a 100-dimensional vector. Everything we do to define our models will be done with Keras. So, we load the Keras model at this step. We then define our input shape as a vector with 100 values.

2. Then, we will pass a vector to this model. In this step, we tell the model what we will be passing in the later step. Using the following code, we declare that the input to this model will be a vector with 100 values that we will later populate with random values:

```
library(keras)
generator_in <- layer_input(shape = c(100))
```

3. After running this step, we can see that we have a special data object, called `Tensor`, in our data environment. The object contains the type, name, shape, and data type of the layer. Your data environment will look as in the following screenshot:

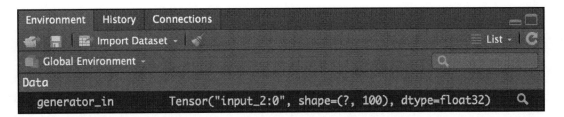

4. After this, we define how our random values will be processed, transformed, and reshaped to create a synthetic array that matches our target arrays. The code to do this is long, but many of the parts are repeated. There are a few lines that are required while others can be modified. The `layer_dense` layer needs to contain the number of units that will appear later in the `layer_reshape` layer. In this case, we will create a shape that has a width and height of 25 and a depth of 128. The depth is modifiable; however, the width and height must be set at half the size of the final image's dimensions when using one transposed convolution layer, as follows:

```
generator_out <- generator_in %>%
    layer_dense(units = 128 * 25 * 25) %>%
    layer_reshape(target_shape = c(25, 25, 128))
```

5. The `layer_conv_2d_transpose` layer uses a 2 x 2 stride to upsample and double the shape of the layer. In this step, the shape changes from 25 x 25 to 50 x 50:

```
generator_out <- generator_in %>%
    layer_dense(units = 128 * 25 * 25) %>%
    layer_reshape(target_shape = c(25, 25, 128)) %>%
    layer_conv_2d(filters = 512, kernel_size = 5,
                  padding = "same")
```

6. The convolution applies filters that look for patterns and the normalization takes the results of the convolution step and normalizes the values. So the mean is close to 0 and the standard deviation is close to 1, and ReLU is used as our activation function. We will add these layers after our dense layer and our convolution layer using the following code:

```
generator_out <- generator_in %>%
    layer_dense(units = 128 * 25 * 25) %>%
    layer_batch_normalization(momentum = 0.5) %>%
    layer_activation_relu() %>%
    layer_reshape(target_shape = c(25, 25, 128)) %>%
    layer_conv_2d(filters = 512, kernel_size = 5,
                  padding = "same") %>%
```

```
layer_batch_normalization(momentum = 0.5) %>%
layer_activation_relu()
```

7. After this, we can continue to add additional convolution layers using the same pattern of convolution, normalization, and activation. Here, we will add four additional series of layers using the pattern we just described:

```
generator_out <- generator_in %>%
    layer_dense(units = 128 * 25 * 25) %>%
    layer_batch_normalization(momentum = 0.5) %>%
    layer_activation_relu() %>%
    layer_reshape(target_shape = c(25, 25, 128)) %>%
    layer_conv_2d(filters = 512, kernel_size = 5,
                  padding = "same") %>%
    layer_batch_normalization(momentum = 0.5) %>%
    layer_activation_relu() %>%
    layer_conv_2d_transpose(filters = 256, kernel_size = 4,
                            strides = 2, padding = "same") %>%
    layer_batch_normalization(momentum = 0.5) %>%
    layer_activation_relu() %>%
    layer_conv_2d(filters = 256, kernel_size = 5,
                  padding = "same") %>%
    layer_batch_normalization(momentum = 0.5) %>%
    layer_activation_relu() %>%
    layer_conv_2d(filters = 128, kernel_size = 5,
                  padding = "same") %>%
    layer_batch_normalization(momentum = 0.5) %>%
    layer_activation_relu() %>%
    layer_conv_2d(filters = 64, kernel_size = 5,
                  padding = "same") %>%
    layer_batch_normalization(momentum = 0.5) %>%
    layer_activation_relu()
```

8. In the very last step, the `filters` argument needs to be set to the number of channels for the image—in this case, three for the red, green, and blue channels of a color image. This completes the definition of our generator model. The entire generator model is defined using the following code:

```
generator_out <- generator_in %>%
    layer_dense(units = 128 * 25 * 25) %>%
    layer_batch_normalization(momentum = 0.5) %>%
    layer_activation_relu() %>%
    layer_reshape(target_shape = c(25, 25, 128)) %>%
    layer_conv_2d(filters = 512, kernel_size = 5,
                  padding = "same") %>%
    layer_batch_normalization(momentum = 0.5) %>%
    layer_activation_relu() %>%
```

```
layer_conv_2d_transpose(filters = 256, kernel_size = 4,
                        strides = 2, padding = "same") %>%
layer_batch_normalization(momentum = 0.5) %>%
layer_activation_relu() %>%
layer_conv_2d(filters = 256, kernel_size = 5,
              padding = "same") %>%
layer_batch_normalization(momentum = 0.5) %>%
layer_activation_relu() %>%
layer_conv_2d(filters = 128, kernel_size = 5,
              padding = "same") %>%
layer_batch_normalization(momentum = 0.5) %>%
layer_activation_relu() %>%
layer_conv_2d(filters = 64, kernel_size = 5,
              padding = "same") %>%
layer_batch_normalization(momentum = 0.5) %>%
layer_activation_relu() %>%
layer_conv_2d(filters = 3, kernel_size = 7,
              activation = "tanh", padding = "same")
```

9. After running this code, we will now see two objects in our environment. We have defined the connected tensors for input and the connected input for the output. Setting up our tensors in this way allows data to be input in batches using the `keras_model` function. Your data environment should look like the following now:

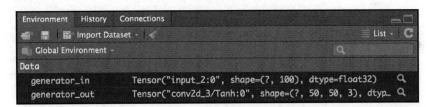

10. After, we define that the input will be 100 random values and the output will be random values mapped to a data object with the same dimensions as our target image.

11. We can then define `keras_model`, which takes the input and output as arguments, specifically. We pass in these defined tensor layers, at this point, to complete the definition of our model.

12. After defining the model, we can run the `summary` function on the generator model to helpfully see what is happening to the data at each layer. We define our generator and view the summary using the following code:

```
generator <- keras_model(generator_in, generator_out)
summary(generator)
```

13. After running the `summary` function, we will see details about our model printed to our console, which looks like this:

```
Layer (type)                      Output Shape              Param #
=================================================================
input_28 (InputLayer)             (None, 100)               0
_____
dense_17 (Dense)                  (None, 80000)             8080000
_____
batch_normalization_v1_59 (BatchNormal (None, 80000)        320000
_____
re_lu_35 (ReLU)                   (None, 80000)             0
_____
reshape_8 (Reshape)               (None, 25, 25, 128)       0
_____
conv2d_70 (Conv2D)                (None, 25, 25, 512)       1638912
_____
batch_normalization_v1_60 (BatchNormal (None, 25, 25, 512)  2048
_____
re_lu_36 (ReLU)                   (None, 25, 25, 512)       0
_____
conv2d_transpose_8 (Conv2DTranspose) (None, 50, 50, 256)    2097408
_____
batch_normalization_v1_61 (BatchNormal (None, 50, 50, 256)  1024
_____
re_lu_37 (ReLU)                   (None, 50, 50, 256)       0
_____
conv2d_71 (Conv2D)                (None, 50, 50, 256)       1638656
_____
batch_normalization_v1_62 (BatchNormal (None, 50, 50, 256)  1024
_____
re_lu_38 (ReLU)                   (None, 50, 50, 256)       0
_____
conv2d_72 (Conv2D)                (None, 50, 50, 128)       819328
_____
batch_normalization_v1_63 (BatchNormal (None, 50, 50, 128)  512
_____
re_lu_39 (ReLU)                   (None, 50, 50, 128)       0
_____
conv2d_73 (Conv2D)                (None, 50, 50, 64)        204864
_____
batch_normalization_v1_64 (BatchNormal (None, 50, 50, 64)   256
_____
re_lu_40 (ReLU)                   (None, 50, 50, 64)        0
_____
conv2d_74 (Conv2D)                (None, 50, 50, 3)         9411
=================================================================
Total params: 14,813,443
Trainable params: 14,651,011
Non-trainable params: 162,432
```

14. From the console output, we can see that we start with one fully connected layer and after numerous intermediate layers, we end up with a final layer that matches the shape of our target image data.

We now have our generator completely defined. We have seen how we can insert random values and how those random values are then transformed to produce a synthetic image. The process of passing data to this model occurs later in the process. With a system in place to produce fake images, we now move on to defining the discriminator model, which will determine whether a given array of pixel data is a real or fake image.

Defining the discriminator model

The discriminator model is the neural network that evaluates the synthetic target data and the real target data to determine which is the real one.

The discriminator, in this case, is a CNN model; it takes a three-dimensional array as input. Often with CNNs, convolving layers and pooling layers are used to reshape the dimensions of the input—ultimately, to a fully connected layer. However, when using these layers to define a discriminator model in the context of creating a GAN, we instead use 2 x 2 strides in the convolving layers to reshape the input dimensions. In the end, a fully connected layer with one unit is passed through the sigmoid activation function to calculate the probability that a given input is real or fake. Let's follow the following lines of code to define the discriminator model:

1. As we did in the generator model, let's start by defining the input shape. While the generator model started with a vector of 100 random values, our discriminator starts with input in the shape of our image data as that is what will be passed to the model. The dimensions for the image are used as arguments to define the input shape using the following code:

    ```
    discriminator_in <- layer_input(shape = c(50, 50, 3))
    ```

2. Running this code adds another object to our data environment. Your **Environment** pane will now look as in the following screenshot:

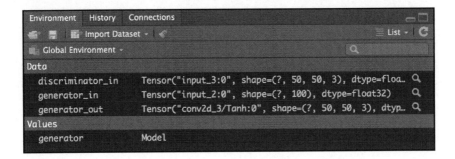

3. Next, we process and transform our data. While the generator took a one-dimensional vector and created a three-dimensional array in the size of our image data, here we will do the opposite. We start with data that is in the shape of our image data as the first layer, as in the following code:

```
discriminator_out <- discriminator_in %>%
    layer_conv_2d(filters = 256, kernel_size = 3)
```

4. The next layer that we will add to the discriminator is an activation layer. For the discriminator, we will use a Leaky ReLU activation function. The activation layer is added after our first convolution layer so that our code now looks like the following:

```
discriminator_out <- discriminator_in %>%
    layer_conv_2d(filters = 256, kernel_size = 3) %>%
    layer_activation_leaky_relu()
```

5. In our next convolution layer, we use strides of 2 to halve the height and width while doubling the depth:

```
discriminator_out <- discriminator_in %>%
    layer_conv_2d(filters = 256, kernel_size = 3) %>%
    layer_activation_leaky_relu() %>%
    layer_conv_2d(filters = 256, kernel_size = 5, strides = 2)
```

6. We can now continue to add more layers, using the same sequence of convolution layers, to the Leaky ReLU activation layer. The constraint is that—as mentioned—at each layer, the height and width are halved and the depth is doubled, so the height and width dimensions need to be such that they can be halved, with the output containing whole numbers, or you will receive an error. In our case, we will add three more sequences of layers so that our code now looks like this:

```
discriminator_out <- discriminator_in %>%
    layer_conv_2d(filters = 256, kernel_size = 3) %>%
    layer_activation_leaky_relu() %>%
    layer_conv_2d(filters = 256, kernel_size = 5, strides = 2) %>%
    layer_activation_leaky_relu() %>%
    layer_conv_2d(filters = 256, kernel_size = 5, strides = 2) %>%
    layer_activation_leaky_relu() %>%
    layer_conv_2d(filters = 256, kernel_size = 3, strides = 2) %>%
    layer_activation_leaky_relu()
```

7. We now need to add a layer to flatten our values to one dimension in preparation for our final output layer. When we add this layer, our code will look like the following:

```
discriminator_out <- discriminator_in %>%
    layer_conv_2d(filters = 256, kernel_size = 3) %>%
layer_activation_leaky_relu() %>%
layer_conv_2d(filters = 256, kernel_size = 5, strides = 2) %>%
layer_activation_leaky_relu() %>%
layer_conv_2d(filters = 256, kernel_size = 5, strides = 2) %>%
layer_activation_leaky_relu() %>%
layer_conv_2d(filters = 256, kernel_size = 3, strides = 2) %>%
layer_activation_leaky_relu() %>%
layer_flatten()
```

8. After this, we add a `dropout` layer that removes some data at random, which forces the model to work harder and slows down training, which produces a better generalizer. Adding this layer results in the following code:

```
discriminator_out <- discriminator_in %>%
    layer_conv_2d(filters = 256, kernel_size = 3) %>%
layer_activation_leaky_relu() %>%
layer_conv_2d(filters = 256, kernel_size = 5, strides = 2) %>%
layer_activation_leaky_relu() %>%
layer_conv_2d(filters = 256, kernel_size = 5, strides = 2) %>%
layer_activation_leaky_relu() %>%
layer_conv_2d(filters = 256, kernel_size = 3, strides = 2) %>%
layer_activation_leaky_relu() %>%
layer_flatten() %>%
    layer_dropout(rate = 0.5)
```

9. Lastly, we add a `dense` layer with just 1 unit, representing the probability that an image is real or fake. Adding this last layer will complete our discriminator model. The final discriminator model is defined with the following code:

```
discriminator_out <- discriminator_in %>%
    layer_conv_2d(filters = 256, kernel_size = 3) %>%
layer_activation_leaky_relu() %>%
layer_conv_2d(filters = 256, kernel_size = 5, strides = 2) %>%
layer_activation_leaky_relu() %>%
layer_conv_2d(filters = 256, kernel_size = 5, strides = 2) %>%
layer_activation_leaky_relu() %>%
layer_conv_2d(filters = 256, kernel_size = 3, strides = 2) %>%
layer_activation_leaky_relu() %>%
layer_flatten() %>%
    layer_dropout(rate = 0.5) %>%
    layer_dense(units = 1, activation = "sigmoid")
```

After running the code, there are now four defined tensors in our data environment. Your data environment will look as in the following screenshot:

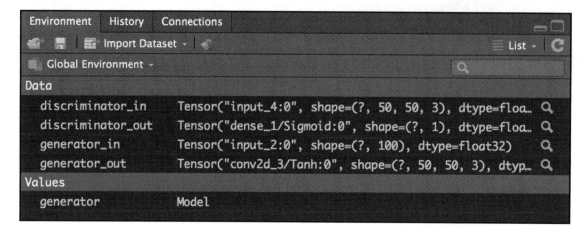

10. After defining the input and output, both objects are passed as arguments to the `keras_model` function, as before, with the generator model. We define the discriminator model using the input and output definitions from the previous steps and then run the `summary` function to see the details of the model, using the following code:

```
discriminator <- keras_model(discriminator_in, discriminator_out)
summary(discriminator)
```

After running the preceding code, you will have details about the model printed to your console. The output to your console will look as in the following screenshot:

Layer (type)	Output Shape	Param #
input_30 (InputLayer)	(None, 50, 50, 3)	0
conv2d_80 (Conv2D)	(None, 48, 48, 64)	1792
batch_normalization_v1_71 (BatchNormal	(None, 48, 48, 64)	256
leaky_re_lu_42 (LeakyReLU)	(None, 48, 48, 64)	0
conv2d_81 (Conv2D)	(None, 23, 23, 128)	131200
batch_normalization_v1_72 (BatchNormal	(None, 23, 23, 128)	512
leaky_re_lu_43 (LeakyReLU)	(None, 23, 23, 128)	0
conv2d_82 (Conv2D)	(None, 10, 10, 256)	524544
batch_normalization_v1_73 (BatchNormal	(None, 10, 10, 256)	1024
leaky_re_lu_44 (LeakyReLU)	(None, 10, 10, 256)	0
conv2d_83 (Conv2D)	(None, 4, 4, 512)	2097664
batch_normalization_v1_74 (BatchNormal	(None, 4, 4, 512)	2048
leaky_re_lu_45 (LeakyReLU)	(None, 4, 4, 512)	0
flatten_9 (Flatten)	(None, 8192)	0
dropout_9 (Dropout)	(None, 8192)	0
dense_19 (Dense)	(None, 1)	8193

Total params: 2,767,233
Trainable params: 2,765,313
Non-trainable params: 1,920

11. To view the details of our model, we can see the dimensions shifting as the input passes through convolution layers. We start with the input in the shape of our image data and at each layer, two dimensions are reduced while the third dimension is increased. In the end, we have one fully connected layer. We see that if we had added a few more convolution layers, we would have gotten to a point where we could no longer halve our data and still have a whole unit remaining.

12. During this step, we will also define our optimizer, which is how the model will pass data back to improve future iterations of the model. We will calculate performance using `binary_crossentropy` and then use the `adam` optimizer to feed data back to the model from the error rate gradients. We define how we evaluate and incrementally improve our discriminator model using the following code:

```
discriminator_optimizer <- optimizer_adam(
   lr = 0.0008
)
discriminator %>% compile(
   optimizer = discriminator_optimizer,
   loss = "binary_crossentropy"
)
```

We now have our generator model and discriminator defined. These are the two main building blocks for our GAN. In the next step, we will load in the real images and show you how to convert the images to numeric data. This is the third and final piece that we need before we assemble everything together to train our GAN and begin generating synthetic images.

Preparing and preprocessing a dataset

For this chapter, we will use a small subset of images from the labeled faces in the wild dataset. Specifically, we will use images of former United States president George W. Bush, since this is the image object that occurs most often in the dataset. Using the following code, we will bring in the image data and convert it to a format that can be inputted into our model. We start by loading the libraries and data files required.

Loading the libraries and data files

We will begin by using the following steps:

1. First, we load all the libraries that we will use. We will use just one function from each of these libraries but we need each one to get our data in the proper format. The `jpeg` library will be used to read in the image data and store it as a matrix. The `purrr` package will be used to apply a function to our list of arrays. The `abind` package will be used to convert the list of arrays into one array. Finally, `OpenImageR` will be used to resize our data. We load all the libraries needed to bring in images and convert them to the proper format using the following code:

```
library(jpeg)
library(purrr)
library(abind)
library(OpenImageR)
```

3. After loading the libraries, the next step is to bring over all the image files. The first step in this process is to change the working directory, for convenience, to the folder containing all the image files.

4. Once you have navigated to this folder, use the `list.files` function to bring over a vector of all the filenames. Lastly, we use the `map()` function from the `purrr` package to perform functions on every element in our vector and pass the results to a list.

5. In this case, every element in our vector is a file path. We pass each file path as an argument to the `readJPEG` function from the `jpeg` package. This function returns an array for every image, with all the pixel values represented as normalized values between 0 and 1. This is convenient because this is the format we want for our neural networks. As noted before, the pixel values are ordinarily stored as integers between 0 and 255; however, values bound between 0 and 1 work better when planning to pass data through a neural network. We import our images, convert all the pixel values to normalized values between 0 and 1, and store all the formatted image data in a list of arrays using the following code:

```
setwd('data/faces')
filename_vector = list.files(pattern="*.jpg")
image_list <- purrr::map(filename_vector, jpeg::readJPEG)
```

6. After running the code, we now have the list of arrays in our data environment. If we expand the object, we can see a sample of pixel values for the images in this set. After expanding the data object in your environment, it will look as in the following screenshot:

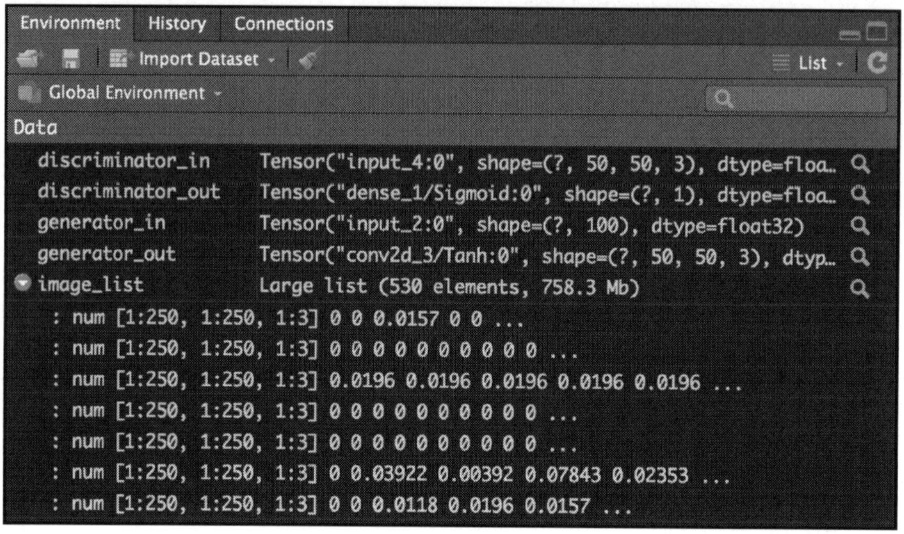

Resizing our images

We will resize the images using the following steps:

1. This step is done for the purposes of this book to speed up the model execution time. In a real-world example, this step may not be necessary or desirable. However, knowing how to resize images is helpful in any case. We can resize every image by once again using the map function from the purrr package and also the resizeImage function from the OpenImageR package. In this case, map takes every element from the image_list object and passes it as an argument through the resizeImage function. So, every array will change from having dimensions of 250 x 250 to 50 x 50. We resize every image by running the following code:

```
image_list <- purrr::map(image_list, ~OpenImageR::resizeImage(.,
width=50, height=50, method = "nearest"))
```

2. After running this code, we can see the dimensions of our images have changed. If `image_list` is still expanded in the data **Environment** pane, then it will now look as in the following screenshot:

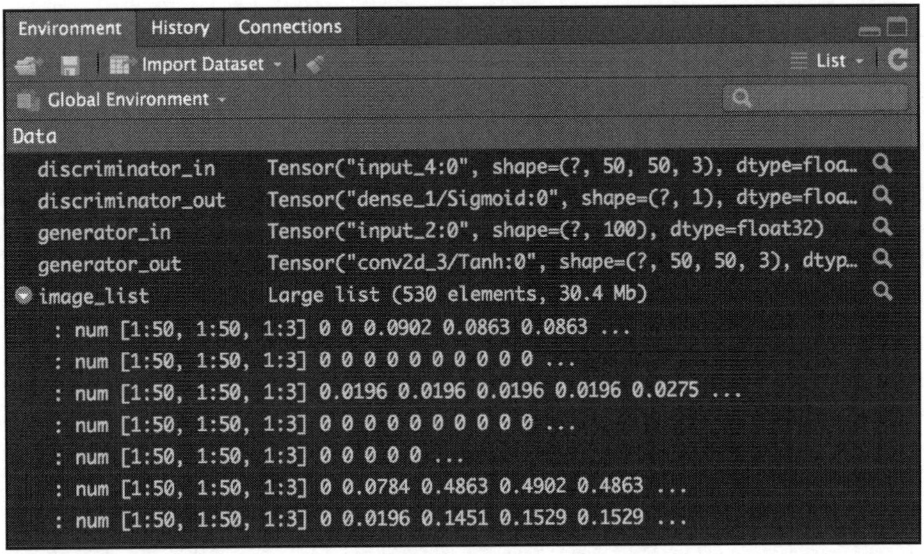

Merging arrays

Now that we are done resizing, we will start merging the arrays:

1. After our images are resized, there is just one last step to get the data in the proper format. The data is currently stored in a list of arrays; however, we need the data to all be in one four-dimensional array. The following code takes all our three-dimensional arrays and combines them along a new fourth dimension. We can combine all of our three-dimensional arrays into one four-dimensional array and then view the dimensions using the following code:

```
image_array <- abind::abind( image_list, along = 0)
dim(image_array)
```

2. This code will print details about our image dimensions to the console, so we can now see the new shape of our four-dimensional array and how the fourth dimension corresponds with the number of image objects we have. You will see the following printed to your console:

3. Our data is now in the proper format and we can just do two last clean-up steps. We remove the list of arrays and the vector of file path names, since we no longer need these, and reset our working directory back to the root for our project:

```
rm(image_list,filename_vector)

setwd('../..')
```

4. After running this code, we have all the objects that we need to begin assembling our GAN model. Your data environment will look as in the following screenshot:

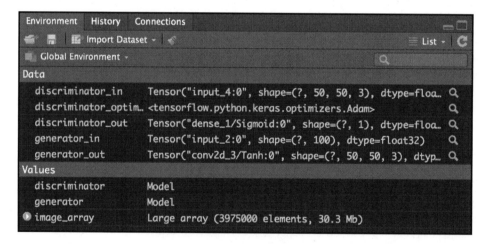

With the data now imported to the environment and converted into the proper format, we are now ready to put everything together to create our GAN model. The data we just loaded is used with the discriminator model, along with the array created by the generator model. We will now write the code that combines the data, generator, and discriminator to create our GAN model.

Training and evaluating the model

Now that the data is in the proper format and we have our discriminator and generator defined, we can put it all together to train our GAN. The final GAN model takes input from our target image dataset and the output is the probability that this is a real image after the real image data and the fake image data have been passed as input to the discriminator. We train our GAN model by running the following sections.

Defining the GAN model

We define the GAN model as follows:

1. The first step that we will perform is calling the `freeze_weights` function on the discriminator model. This is so that the weights for the discriminator model do not update during the training process. We want the weights to update for the generator and not for the discriminator:

```
freeze_weights(discriminator)
```

2. The next step is to define the input and output for `keras_model`, as we did with the generator and the discriminator. In this case, `keras_model` will be our final GAN model. Note here that the input will contain 100 values, which is the same as our generator, since the input to our GAN model will pass through our generator model and then continue through to our discriminator model, which will then produce the output for our model. We define the GAN model using the following code:

```
gan_in <- layer_input(shape = c(100))
gan_out <- discriminator(generator(gan_in))
gan <- keras_model(gan_in, gan_out)
```

3. After running this code, we now have the following objects in our data environment. We can see in all the details about the different tensor layers the path of the data through the entire GAN model pipeline. Your **Environment** pane will look like the following:

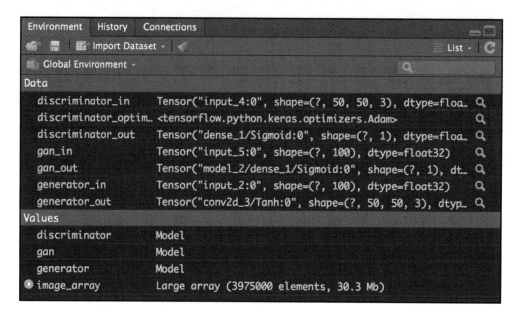

4. Similar to the discriminator model, we need to define the compile step. We set it up in the same way that we did with the discriminator. The error is computed using the `binary_crossentropy` loss function and `adam` is used to iteratively improve the model. Defining how the final GAN model is compiled is done using the following code:

```
gan_optimizer <- optimizer_adam(
    lr = 0.0004
)
gan %>% compile(
    optimizer = gan_optimizer,
    loss = "binary_crossentropy"
)
```

Passing data to the GAN model

Now, we will pass data to the model as follows:

1. With this, our model is ready and we can begin to pass data through to generate synthetic images. In order to store these data objects, we will need to create a directory within our project folder. We create a directory to hold our real and fake images by using the following code:

```
image_directory <- "gan_images"
  dir.create(image_directory)
```

2. After running this code, you will see a new folder in your main project folder with the name gan_images.

Training the GAN model

Now that we have prepared our model, it is time to train it, using the following steps:

1. Training our GAN model is an iterative process and we will need to create a loop that selects and creates image arrays and then passes them through our GAN, which will calculate the probability that each image array belongs to the target class. However, if we start a loop here, then the effects on every line of code will not be seen until the entire code completes. For that reason, we will first walk through every line of code inside the loop and then, we will show the entire code wrapped in the for loop.

2. Before entering the loop, we declare one variable that we will need inside our loop. The following code sets a value for the first_row variable. This will be used later when we subset our array. We start with the first three-dimensional array within our four-dimensional array. Later, when the following code is run in a loop, the value for first_row will change during every iteration to ensure a different subset of real images is passed to the discriminator model. We set the value of first_row for the first iteration of the loop by running the following code:

```
first_row <- 1
```

Generating random images

After training, we will use the model to create random images, as follows:

1. The next step is to create a matrix of random variables. The number of random variables should be set at the batch size times the size of the input shape for our generator model. The dimensions are then set so that the number of rows is equal to the batch size and the number of columns is equal to the length of the input shape defined here. In this case, `20` is used as the batch size and `100` is used as the length of the vector to be passed to the generator model. Both of these values are modifiable. Increasing either or both provides more data to the model, which could improve performance but will also increase runtime. We create our matrix of random values from a normal distribution by using the following code:

```
random_value_matrix <- matrix(rnorm(20 * 100),
                                    nrow = 20, ncol = 100)
```

2. After running the code, a matrix will be created consisting of values selected from a normal (Gaussian) distribution. Every row in the matrix will be used to generate an image. The images are created by using random values. By selecting the object in our data environment, we can view it. After selecting the data object from the environment, you will see something like the following:

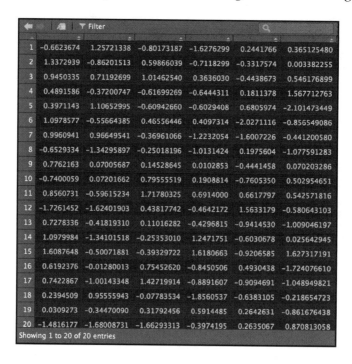

3. Next, using our matrix of random values, we will generate fake images. These fake images are created using the generator model that we defined earlier. The model takes the random values as input and the output is a four-dimensional array. The first dimension of the array corresponds with the batch size, which in this case is 20, and the other three dimensions correspond to the dimensions of our image data. After generating synthetic data, we will sample a few values to show that the arrays have been created and populated with the random values. We create the array and view a portion of it by running the following code:

```
fake_images <- generator %>% predict(random_value_matrix)
fake_images[1,1:5,1:5,1]
```

4. After running the preceding code, we see a small section of the array that we created. Since this has a value of 1 for the first dimension and a value of 1 for the fourth dimension, then we know that the values will be used to represent the intensity of the red values for the first image. The preceding code prints values to the console. You will see something like the following printed to your console:

```
> fake_images[1,1:5,1:5,1]
              [,1]          [,2]         [,3]         [,4]         [,5]
[1,] -0.001943786 -0.0003296182 -0.002263287 -0.003480832 -0.001259800
[2,] -0.006301089 -0.0020882732 -0.002275479 -0.003319296 -0.004303632
[3,] -0.001468549 -0.0032615596  0.002270642 -0.002021129 -0.004150799
[4,] -0.006161732 -0.0007549439 -0.003263999 -0.001655906 -0.003575346
[5,] -0.003726891  0.0008677171 -0.003815699 -0.005067361  0.003351704
>
```

5. Earlier, we set the `first_row` value to indicate where we would like row-wise subsets to begin for every iteration. Next, we need to define the last row, which is equal to the value of the first row plus one less than the batch size. In this case, the batch size is 20, so we use 19. Also, while the `first_row` value begins at 1, it will change dynamically throughout the iterations. We set the value of the last row for subsetting our data by running the following code:

```
last_row <- first_row + 19
```

Selecting real images

Now, we select the real images, as follows:

1. Next, we use the values for `first_row` and `last_row` to create a subset of the array containing our real target images. We will also run two lines to remove attributes from our data objects. This is not strictly necessary and at times, you may want data that is stored here. However, for demonstration purposes, we will remove it now so we can see the dimensions of all the arrays in the data environment window. The array of real images equal to the batch size to be used in an iteration of the model is created using the following line of code:

```
real_images <- image_array[first_row:last_row,,,]

attr(real_images, "dimnames") <- NULL
attr(image_array, "dimnames") <- NULL
```

2. After running these lines, we can now see that `real_images` and `fake_images` are arrays of the same size. Expand both data objects in your **Environment** pane and you will see that your environment now looks like the following:

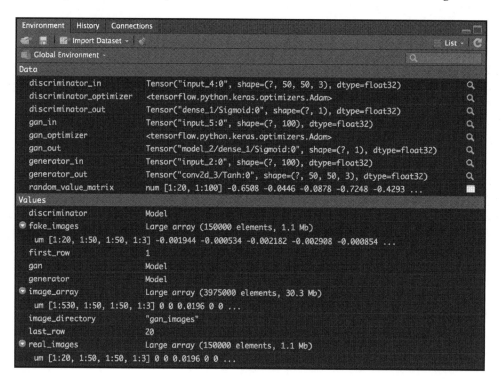

Combining real and fake images

After differentiating the real and fake images, we will now merge them using the following steps:

1. In our next step, we create an array with all the 0 values in the shape of our real images stacked on top of our fake images. That is to say, the first dimension is equal to twice the batch size, which in this case is 40, and the remaining three dimensions are equal to the size of our image arrays. We create this placeholder array of zeroes by running the following code:

```
combined_images <- array(0, dim = c(nrow(real_images) * 2,
50,50,3))
```

2. After running this code, we will see a new object in our **Environment** window and we can see that it does have a first dimension that is twice the size of the other two arrays that we created. Your environment will now look like this:

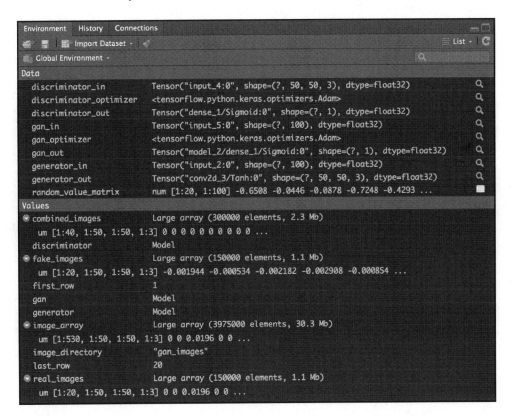

3. Next, we will populate our placeholder array. For the top half of this array, we assign the values from the fake images that we generated and for the bottom half, we assign the values for the real images. We populate our array with values from the fake and real image data using the following code:

```
combined_images[1:nrow(real_images),,,] <- fake_images
combined_images[(nrow(real_images)+1):(nrow(real_images)*2),,,] <-
real_images
```

4. After running this code, we will see that even for the small sample of data available in the **Environment** window, the values for `combined_images` have changed from all the zeroes, as seen earlier, to random values from our `fake_images` array. Your **Environment** window will now look as in the following screenshot:

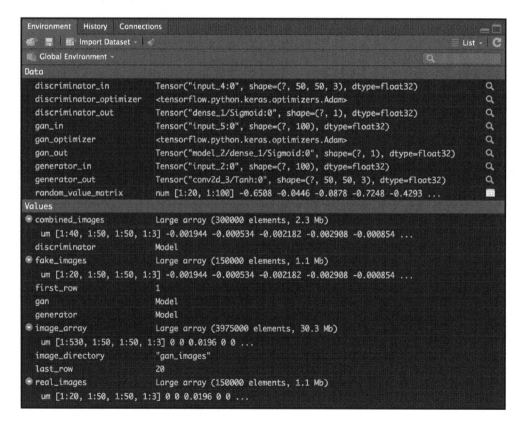

Creating target labels

Now, we create target labels for all the images using the following steps:

1. We need to create a matrix of labels; this is simply a matrix of binary values. We add 20 rows with values of 1 to label the fake images and 20 rows with values of 0 to label the real images. We create our matrix of label data using the following code:

```
labels <- rbind(matrix(1, nrow = 20, ncol = 1),
                matrix(0, nrow = 20, ncol = 1))
```

2. After running this code, let's click on the labels object to view it. We can see that it does contain 20 rows with a value of 1 and 20 rows with a value of 0. The following is an image that you will see near the midpoint when viewing this matrix:

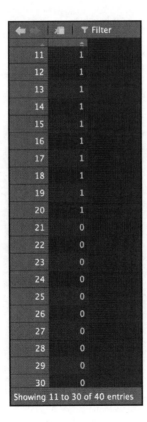

3. The next step is to add some noise to the labels. Just like using the dropout layer earlier, we want to introduce some noise and randomness throughout the modeling process to try to force the discriminator to generalize more and avoid overfitting. We add noise by applying a constant value to an array of random values selected from a uniform distribution that is the same length as our labels object and then adding it to the current values in the labels matrix. We add noise to our labels using the following code:

```
labels <- labels + (0.1 * array(runif(prod(dim(labels))),
                                dim = dim(labels)))
```

4. After we do this, we can look at the same subset of rows from the `labels` object and see that the values are now all slightly modified. The values in your `labels` object will be similar to the following screenshot:

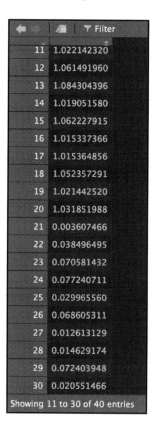

Passing input to the discriminator model

Now, we will pass the inputs to the discriminator model using the following steps:

1. Next, we pass our combined images, containing a mix of real and fake images, as input to our discriminator model and we pass along the labels as the target variable for the model. We feed our independent and dependent variables to the input and output layers of our discriminator model using the following code:

```
d_loss <- discriminator %>% train_on_batch(combined_images, labels)

d_loss
```

2. The result of running this code is the error rate for the discriminator. We can just run the name of the object to have this value printed to our console. After running the preceding code, your console will look as in the following screenshot, though the value may be slightly different:

3. Our next step will be to create another random matrix, which we will use as input to our GAN. It goes to the generator and in turn, the discriminator, as defined in our GAN model definition. We create the input for our GAN model using the following code:

```
random_value_matrix <- matrix(rnorm(20 * 100),
                              nrow = 20, ncol = 100)
```

4. After this, we create an array that is the size of our batch. It is set to state that all the data objects are true:

```
fake_target_array <- array(0, dim = c(20, 1))
```

5. We pass this matrix of random variables and the array to the GAN model:

```
a_loss <- gan %>% train_on_batch(
    random_value_matrix,
    fake_target_array
  )

a_loss
```

6. The result of running this code is a calculation of the error rate for the GAN. If many of the true target images were correctly identified, then the generator will make larger changes and if the generator creates images that are selected as real images, then fewer changes will be made during future iterations. If we run the line that only contains the object name, then we will receive a print out to our console. Your console will look similar to the following screenshot:

Updating the row selector

Next, we will update the row selector with the following steps:

1. Our next step will be to reset the `first_row` value to get a different subset of the `real_image` data during the subsequent iteration. We reset the `first_row` value using the following code:

```
first_row <- first_row + 20
  if (first_row  > (nrow(image_array)  - 20))
    first_row <- sample(1:10,1)

first_row
```

2. After this code is run, the `first_row` value will either be set to the previous value plus the batch size of `20`, or if that number would result in a subset that is out of bounds, then the `first_row` value is set to a randomly drawn value between `1` and `10`. In this case, the value will be set to `21`. You will see a printout to your console, as in the following screenshot:

Evaluating the model

Finally, we will evaluate the model using the following steps:

1. The last step is to periodically print model diagnostics along with real and generated images for comparison and to track whether the synthetic images are being generated as expected. We print the model iteration and error rates and also save one real and one fake image in the directory that we created earlier using the following code:

```
if (i %% 100 == 0) {
    cat("step:", i, "\n")
    cat("discriminator loss:", d_loss, "\n")
    cat("adversarial loss:", a_loss, "\n")
    image_array_save(
      fake_images[1,,,] * 255,
      path = file.path(image_directory, paste0("fake_gwb", i,
".png"))
    )
    image_array_save(
      real_images[1,,,] * 255,
      path = file.path(image_directory, paste0("real_gwb", i,
".png"))
    )
}
```

2. After running the code, we can see model diagnostics printed to our console. Your console will look as in the following screenshot:

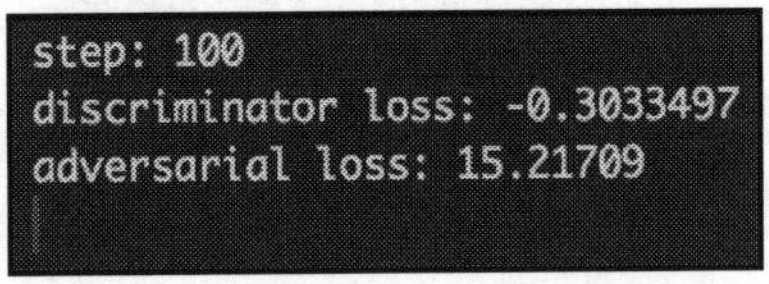

```
step: 100
discriminator loss: -0.3033497
adversarial loss: 15.21709
```

3. In addition, we can see generated and real images in the folder we created earlier. It will take quite a large number of rounds or epochs for any images to look like realistic faces, as in our real images set. However, even in earlier rounds, we can see the GAN begin to find features. The following is an original photo from our dataset:

4. This is a generated image:

This early synthetic image has captured a number of features already.

For convenience, the entire `for` loop for iteratively training our model is included in the GitHub repository.

Our GAN model is complete. You can continue to make a number of adjustments to see how it affects the synthetic images created. All through the model pipeline creation, we noted the values that need to be present in order to make the model work. However, huge portions can be modified. All modifications will result in different generated images. As noted before, there is no metric for a successful GAN. It will all depend on the end user's interpretation of the generated data. Adding more layers to the generator or discriminator, as well as adjusting the filter size, layer parameters, and learning rate, are all good options for modification as you continue to explore developing this particular type of deep learning model.

Summary

In this chapter, we created a model that can take images of faces as input and generate faces as output. We used images from the labeled faces in the wild dataset. Using a GAN model, we generated an image with random values and then sampled an actual image. To generate an image, we took random values and reshaped them to the dimensions of the images in our dataset. We then fed this image—composed of random values—along with an actual image, to a model that reshaped the data down to a simple probability score, representing the likelihood that an image is real or fake. Through multiple iterations, the generator was trained to create images that were increasingly likely to be classified as real by the discriminator model.

In our next chapter, we will learn about another unsupervised deep learning technique called **reinforcement learning**. It is similar to GANs in that an agent performs a task and continually learns from failing until it can perform the task successfully. We will dive into the details of reinforcement learning in the next chapter.

3
Section 3: Reinforcement Learning

This section will demonstrate reinforcement learning and deep reinforcement learning. The reader will learn how reinforcement learning differs from both supervised and unsupervised learning algorithms. The reader will use this machine learning technique in a number of situations to solve problems where discrete actions lead to an increased or reduced probability of a positive outcome.

This section comprises the following chapters:

- Chapter 10, *Reinforcement Learning for Gaming*
- Chapter 11, *Deep Q-learning for Maze Solving*

10
Reinforcement Learning for Gaming

In this chapter, we will learn about reinforcement learning. As the name suggests, with this method, optimal strategies are discovered through reinforcing or rewarding certain behavior and penalizing other behavior. The basic idea for this type of machine learning is to use an agent that performs actions towards a goal in an environment. We will explore this machine learning technique by using the `ReinforcementLearning` package in R to compute a policy for the agent to win a game of tic-tac-toe.

While this may seem like a simple game, it is a good environment for investigating reinforcement learning. We will learn how to structure input data for reinforcement learning, which is the same format for tic-tac-toe as for more complex games. We will learn how to compute a policy using the input data to provide the agent with the optimal strategy for the environment. We will also look at the hyperparameters available with this type of machine learning and the effect of adjusting these values.

Throughout this chapter, we will complete the following tasks:

- Understanding the concept of reinforcement learning
- Preparing and preprocessing data
- Configuring a reinforcement learning agent
- Tuning hyperparameters

Technical requirements

You can find the code files of this chapter at GitHub link at `https://github.com/PacktPublishing/Hands-on-Deep-Learning-with-R`.

Understanding the concept of reinforcement learning

Reinforcement learning is the last of the three most broad categories of machine learning. We have already studied supervised learning and unsupervised learning. Reinforcement learning is the third broad category and differs from the other two types in significant ways. Reinforcement learning neither trains on labeled data nor adds labels to data. Instead, it seeks to find an optimal solution for an agent to receive the highest reward.

The environment is the space where the agent completes its task. In our case, the environment will be the 3 x 3 grid used to play the game tic-tac-toe. The agent performs tasks within the environment. In this case, the agent places the X's or O's on the grid. The environment also contains rewards and penalties—that is, the agent needs to be rewarded for certain actions and penalized for others. In tic-tac-toe, if a player places marks (X or O) in three consecutive spaces either horizontally, vertically, or diagonally, then they win and conversely the other player loses. This is the simple reward and penalty structure for this game. The policy is the strategy that dictates which actions the agent should take to lead to the greatest probability for success given any set of previous actions.

To determine the optimal policy, we will be using Q-learning. The Q in Q-learning stands for quality. It involves developing a quality matrix to determine the best course of action. This involves using the Bellman equation. The interior of the equation calculates the reward value plus the discounted maximum value of future moves minus the current quality score. This calculated value is then multiplied by the learning rate and added to the current quality score. Later, we will see how to write this equation using R.

In this chapter, we are using Q-learning; however, there are other ways to perform reinforcement learning. Another popular algorithm is called **actor–critic** and it differs from Q-learning in significant ways. The following paragraph is a comparison of the two to better show the different approaches to pursuing the same type of machine learning.

Q-learning computes a value function, so it requires a finite set of actions, such as the game tic-tac-toe. Actor–critic works with a continuous environment and seeks to optimize the policy without a value function like Q-learning does. Instead, actor–critic has two models. One of them, the actor, performs actions while the other, the critic, calculates the value function. This takes place for each action, and over numerous iterations, the actor learns the best set of actions. While Q-learning works well for solving a game like tic-tac-toe, which has a finite space and set of moves, actor–critic works well for environments that are not constrained or that change dynamically.

In this section, we quickly reviewed the different methods for performing reinforcement learning. Next, we will begin to implement Q-learning on our tic-tac-toe data.

Preparing and processing data

For our first task, we will use the tic-tac-toe dataset from the `ReinforcementLearning` package. In this case, the dataset is built for us; however, we will investigate how it is made to understand how to get data into the proper format for reinforcement learning:

1. First, let's load the tic-tac-toe data. To load the dataset, we first load the `ReinforcementLearning` library and then call the `data` function with `"tictactoe"` as the argument. We load our data by running the following code:

    ```
    library(ReinforcementLearning)

    data("tictactoe")
    ```

    After running these lines, you will see the data object in the data **Environment** pane. Its current type is `<Promise>`; however, we will change that in the next step to see what is contained in this object. For now, your **Environment** pane will look like the following screenshot:

2. Now, let's look at the first few rows to evaluate what the dataset contains. We will use the `head` function to print the first few rows to the console and this will also convert the object in our **Environment** pane from `<Promise>` to an object that we can interact with and explore. We print the first five rows to our console using the following code:

    ```
    head(tictactoe, 5)
    ```

After running the code, your console will look like the following:

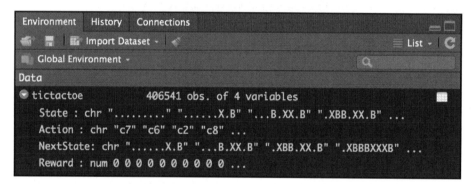

```
> head(tictactoe, 5)
      State Action NextState Reward
1 .........    c7  ......X.B      0
2 ......X.B    c6  ...B.XX.B      0
3 ...B.XX.B    c2  .XBB.XX.B      0
4 .XBB.XX.B    c8  .XBBBXXXB      0
5 .XBBBXXXB    c1  XXBBBXXXB      0
```

In addition, the object in the **Environment** pane will now look like the following:

```
Environment   History   Connections
      Import Dataset -                          List -  C
  Global Environment -                     Q
Data
  tictactoe            406541 obs. of 4 variables
     State : chr "........." "......X.B" "...B.XX.B" ".XBB.XX.B" ...
     Action : chr "c7" "c6" "c2" "c8" ...
     NextState: chr "......X.B" "...B.XX.B" ".XBB.XX.B" ".XBBBXXXB" ...
     Reward : num 0 0 0 0 0 0 0 0 0 ...
```

As we look at these images, we can see the way that this data is set up. In order to conduct reinforcement learning, we need our data to be in the format where one column is the current state, another is the action, and then the subsequent state, and lastly the reward. Let's take the first row and explain exactly what the value means.

The State is "`.........`". The dots indicate that the space on the 3 x 3 grid is blank, so this character string represents a blank tic-tac-toe board. The Action is "`c7`". This means that the agent who is playing as X will place an X in the seventh spot, which is the bottom-left corner. The NextState is "`......X.B`", which means that in this scenario, for this row, the opponent has placed an O in the bottom-right corner. The Reward is 0 because the game has not ended and the value of 0 for Reward indicates a neutral state where the game will continue. A row like this will exist for every possible combination of values for State, Action, NextState, and Reward.

3. Using only the top five rows, we can see that all possible moves are nonterminal, which is to say that the game continues after the move. Let's now look at the moves that lead to the conclusion of the game:

```
tictactoe %>%
  dplyr::filter(Reward == 1) %>%
  head()
```

```
tictactoe %>%
  dplyr::filter(Reward == -1) %>%
  head()
```

After running the preceding code, we will see the following rows printed to our console for actions that lead to victory:

```
    State Action NextState Reward
1 ..X.X..BB     c7 ..X.X.XBB      1
2 XBB...XXB      c4 XBBX..XXB      1
3 BXXXXBB.B      c8 BXXXXBBXB      1
4 .BBX.B.XX      c7 .BBX.BXXX      1
5 B..XXBXB.      c3 B.XXXBXB.      1
6 XBB.B.X.X      c8 XBB.B.XXX      1
```

We will also see these rows printed to our console for moves that lead to defeat:

```
    State Action NextState Reward
1 .XXBBX..B     c8 BXXBBX.XB     -1
2 X...X..BB      c6 X...XXBBB     -1
3 ...XB..BX      c7 .B.XB.XBX     -1
4 .X...BX.B      c5 .XB.XBX.B     -1
5 X..XBBB.X      c8 X.BXBBBXX     -1
6 XB..B...X      c4 XB.XB..BX     -1
```

Let's look at the first row from the subset that leads to victory. In this case, the agent already has an X in the top-right corner and the center of the game board. Here, the agent places an X in the bottom-left corner, and this results in three consecutive X's along a diagonal, which means the agent has won the game, which we see reflected in the Reward column.

4. Next, let's look at a given state and see all possible moves:

```
tictactoe %>%
  dplyr::filter(State == 'XB..X.XBB') %>%
  dplyr::distinct()
```

Subsetting our data this way, we start from a given state and see all possible options. The printout to your console will look like the following:

```
  State    Action NextState  Reward
1 XB..X.XBB    c3 XBX.X.XBB        1
2 XB..X.XBB    c6 XB.BXXXBB        0
3 XB..X.XBB    c4 XB.XX.XBB        1
4 XB..X.XBB    c6 XBB.XXXBB        0
```

In this case, there are only three spaces left on the game board. We can see that two moves lead to victory for the agent. If the agent selects the other space on the game board, then there are two remaining spaces on the board, and we can see that, regardless of which one the opponent chooses, the game continues.

From this investigation, we can see how to prepare a dataset for reinforcement learning. Even though this one was done for us, we could see just how we would make one ourselves. If we wanted to code our tic-tac-toe board differently, we could use the values from the game Number Scramble. Number Scramble is isomorphic to tic-tac-toe, but involves choosing numbers rather than placing marks on a grid; however, the number values match perfectly to the grid, so the values can be swapped. The game of Number Scramble involves selecting numbers between 1 and 15 between two players, where no number can be selected twice and the winner is the first to select numbers that sum up to 15. With this in mind, we could rewrite the first row that we looked at like this:

```
State <- '0,0'
Action <- '4'
NextState <- '4,8'
Reward <- 0

numberscramble <- tibble::tibble(
  State = State,
  Action = Action,
  NextState = NextState,
  Reward = Reward
)

numberscramble
```

After running this, we would get the following printed to our console:

From this, we can see that the values for `State`, `Action`, and `NextState` can be encoded in any way that we like as long as a consistent convention is used so that the reinforcement learning process can traverse from state to state to discover the optimal path to reward.

Now that we know how to set up our data, let's move on to looking at exactly how our agent will find the best way to reach the reward.

Configuring the reinforcement agent

Let's go into the details of what is happening to configure a reinforcement agent using Q-learning. The goal of Q-learning is to create a state–action matrix where a value is assigned for all state–action combinations—that is, if our agent is at any given state, then the values provided determine the action the agent will take to obtain maximum value. We are going to enable the computation of the best policy for our agent by creating a value matrix that provides a calculated value for every possible move:

1. To start, we need a set of state and action pairs that all have a value of 0. As a best practice, we will use hashing here, which is a more efficient alternative to large lists for scaling up to more complex environments. To begin, we will load the hash library and then we will use a `for` loop to populate the hash environment. The `for` loop starts by getting every unique state from the data, and for every unique state, it then appends every unique action to create all possible state–action pairs and assigns all pairs a value of 0. We generate this hash environment that will hold the values calculated during the Q-learning phase by running the following code:

```
library(hash)

Q <- hash()

for (i in unique(tictactoe$State)[!unique(tictactoe$State) %in%
names(Q)]) {
  Q[[i]] <- hash(unique(tictactoe$Action), rep(0,
length(unique(tictactoe$Action))))
}
```

After running the code, we will see that our **Environment** pane now looks like the following screenshot:

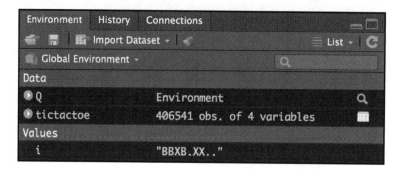

We have a hash environment, Q, that contains every state-action pair.

2. The next step is to define the hyperparameters. For now, we will use the default values; however, we will soon tune these to see the impact. We set the hyperparameters to their default values by running the following code:

```
control = list(
  alpha = 0.1,
  gamma = 0.1,
  epsilon = 0.1
  )
```

After running the code, we can now see that we have a list with our hyperparameter values in our **Environment** pane, which now looks like the following:

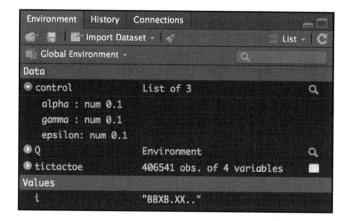

3. Next, we begin to populate our Q matrix. This again takes place within a `for` loop; however, we will look at one isolated iteration. We start by taking a row and moving the elements from this row to discrete data objects using the following code:

```
d <- tictactoe[1, ]
state <- d$State
action <- d$Action
reward <- d$Reward
nextState <- d$NextState
```

After running the code, we can see the changes to our **Environment** pane, which now contains the discrete elements from the first row. The **Environment** pane will look like the following:

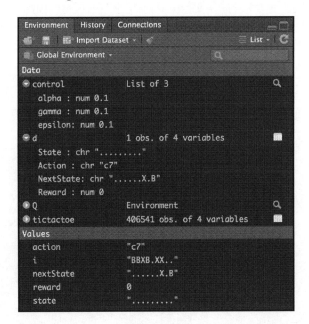

4. Next, we get a value for the current Q-learning score if there is one. If there isn't a value, then `0` is stored as the current value. We set this initial quality value score by running the following code:

```
currentQ <- Q[[state]][[action]]
if (has.key(nextState,Q)) {
  maxNextQ <- max(values(Q[[nextState]]))
} else {
  maxNextQ <- 0
}
```

After running this code, we now have a value for `currentQ`, which is `0` in this case because all values in Q for the state `'......X.B'` are `0`, as we have set all values to `0`; however, in the next step, we will begin to update the Q values.

5. Lastly, we update the Q value by using the Bellman equation. This is also called **temporal difference learning**. We write out this step for computing values with this equation for R using the following code:

```
## Bellman equation
Q[[state]][[action]] <- currentQ + control$alpha *
    (reward + control$gamma * maxNextQ - currentQ)

q_value <- Q[[tictactoe$State[1]]][[tictactoe$Action[1]]]
```

After running the following code, we can pull out the updated value for this state–action pair; we can see it in the field labeled `q_value`. Your **Environment** pane will look like the following screenshot:

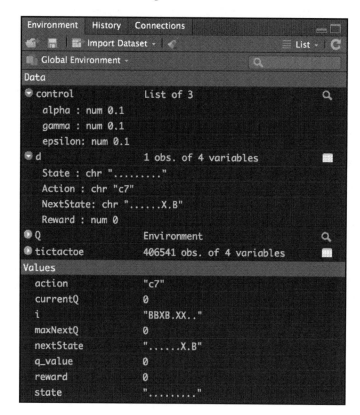

We note here that the q_value is still 0. Why is this the case? If we look at our equation, we will see that the reward is part of the equation and our reward is 0, which makes the entire calculated value 0. As a result, we will not begin to see updated Q values until our code encounters a row with a nonzero reward.

6. We can now put all of these steps together and run them over every row to create our Q matrix. We create the matrix of values that we will use to select the policy for optimal strategy by running the following code, which wraps all the previous code together in a `for` loop:

```
for (i in 1:nrow(tictactoe) {
  d <- tictactoe[i, ]
  state <- d$State
  action <- d$Action
  reward <- d$Reward
  nextState <- d$NextState
  currentQ <- Q[[state]][[action]]
  if (has.key(nextState,Q)) {
    maxNextQ <- max(values(Q[[nextState]]))
  } else {
    maxNextQ <- 0
  }
  ## Bellman equation
  Q[[state]][[action]] <- currentQ + control$alpha *
    (reward + control$gamma * maxNextQ - currentQ)
}

Q[[tictactoe$State[234543]]][[tictactoe$Action[234543]]]
```

After looping through all the rows, we see that some state–action pairs do now have a value in the Q matrix. Running the following code, we will see the following value printed to our console:

```
> Q[[tictactoe$State[234543]]][[tictactoe$Action[234543]]]
[1] 0.05877852
>
```

At this point, we have now created our matrix for Q-learning. In this case, we are storing the value in a hash environment with values for every key-value pairing; however, this is equivalent to storing the values in a matrix—it is just more efficient for scaling up later. Now that we have these values, we can compute a policy for our agent that will provide the best path to a reward; however, before we compute this policy, we will make one last set of modifications, and that is to tune the hyperparameters that we set earlier to their default values.

Tuning hyperparameters

We have now defined our environment and iterated over all possible actions and results from any given state to calculate the quality value of every move and stored these values in our Q object. At this point, we can now begin to tune the options for this model to see how it impacts performance.

If we recall, there are three parameters for reinforcement learning, and these are alpha, gamma, and epsilon. The following list describes the role of each parameter and the impact of adjusting their value:

- **Alpha**: The alpha rate for reinforcement learning is the same as the learning rate for many other machine learning models. It is the constant value used to control how quickly probabilities are updated as calculations are made based on exploring rewards for the agent taking certain actions.
- **Gamma**: Adjusting gamma adjusts how much the model values future rewards. When gamma is set to 1, then all rewards current and future are valued equally. This means that a reward that is several steps away is worth as much as a reward that is earned at the next step. Practically, this is almost never what we want since we want future rewards to be more valuable since it takes more effort to earn them. By contrast, setting gamma to 0 means that only rewards from the next action will have any value. Future rewards have no value at all. Again, aside from special cases, this is not desirable. When adjusting gamma, you have to seek the balance in weighting among future rewards that leads the agent to make an optimal selection of actions.
- **Epsilon**: The epsilon parameter is used to introduce randomness when selecting future actions. Setting epsilon to 0 is referred to as greedy learning. In this case, the agent will always take the path with the highest probability of success; however, in this case, as with other machine learning, it is easy for an agent to get lost in some local minima and never discover an optimal strategy. By introducing some randomness, different actions will be pursued over different iterations. Adjusting this value optimizes the exploration to exploit balance. We want the model to exploit what has been learned to choose the best future action; however, we also want the model to explore and continue learning.

Using what we know about these hyperparameters, let's see how the values change as we make adjustments to these parameters:

1. First, we will make adjustments to the value of `alpha`. As noted, the `alpha` value is the learning rate value, which we may be familiar with from learning about other machine learning topics. It is just the constant value that controls how quickly the algorithm makes adjustments. Currently, we have an `alpha` rate set at `0.1`; however, let's set our `alpha` rate at `0.5`. This is higher than we would usually ever want it to be in practice and is used here simply to explore the impact of changing these values. We will need to reset Q to all zeroes and restart the learning process to see what happens. The following code block takes everything we just did previously and runs it all again with the one adjustment to `alpha`. We tune the `alpha` value and see the effect by running the following code:

```
Q <- hash()

for (i in unique(tictactoe$State)[!unique(tictactoe$State) %in%
names(Q)]) {
  Q[[i]] <- hash(unique(tictactoe$Action), rep(0,
length(unique(tictactoe$Action))))
}

control = list(
  alpha = 0.5,
  gamma = 0.1,
  epsilon = 0.1
)

for (i in 1:nrow(tictactoe)) {
  d <- tictactoe[i, ]
  state <- d$State
  action <- d$Action
  reward <- d$Reward
  nextState <- d$NextState
  currentQ <- Q[[state]][[action]]
  if (has.key(nextState,Q)) {
    maxNextQ <- max(values(Q[[nextState]]))
  } else {
   maxNextQ <- 0
  }
  ## Bellman equation
  Q[[state]][[action]] <- currentQ + control$alpha *
    (reward + control$gamma * maxNextQ - currentQ)
```

```
}
```

```
Q[[tictactoe$State[234543]]][[tictactoe$Action[234543]]]
```

We can see from this tuning that we get a different value for the Q value at 234543. You will see the following printed out to your console:

```
> Q[[tictactoe$State[234543]]][[tictactoe$Action[234543]]]
[1] 0.08660724
```

As we might have expected, since we increased the value for alpha, we, as a result, ended up with a larger value for the Q value at the same point that we looked at previously. In other words, our algorithm learned faster and the quality value received a greater amount of weight.

2. Next, let's tune the value for gamma. If we recall, adjusting this value for gamma will alter how much the agent values future rewards. Our value is currently set at 0.1, which means that future rewards do have value, but the level at which they are valued is relatively small. Let's boost this up to 0.9 and see what happens. We go through the same operation as we did when we adjusted alpha. We start by resetting the Q hash environment so that all state–action pairs have a value of 0 and then we repopulate this hash environment by looping through all options, applying the Bellman equation by making our own changes to the gamma value. We assess what happens when we change the gamma value by running the following code:

```
library(hash)

Q <- hash()

for (i in unique(tictactoe$State)[!unique(tictactoe$State) %in%
names(Q)]) {
  Q[[i]] <- hash(unique(tictactoe$Action), rep(0,
length(unique(tictactoe$Action))))
}

control = list(
  alpha = 0.1,
  gamma = 0.9,
  epsilon = 0.1
)

for (i in 1:nrow(tictactoe)) {
  d <- tictactoe[i, ]
```

```
state <- d$State
action <- d$Action
reward <- d$Reward
nextState <- d$NextState
currentQ <- Q[[state]][[action]]
if (has.key(nextState,Q)) {
  maxNextQ <- max(values(Q[[nextState]]))
} else {
  maxNextQ <- 0
}
## Bellman equation
Q[[state]][[action]] <- currentQ + control$alpha *
  (reward + control$gamma * maxNextQ - currentQ)
}

Q[[tictactoe$State[234543]]][[tictactoe$Action[234543]]]
```

After running this code, you will see the following code printed on your console:

```
> Q[[tictactoe$State[234543]]][[tictactoe$Action[234543]]]
[1] 0.5290067
>
```

From this, we can make the following observations:

- We can see that our value increased quite significantly
- From this state and taking this action, there is value, but when considering future rewards there is even more value
- However, with a game like tic-tac-toe, we need to consider that there are never many steps between any state and a reward; however, we can see that from this state and this action, there will be a good probability of getting a reward

3. For our final adjustment, we will adjust the `epsilon`. The value of `epsilon` relies on how much previous knowledge is used compared with how much exploration is done to gather knowledge. For this adjustment, we will go back to using the function from the `ReinforcementLearning` package, since it relies on not only looping through the Bellman equation, but also storing these values for reference over multiple iterations. To adjust `epsilon`, we use the following code:

```
# Define control object
control <- list(
alpha = 0.1,
gamma = 0.1,
```

```
        epsilon = 0.9
        )

        # Perform reinforcement learning
        model <- ReinforcementLearning(data = tictactoe,
                                       s = "State",
                                       a = "Action",
                                       r = "Reward",
                                       s_new = "NextState",
                                       iter = 5,
                                       control = control)

        model$Q_hash[[tictactoe$State[234543]]][[tictactoe$Action[234543]]]
```

After running this code, we will see that our Q value has changed. You will see the following value printed to the console:

```
> model$Q_hash[[tictactoe$State[234543]]][[tictactoe$Action[234543]]]
[1] 0.06911028
>
```

From this, we can make the following observations:

- Our value is similar to the value that we had when we were using our default values for parameters, but slightly larger
- In this case, we have introduced a relatively large amount of randomness to force our agent to continue exploring; as a result, we can see that we have not lost so much value with this randomness, and this action retains a similar value even when it leads to different sets of subsequent actions

4. After tuning the parameters to the desired settings, we can now view the policy for a given state. First, let's take a look at the model object in our **Environment** pane. Your **Environment** pane will look like the following:

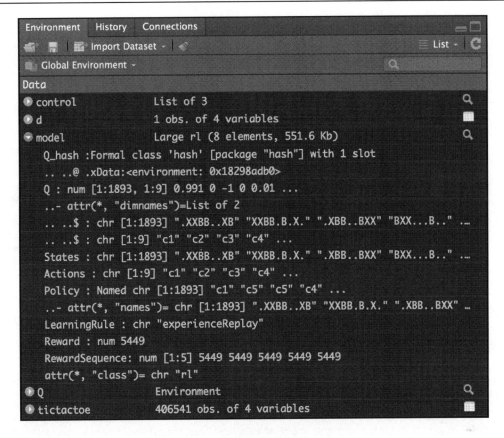

Let's look more in-depth at every element in the model object:

- Q_hash: The hash environment, just like we created earlier, which includes every state–action pair, along with a Q value
- Q: A named matrix that contains the same data as the hash environment, except in the form of a named matrix
- States: The named rows from our matrix
- Actions: The named columns from our matrix
- Policy: A named vector that contains the optimal action that the agent should take from any state
- Reward and RewardSequence: These are the number of rows from the dataset that lead to a reward less than the number that lead to a penalty

We can use the values from here to see the value of all actions at any given state and judge which is the best move to make. Let's start with a brand new game and see which move has the most value. We can see the value of every action from this state and note which action is best by running the following code:

```
sort(model$Q['.........',1:9], decreasing = TRUE)

model$Policy['.........']
```

After running this code, we will see the following printed to the console:

```
> sort(model$Q['.........',1:9], decreasing = TRUE)
         c5           c1           c7           c3           c9           c8           c4
0.008944695 0.006566869 0.005913829 0.005434826 0.005105148 0.002777202 0.002715441
         c2           c6
0.001756248 0.001398193
>
> model$Policy['.........']
.........
    "c5"
>
```

We can see that our first line lists every possible action along with their respective values in descending order. We can see that from this named vector, the move "c5", which is a mark at the center of the grid, has the highest value. Consequently, when we view the policy for our agent when it is at that state, we see that it is "c5". In this way, we can now use the results of reinforcement learning to choose the optimal move from any given state:

- We just adjusted all the parameters to note the effects of changing these variables
- Then, in the last step, we saw how to select the best policy based on the grid being in any state
- Through trying every possible combination of actions, we calculated the value of moves based on immediate and future rewards
- We decided to weigh the Q value by adjusting our parameters and decided upon a method to solve games

Summary

In this chapter, we have coded a reinforcement-learning system using Q-learning. We defined our environment or playing surface and then looked at the dataset containing every possible combination of states, actions, and future states. Using the dataset, we calculated the value of every state–action pair, which we stored in a hash environment and also as a matrix. We then used this matrix of values as the basis of our policy, which selects the move with the most value.

In our next chapter, we will expand on Q-learning by adding neural networks to create deep Q-learning networks.

Deep Q-Learning for Maze Solving

11

In this chapter, you will learn how to use R to implement reinforcement learning techniques within a maze environment. In particular, we will create an agent to solve a maze by training the agent to perform actions and learn from failed attempts. We will learn how to define the maze environment and configure the agent to travel through it. We will also be adding neural networks to Q-learning. This provides us with an alternative way of getting the value for all the state-action pairs. We are going to iterate over our model numerous times to create the policy to get through the maze.

This chapter will cover the following topics:

- Creating an environment for reinforcement learning
- Defining an agent to perform actions
- Building a deep Q-learning model
- Running the experiment
- Improving performance with policy functions

Technical requirements

You can find the code files used in this chapter at https://github.com/PacktPublishing/Hands-on-Deep-Learning-with-R.

Creating an environment for reinforcement learning

In this section, we will define an environment for reinforcement learning. We could think of this as a typical maze where an agent needs to navigate the two-dimensional grid space to get to the end. However, in this case, we are going to use more of a physics-based maze. We will represent this using the mountain car problem. An agent is in a valley and needs to get to the top; however, it cannot simply go up the hill. It has to use momentum to get to the top. In order to do this, we need two functions. One function will start or reset the agent to a random point on the surface. The other function will describe where the agent is on the surface after a step.

We will use the following code to define the `reset` function to provide a place for the agent to start:

```
reset = function(self) {
  position = runif(1, -0.6, -0.4)
  velocity = 0
  state = matrix(c(position, velocity), ncol = 2)
  state
}
```

We can see that with this function, the first thing that happens is that the `position` variable is defined by taking one random value from a uniform distribution between -0.6 and -0.4. This is the point on the surface where the agent will be placed. Next, the variable velocity is set to 0, since our agent is not moving yet. The `reset` functions act merely to place the agent at a starting point. The `position` variable and the `velocity` variable are now added to a 1 x 2 matrix and this `matrix` variable is the starting spot and starting speed for our agent.

The next function takes a value for every action and calculates the next step that the agent will take. To code this function, we use the following code:

```
step = function(self, action) {
position = self$state[1]
velocity = self$state[2]
velocity = (action - 1L) * 0.001 + cos(3 * position) * (-0.0025)
velocity = min(max(velocity, -0.07), 0.07)
position = position + velocity
if (position < -1.2) {
  position = -1.2
  velocity = 0
}
state = matrix(c(position, velocity), ncol = 2)
```

```
    reward = -1
    if (position >= 0.5) {
      done = TRUE
      reward = 0
    } else {
      done = FALSE
    }
    list(state, reward, done)
  }
```

In this function, the first part defines the position and velocity. In this case, this is taken from the `self` object, which we will cover next. The `self` variable contains details about the agent. Here, the `position` and `velocity` variables are taken from `self` and represent where the agent currently is on the surface and the current velocity. Then, the `action` argument is used to calculate the velocity. The next line constrains `velocity` between -0.7 and 0.7. After this, we calculate the next position by adding the velocity to the current position. Then, there is one more constraint line. If `position` goes past -1.2, then the agent is out of bounds and gets reset to the -1.2 position with no velocity. Finally, a check is carried out to see whether the agent has reached its goal. If the state is greater than 0.5, then the agent wins; otherwise, the agent keeps moving and attempts to reach the goal.

When we finish with the two coding blocks, we will see that we have two functions defined in our **Environment** pane. Your **Environment** pane will appear as in the following screenshot:

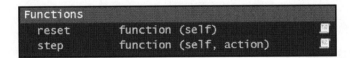

The combination of these two functions defines the shape of the surface and the location of the agent on the surface, as well as the placement of the target spot on that surface. The `reset` function is the initial placement of the agent and the `step` function defines the step the agent takes at every iteration. With these two functions, we have a way of defining the shape and boundaries of our environment and a mechanism for placing and moving our agent within this environment. Next, let's define our agent.

Defining an agent to perform actions

In this section, we will define our agent for deep Q-learning. We have already seen how the preceding environment functions define how the agent moves. Here, we define the agent itself. In the previous chapter, we used Q-learning and were able to apply the Bellman equation to the new state that was the result of a given action. In this chapter, we will augment that portion of Q-learning with a neural network, which is what takes standard Q-learning and makes it deep Q-learning.

In order to add this neural network model to the process, we need to define a class. This is something that is often done in object-oriented programming; however, it is done less often in a programming language such as R. To accomplish this, we will use the R6 package for class creation. We will break up the creation of this R6 class into numerous parts to make it easier to understand. A class provides instructions for instantiating and operating on a data object. In this case, our class will use declared variables to instantiate the data object and a series of functions, which are referred to as methods within a class context, to operate on the data object. In the following steps, we will just look at the individual parts of our class one by one to make it easier to understand the parts of the class that we are creating. However, running parts of the code will result in errors. After walking through all the parts, we will wrap everything in a function to create our class and this final, longer R6 code that includes everything that you will run. To get started, we will set up the initial values using the following code:

```
portable = FALSE,
lock_objects = FALSE,
public = list(
   state_size = NULL,
   action_size = NA,
   initialize = function(state_size, action_size) {
       self$state_size = state_size
       self$action_size = action_size
       self$memory = deque()
       self$gamma = 0.95
       self$epsilon = 1.0
       self$epsilon_min = 0.01
       self$epsilon_decay = 0.995
       self$learning_rate = 0.001
       self$model = self$build_model()
   }
)
```

When creating a class for this purpose using R, we first set two options. First, we set `portable` to `FALSE`, which means other classes cannot inherit methods or functions from this class. However, it also means that we can use the `self` keyword. Second, we set `lock_objects` to `FALSE`, since we will need to modify objects within this class.

Next, we define our initial values. We use `self` here, which is a special keyword that refers to the object created. Remember that a class is not an object—it is a constructor for creating an object. Here, we will create an instance of our class and this object will be the agent. The agent will initialize with the following values. The state size and action size will be passed in as arguments when creating the environment. The next memory is an empty deque. A **deque** is a special object type, which is double-ended so that values can be added to and removed from both sides. We will use this to store the steps the agent takes while trying to reach the goal. Gamma is the discount rate. Epsilon is the exploration rate. As we know, with deep learning, the goal is to balance exploration and exploitation, so we begin with an aggressive exploration rate. However, we then define an epsilon decay, which is how much the rate will be reduced, and an epsilon minimum, so the rate never reaches 0. Lastly, the learning rate is just the constant value used when adjusting weights and the model takes the result of running our neural network model, which we will get to next.

Next, we will give the class the power to act on variables by adding a function. In particular, we will add the `build_model` function to run the neural network:

```
build_model = function(...){
        model = keras_model_sequential() %>%
        layer_dense(units = 24, activation = "relu", input_shape =
self$state_size) %>%
        layer_dense(units = 24, activation = "relu") %>%
        layer_dense(units = self$action_size, activation = "linear")
        compile(model, loss = "mse", optimizer = optimizer_adam(lr =
self$learning_rate), metrics = "accuracy")

        return(model)
    }
```

The model takes the current state as input and the output will be one of the actions available when we predict the model. However, this function just returns the model because we will pass a different state argument to the model, depending on what part of the deep Q-learning path we are on when it is called. The model is called in two different scenarios, which we will cover shortly.

Next, we include a function for memory. The memory portion of this class will be a function to store the state, action, reward, and next state details as the agent attempts to solve the maze. We store those values in the agent's memory by adding them to the deque using the following code:

```
memorize = function(state, action, reward, next_state, done){
        pushback(self$memory,state)
        pushback(self$memory,action)
        pushback(self$memory,reward)
        pushback(self$memory, next_state)
        pushback(self$memory, done)
    }
```

We use the `pushback` function to add a given value to the first position in the deque and move all the existing elements back by one. We do this for state, action, reward, and next state, and the flag that shows whether or not the puzzle is complete. This sequence is stored in the agent's memory, so it can exploit what it already knows by accessing this sequence in memory rather than continuing to explore when the exploration-versus-exploitation formula selects the exploitation option.

Next, we will add some code to select the next action. To perform this task, we will use a check on the decaying epsilon value. Depending on whether or not the decaying epsilon is greater than a randomly selected value from a uniform distribution, one of two actions will take place. We set up the function for deciding on the next action by using the following code:

```
act = function(state){
        if (runif(1) <= self$epsilon){
            return(sample(self$action_size, 1))
            } else {
        act_values <- predict(self$model, state)
        return(which(act_values==max(act_values)))
            }
    }
```

As noted previously, there are two possible outcomes from this action function. First, if the randomly selected value from the uniform distribution is less than or equal to epsilon, then a value will be selected between the full range of active movements. Otherwise, the current state is used to predict the next action using the model we defined earlier, which results in weighted probabilities that any of these actions are correct. The action with the highest probability is selected. This is a balance between two different forms of exploration in seeking the correct next step.

Having covered exploration steps previously, we will now write our `replay()` function, which will exploit what the agent already knows and has stored in memory. We code this exploitation function using the following code:

```
replay = function(batch_size){
        minibatch = sample(length(self$memory), batch_size)
            state = minibatch[1]
            action = minibatch[2]
            target = minibatch[3]
            next_state = minibatch[4]
            done = minibatch[5]
            if (done == FALSE){
                target = (target + self$gamma *
                            max(predict(self$model, next_state)))
            target_f = predict(self$model, state)
            target_f[0][action] = target
            self$model(state, target_f, epochs=1, verbose=0)
            }
        if (self$epsilon > self$epsilon_min){
            self$epsilon = self$epsilon * self$epsilon_decay
            }
    }
```

Let's break apart the function for leveraging what the agent already knows to help solve the puzzle. The first thing we will do is select a random sequence from the memory deque. We will then place each element from our sample into a given part of a sequence for the agent: state, action, target, next state, and the done flag to indicate whether the maze is solved. Next, we will add some code to change the way that our model predicts. We start by defining the target using the resulting state from the sequence, leveraging what we have already learned from attempting this sequence.

Next, we predict on the state to get all the possible values the model would predict. We then insert the calculated value into that vector. When we run the model once more, we help train the model based on experience. This is also the step where epsilon is updated, which will result in more exploitation and less exploration during future iterations.

The very last step is to add a method or function for saving and loading our model. We add the means to save and load our model using the following code:

```
load = function(name) {
    self$model %>% load_model_tf(name)
},
save = function(name) {
    self$model %>% save_model_tf(name)
}
```

With these methods, we are now able to save the model that we defined earlier, as well as load the trained models.

We will now need to take everything that we have covered and place it all in a overarching function that will take all the declared variables and functions and use them to create an R6 class. To create our R6 class, we will take all the code that we have just written and put it all together.

After running the complete code, we will have an R6 class in our environment. It will have a class of `Environment`. If you click on it, you can see all the attributes of the class. You will notice that there are many attributes associated with creating a class that we did not specifically define; however, take a look at the following screenshot. We can see that the class is not portable, we can see the public fields where we will assign values, and we can see all the functions we defined, which are called methods when included as part of a class:

Name	Type	Value
portable	logical [1]	FALSE
private_fields	NULL	Pairlist of length 0
private_methods	NULL	Pairlist of length 0
public_fields	list [2]	List of length 2
state_size	NULL	Pairlist of length 0
action_size	logical [1]	NA
public_methods	list [8]	List of length 8
initialize	function	function(state_size, action_size) { ... }
build_model	function	function(...) { ... }
memorize	function	function(state, action, reward, next_state, done) { ... }
act	function	function(state) { ... }
replay	function	function(batch_size) { ... }
load	function	function(name) { ... }
save	function	function(name) { ... }
clone	function	function(deep = FALSE) { ... }
self	environment [24] (S3: R6ClassGe	<environment: 0x000002bd83644f08>

With this step, we have completely created an R6 class to act as our agent. We have provided it with various means to take an action based on the current state and an element of randomness, and we have also provided a way for our agent to explore the surface of this maze to find the target location. We have also provided a means for the agent to recall what it has already learned from past experience and use that to inform future decisions. Altogether, we have a complete reinforcement learning agent that learns through trial and error and, importantly, learns from past mistakes and from continually taking actions at random.

Building a deep Q-learning model

At this point, we have defined the environment and our agent, which will make running our model quite straightforward. Remember that to get set up for reinforcement learning using R, we used a technique from object-oriented programming, which is not used very often in a programming language such as R. We created a class that describes an object, but is itself not an object. To create an object from a class, we must instantiate it. We set our initial values and instantiate an object using our DQNAgent class by using the following code:

```
state_size = 2
action_size = 20
agent = DQNAgent(state_size, action_size)
```

After running this block of code, we will see an agent object in our environment. The agent has a class of Environment; however, if we click on it, we will see something similar to the following screenshot, which contains some differences compared with our class:

Name	Type	Value
act	function	function(state) { ... }
action_size	double [1]	20
build_model	function	function(...) { ... }
clone	function	function(deep = FALSE) { ... }
epsilon	double [1]	1
epsilon_decay	double [1]	0.995
epsilon_min	double [1]	0.01
gamma	double [1]	0.95
initialize	function	function(state_size, action_size) { ... }
learning_rate	double [1]	0.001
load	function	function(name) { ... }
memorize	function	function(state, action, reward, next_state, done) { ... }
memory	externalptr (S3: deque)	<pointer: 0x000002bd805dbfd0>
model	function (S3: keras.engine.sequer	function(object) { ... }
replay	function	function(batch_size) { ... }
save	function	function(name) { ... }
self	environment [19] (R6: DQNAgent	R6 object of class DQNAgent
state_size	double [1]	2

After running this line, we will now have an object that has inherited all the attributes defined in the class. We pass in a state size of 2 as an argument because, for this environment, the state is two-dimensional. The two dimensions are position and velocity. We see the value that we passed is reflected alongside the state_size field. We pass in an action size of 20 as an argument because for this game, we will allow the agent to use up to 20 units of force to propel forward or backward. We can see this value as well. We also can see all the methods; however, they are no longer nested under various methods—they are now all just inherited by the agent object.

To create our environment, we use the makeEnvironment function from the reinforcelearn package, which allows for custom environment creation. We use the following code to pass the step and reset functions as arguments to create the custom environment for the agent to navigate:

```
env = makeEnvironment(step = step, reset = reset)
```

After running the preceding line of code, you will see an env object in your **Environment** pane. Note that this object also has a class of Environment. When we click on this object, we will see the following:

Name	Type	Value
env	environment [17] (R6: Environme	R6 object of class Environment
._enclos_env__	environment [2]	<environment: 0x000002bdfe8d5930>
action.names	NULL	Pairlist of length 0
clone	function	function(deep = FALSE) { ... }
discount	double [1]	1
done	logical [1]	FALSE
episode	integer [1]	0
episode.return	double [1]	0
episode.step	integer [1]	0
initialize	function	function(step, reset, visualize = , discount, action.names =) { ... }
n.step	integer [1]	0
previous.state	NULL	Pairlist of length 0
reset	function	function() { ... }
resetEverything	function	function() { ... }
reward	NULL	Pairlist of length 0
state	double [1 x 2]	−0.484 0.000
step	function	function(action) { ... }
visualize	function	function() { ... }

The preceding line of code used the functions that we created earlier to define an environment. We now have an instance of the environment, which includes a means of initializing a game, while the `step` function defines the range of possible motions that the agent can make every turn. Note that this is also an `R6` class, just like our agent class.

Lastly, we include two additional initial values. We establish the remaining initial values to complete our model setup by running the following code:

```
done = FALSE
batch_size = 32
```

The first value of `FALSE` for `done` denotes that the objective is not yet complete. The batch size of `32` is the size of the exploration attempt or series of moves the agent will make before beginning to leverage what is already known before the next series of moves.

This is the complete model setup for deep Q-learning. We have an instance of our agent, which is an object created with the characteristics we established in the class earlier. We also have an environment defined with the parameters we set up when we created our `step` and `reset` functions. Lastly, we defined some initial values and now, everything is complete. The next step is just to put the agent in motion, which we will do next.

Running the experiment

The last step in reinforcement learning is to run the experiment. To do this, we need to drop the agent into the environment and then allow the agent to take steps until it reaches the goal. The agent is constrained by a limited number of possible moves and the environment also places another constraint—in our case, by setting boundaries. We set up a `for` loop that iterates through rounds of the agent attempting a legal move and then sees whether the maze has been successfully accomplished. The loop stops when the agent reaches the goal. To begin our experiment with our defined agent and environment, we write the following code:

```
state = reset(env)
for (j in 1:5000) {
  action = agent$act(state)
  nrd = step(env,action)
  next_state = unlist(nrd[1])
  reward = as.integer(nrd[2])
  done = as.logical(nrd[3])
  next_state = matrix(c(next_state[1],next_state[2]), ncol = 2)
  reward = dplyr::if_else(done == TRUE, reward, as.integer(-10))
  agent$memorize(state, action, reward, next_state, done)
  state = next_state
```

```
env$state = next_state
if (done == TRUE) {
  cat(sprintf("score: %d, e: %.2f",j,agent$epsilon))
  break
}
if (length(agent$memory) > batch_size) {
  agent$replay(batch_size)
}
if (j %% 10 == 0) {
  cat(sprintf("try: %d, state: %f,%f ",j,state[1],state[2]))
}
}
```

The preceding code runs the experiment that sets our agent in motion. The agent is governed by the values and functions in the class that we defined and is furthered by the environment that we created. As we can see, quite a few steps take place when we run our experiment. We will review each step here:

1. After running the first line in the preceding code, we will see a starting state for our agent. If you view the `state` object, it will look something like this, where the position value is between -0.4 and -0.6 and the velocity is 0:

2. After running the remaining code block, we will see something like the following printed to the console, which shows the state at every tenth round:

```
try: 10, state: -0.388078,0.011088  try: 20, state: -0.333161,0.001659  try: 30, state: -0.298411,-0.000
567  try: 40, state: -0.207550,0.017046  try: 50, state: -0.146665,0.015791  try: 60, state: -0.100613,
0.007631  try: 70, state: -0.042036,0.004524  try: 80, state: -0.006942,0.016506  try: 90, state: 0.0781
95,0.012548  try: 100, state: 0.131279,0.001687  try: 110, state: 0.211107,0.010937  try: 120, state: 0.
253006,0.004165  try: 130, state: 0.304203,0.007427  try: 140, state: 0.363525,0.001833  try: 150, stat
e: 0.420849,0.002226  try: 160, state: 0.466184,0.002553  score: 165, e: 0.45
```

3. When we run this code, the first thing that happens is that the environment is reset and the agent is placed on the surface.

4. Then, the loop is initiated. Every round in the loop has the following sequence of activities:

    1. First, use the `act` function in the `agent` class to take an action. Remember, this function defines the allowable moves for the agent.

    2. Next, we pass the action that the agent takes through to the `step` function to get the results.

    3. The output is the next state, which is where the agent lands after the action, as well as the reward based on whether the action led to a positive result, and finally the `done` flag, which indicates whether the target has been reached successfully.

    4. These three elements are output from the function as a `list` object.

    5. The next steps are to assign them to their own objects. For `reward` and `done`, we just extract them from the list and assign them to an integer and logical data type, respectively. For the next state, it is a little more difficult. We first use `unlist` to extract the two values and then we place them in a 2 x 1 matrix.

    6. After all of the elements in an agent's move are moved to their own objects, the reward is calculated. In our case, there are no intermediate accomplishments that would lead to a reward short of reaching the target, so `reward` and `done` operate in a similar way. Here, we see that if the `done` flag is set to TRUE, then `reward` is set to 0, as defined in the `step` function, when `reward` is TRUE.

    7. Next, all the values that were output from the `step` function are added to the `memory` deque object. The `memorize` function takes each value and pushes it to the first element in the deque while pushing existing values back.

    8. After this, the `state` object is assigned the value of the next state. This is because the next state is now the new current state as the agent takes a new step.

    9. There is then a check to see whether the agent has reached the end of the maze. If so, the loop breaks and the epsilon value is printed to see how much was done through exploration and how much through exploitation. For all the other rounds, there is a secondary check that prints the current state and velocity for every tenth move.

    10. The other conditional is the trigger for the `replay` function. After reaching the threshold, the agent pulls values from the memory deque and the process continues from there.

This is the entire process for running an experiment for reinforcement learning. With this process, we now have a method of reinforcement learning that is more robust than just using Q-learning. While using Q-learning is a good solution when the environment is limited and known, deep Q-learning is required when the environment scales up or changes dynamically. By iterating over a defined agent taking actions in a defined environment, we can see how well the defined agent can solve the problem presented in the environment.

Improving performance with policy functions

We have successfully coded an agent to use a neural network deep learning architecture to solve a problem. Let's now look at a few ways that we could improve our model. Unlike other machine learning, we cannot evaluate to a performance metric as usual, where we try to minimize some chosen error rate. Success in reinforcement learning is slightly more subjective. You may want an agent to complete a task as quickly as possible, to acquire as many points as possible, or to make the fewest mistakes possible. In addition, depending on the task, we may be able to alter the agent itself to see how it impacts results.

We will look at three possible methods for improving performance:

- **Action size**: At times, this will be an option and, at times, it will not. If you are trying to solve a problem where the agent rules and environment rules are set externally, such as trying to optimize performance in a game such as chess, then this will not be an option. However, you can imagine a problem such as setting up a self-driving car and in this case, you could change the agent, if it would work better in this environment. With our experiment, try changing the action size value from 20 to 10 and also to 40 to see what happens.
- **Batch size**: We can also adjust the batch size to see how it impacts performance. Remember that when the move count for the agent reaches the threshold for a batch, the agent then selects values from memory to begin to leverage what is already known. By raising or lowering this threshold, we provide a policy for the agent that, more or less, exploration should be conducted before using what is already known. Change the batch size to 16, 64, and 128 to see which option results in the agent completing the challenge the quickest.

- **Neural network**: The last part of the agent policy that we will discuss modifying is the neural network. In many ways, this is the brain for the agent. By making changes, we can allow our agent to make choices that will lead to a more optimized performance. Within the `AgentDQN` class, add some layers to the neural network and then run the experiment again to see what happens. Then, make some changes to the number of units in each layer and run those experiments to see what happens.

In addition to these changes, we could also make changes to the starting epsilon value, how quickly the epsilon decays, and the learning rate for the neural network model. All of these types of changes will impact the policy functions for the agent. When we change a value that alters the output of the act or replay function, then we modify the policy that the agent uses to solve the problem. We can make a policy for the agent to explore a wider or narrower number of actions if possible, or to use more or less time exploring the environment versus exploiting current knowledge, as well as adjust how quickly the agent learns from every move, how many times an agent may try a similar action to see whether it is always incorrect, and how drastically the agent tries to adjust after trying actions that lead towards failure.

As with any type of machine learning, there are a number of parameters that can be tuned to optimize performance in reinforcement learning. Unlike other problems, there may not be a standard metric to help tune these, and deciding on the values that will work best may be more subjective and rely more on trial and error experimentation.

Summary

In this chapter, we wrote code to conduct reinforcement learning using deep Q-learning. We noted that while Q-learning is a simpler approach, it requires a limited and known environment. Applying deep Q-learning allows us to solve problems at a larger scale. We also defined our agent, which required creating a class. The class defined our agent and we instantiated an object with the attributes defined in our class to solve the reinforcement learning challenge. We then created a custom environment using functions that defined boundaries, as well as the range of moves the agent could take and the target or objective. Deep Q-learning involves adding a neural network to select actions, rather than relying on the Q matrix, as in Q-learning. We then added a neural network to our agent class.

Lastly, we put it all together by placing our agent object in our custom environment and letting it take various actions until it solved the problem. We further discussed some choices we could make to improve the agent's performance. With this framework, you are ready to apply reinforcement learning to any number of environments using any number of possible agents. The process will largely stay consistent; the changes will be in how the agent is programmed to act and learn and what the rules are in the environment.

This completes *Hands-On Deep Learning with R*. Throughout this book, you have learned a wide variety of deep learning methods. In addition, we applied these methods to a diverse set of tasks. This book was written with a bias toward action. The goal of this book was to provide concise code that addresses practical projects. Using what you have learned in this book, I hope that I have prepared you well to begin solving real-world challenges using deep learning.

Other Books You May Enjoy

If you enjoyed this book, you may be interested in these other books by Packt:

Advanced Deep Learning with R
Bharatendra Rai

ISBN: 978-1-78953-877-9

- Learn how to create binary and multi-class deep neural network models
- Implement GANs for generating new images
- Create autoencoder neural networks for image dimension reduction, image de-noising and image correction
- Implement deep neural networks for performing efficient text classification
- Learn to define a recurrent convolutional network model for classification in Keras
- Explore best practices and tips for performance optimization of various deep learning models

Deep Learning with R Cookbook

Swarna Gupta, Rehan Ali Ansari, Et al

ISBN: 978-1-78980-567-3

- Work with different datasets for image classification using CNNs
- Apply transfer learning to solve complex computer vision problems
- Use RNNs and their variants such as LSTMs and Gated Recurrent Units (GRUs) for sequence data generation and classification
- Implement autoencoders for DL tasks such as dimensionality reduction, denoising, and image colorization
- Build deep generative models to create photorealistic images using GANs and VAEs
- Use MXNet to accelerate the training of DL models through distributed computing

Leave a review - let other readers know what you think

Please share your thoughts on this book with others by leaving a review on the site that you bought it from. If you purchased the book from Amazon, please leave us an honest review on this book's Amazon page. This is vital so that other potential readers can see and use your unbiased opinion to make purchasing decisions, we can understand what our customers think about our products, and our authors can see your feedback on the title that they have worked with Packt to create. It will only take a few minutes of your time, but is valuable to other potential customers, our authors, and Packt. Thank you!

Index

D

data
  clustering, into topic groups 201, 203
  exploring, to implement collaborative filtering
    166, 167, 168
  formatting, with tokenization 194, 195, 196
  preparing 273, 274, 276, 277
  preparing, to implement collaborative filtering
    166, 167, 168
  preprocessing, to implement collaborative
    filtering 166, 167, 168
  processing 273, 275, 276, 277
dataset
  preparing 44, 45, 46
decision trees 35
deep belief network
  creating, by stacking RBM 211, 213
deep learning (DL)
  about 10
  comparing, with machine learning (ML) 58, 59
deep learning libraries
  comparing 55, 56
deep learning models, data types
  cross-validation 23
  test data 22
  train data 22
  validation data 22
deep learning models, machine learning metrics
  about 27
  accuracy 27
  Area Under the Curve (AUC) 28
  confusion matrix 27
  Logarithmic Loss (Log-Loss) 28
  Mean Absolute Error (MAE) 27
  Root Mean Squared Error (RMSE) 27
deep learning models, results
  evaluating 26
  improving 28, 29, 31, 32, 34
deep learning models
  data, preparing for 10, 11, 12, 13, 14, 15, 17,
    18, 20, 21
  machine learning algorithms, selecting for 23,
    24, 25, 26
  missing values, handling 21

test data 22
train data 22
training, on prepared data 22
deep Q-learning model
  building 299, 300, 301
deque 295
discriminator model
  about 235, 243, 244, 245, 246, 248
  input, passing to 263, 264
documents
  summarizing, with model results 203, 204, 205
dropout layer
  used, for selecting optimal epochs 131, 132,
    133, 134, 135

E

early stopping function
  used, for selecting optimal epochs 131, 132,
    133, 134, 135
embeddings
  exploring 166
Environment pane 221
Environment tab 221
environment
  creating, for reinforcement learning 292, 293
epsilon parameter 282
evaluation metric
  accuracy 118
  cosine similarity 118
  hinge 118
  KL divergence 118
  mean absolute error 118
  mean square error (mse) 118
  using 118, 119
exploratory data analysis (EDA)
  performing 169, 171, 172, 173, 174, 176
exponential function 128
Exponential Linear Unit (ELU) function 128

F

Fashion MNIST dataset
  using 94
feedforward networks
  about 225
  creating 75

forget gate 225

G

gamma 282
GAN model
  about 253, 254
  data, passing to 255
  evaluating 253, 265, 266, 267
  input, passing to discriminator model 263, 264
  random images, generating 256, 257
  real images, combining with fake images 259, 260
  real images, selecting 258
  row selector, updating 264
  target labels, creating 261, 262
  training 253, 255
generative adversarial networks (GANs)
  about 235
  arrays, merging 251, 252
  data files, loading 249, 250
  dataset, preparing 248
  dataset, preprocessing 248
  images, resizing 250
  libraries, loading 249, 250
  overview 236, 237, 238
generator model 235, 238, 239, 240, 241, 243
Gibbs sampling rate
  defining 207, 208, 209
Gibbs sampling
  speeding up, with contrastive divergence 209, 210
Gradient Boosting Machines (GBM) 36
grid search 28

H

H2O
  example 50, 51, 52
  exploring 50
  functions 50
  installing 42
hard Sigmoid function 128
hidden layers
  activation function, utilizing 61, 62, 64
  bias function, utilizing 61, 62, 64
  selecting 150, 151, 152, 153, 154, 155, 156,
  157, 158, 159
hybrid 164
hyperbolic tangent (tanh) function
  about 128
  investigating 67, 68
hyperparameters
  alpha 282
  epsilon 282
  gamma 282
  tuning 282, 284, 286, 288

I

image recognition model
  enhancing, with convolution layer 119, 122, 124, 127
  enhancing, with pooling layer 119, 122, 124, 127
image recognition, with convolutional neural networks (CNNs)
  about 105, 106, 107, 108, 109, 110, 111, 112, 113, 114, 115
  evaluation metric, using 119
image recognition
  with shallow nets 94, 95, 96, 97, 98, 99, 100, 101, 102, 103, 104
integrated (I) 216
item embeddings
  creating 176

K

k-means clustering 36
k-nearest neighbors (KNN) 21, 36
Keras
  example 47, 48
  exploring 46
  functions 46
  installing 40, 41

L

Latent Dirichlet allocation (LDA) 201
Leaky ReLU activation function
  about 128
  calculating 71, 72
LightGBM 36
linear function 128

Made in the USA
Columbia, SC
11 May 2020